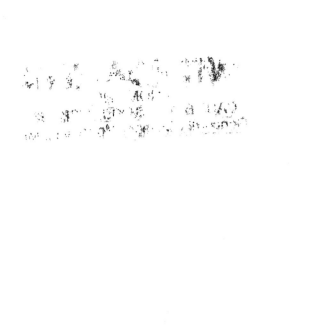

A NEXTEXT ANTHOLOGY

Multicultural
AMERICA

nextext

Cover: © Helen Hardin 1976. Photograph © Cradoc Bragshaw.

Printed in the United States of America.

ISBN 0-618-22204-9

1 2 3 4 5 6 7 — QKT — 08 07 06 05 04 03 02

Part One

Homelands

Part Two

Traditions

Part Three

Growing Up

Part Four

Families

Between Cultures

Part Six

Struggles

Throughout the anthology, vocabulary words appear in boldface type and are footnoted. Specialized or technical words and phrases appear in lightface type and are footnoted.

Homelands

One of the basic and most enduring ties that people possess is to their homes, their neighborhoods, their communities. These homelands are often defined by the ethnic group to which an individual belongs.

◀ This mural appears on a wall in the Chinese neighborhood in San Francisco, California.

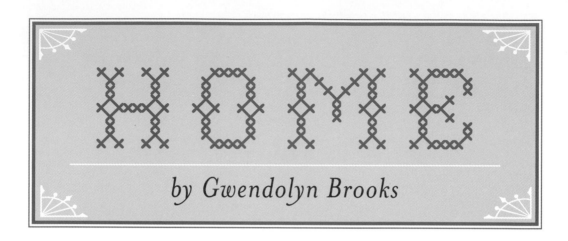

HOME

by Gwendolyn Brooks

About the Author

Gwendolyn Brooks (1917–2000) was born in Topeka, Kansas. She grew up in Chicago, where many of her stories and poems are set. She wrote more than 20 collections of poetry and other books, including a novel and an autobiography. In 1950, Brooks became the first African American to win the Pulitzer Prize, for Annie Allen, her second book of poems. In 1968, she was named Illinois's poet laureate. Through her works, which she called her "family," Brooks hoped to educate readers about urban black culture and the need for harmony among all people.

About the Selections

*The notion of **home** is one that has many layers of meaning. Owning your own home in the United States is regarded as a mark of success. Those who are homeless are pitied and often ignored. Yet a home is more than a house or other shelter. Home signifies different things to different people, but to each person it has an important meaning. For many, it is where they grew up or now live. It is also where they most want to be, where they feel they belong. As you read "Home" and "Knoxville, Tennessee" (page 6), think about the meaning of home to each author.*

What had been wanted was this always, this always to last, the talking softly on this porch, with the snake plant in the jardiniere[1] in the southwest corner, and the **obstinate**[2] slip from Aunt Eppie's magnificent Michigan fern at the left side of the friendly door. Mama, Maud Martha and Helen rocked slowly in their rocking chairs, and looked at the late afternoon light on the lawn, and at the **emphatic**[3] iron of the fence and at the poplar tree. These things might soon be theirs no longer. Those shafts and pools of light, the tree, the graceful iron, might soon be viewed **possessively**[4] by different eyes.

Papa was to have gone that noon, during his lunch hour, to the office of the Home Owners' Loan. If he had not succeeded in getting another **extension,**[5] they would be leaving this house in which they had lived for more than fourteen years. There was little hope. The Home Owners' Loan was hard. They sat, making their plans.

"We'll be moving into a nice flat[6] somewhere," said Mama. "Somewhere on South Park, or Michigan, or in Washington Park Court." Those flats, as the girls and Mama knew well, were burdens on wages twice the size of Papa's. This was not mentioned now.

"They're much prettier than this old house," said Helen. "I have friends I'd just as soon not bring here. And I have other friends that wouldn't come down this far for anything, unless they were in a taxi."

Yesterday, Maud Martha would have attacked her. Tomorrow she might. Today she said nothing. She merely gazed at a little hopping robin in the tree, her tree, and tried to keep the fronts of her eyes dry.

"Well, I do know," said Mama, turning her hands over and over, "that I've been getting tireder and tireder of doing that firing.[7] From October to April, there's firing to be done."

"But lately we've been helping, Harry and I," said Maud Martha. "And sometimes in March and April and in October, and even in

---

[1] jardiniere (JAHRD•uhn•EER)—plant stand or ornamental pot.

[2] **obstinate** (OHB•stuh•niht)—stubborn; difficult to manage.

[3] **emphatic** (ehm•FAT•ihk)—strongly expressive.

[4] **possessively** (puh•ZEHS•ihv•lee)—in a way that shows ownership.

[5] **extension** (eks•TEHN•shuhn)—allowance of extra time, as for repayment of a debt.

[6] flat—apartment.

[7] firing—tending to a furnace.

November, we could build a little fire in the fireplace. Sometimes the weather was just right for that."

She knew, from the way they looked at her, that this had been a mistake. They did not want to cry.

But she felt that the little line of white, somewhat ridged with smoked purple, and all that cream-shot saffron,[8] would never drift across any western sky except that in back of this house. The rain would drum with as sweet a dullness nowhere but here. The birds on South Park were mechanical birds, no better than the poor caught canaries in those "rich" women's sun parlors.

> *The rain would drum with as sweet a dullness nowhere but here.*

"It's just going to kill Papa!" burst out Maud Martha. "He loves this house! He lives for this house!"

"He lives for us," said Helen. "It's us he loves. He wouldn't want the house, except for us."

"And he'll have us," added Mama, "wherever."

"You know," Helen sighed, "if you want to know the truth, this is a relief. If this hadn't come up, we would have gone on, just dragged on, hanging out here forever."

"It might," allowed Mama, "be an act of God. God may just have reached down, and picked up the reins."

"Yes," Maud Martha cracked in, "that's what you always say—that God knows best."

Her mother looked at her quickly, decided the statement was not suspect, looked away.

Helen saw Papa coming. "There's Papa," said Helen.

They could not tell a thing from the way Papa was walking. It was that same dear little staccato[9] walk, one shoulder down, then the other, then repeat, and repeat. They watched his progress. He passed the Kennedys', he passed the vacant lot, he passed Mrs. Blakemore's. They wanted to hurl themselves over the fence, into the street, and shake the truth out of his collar. He opened his gate—the gate—and still his stride and face told them nothing.

---

[8] cream-shot saffron—orange-yellow (saffron) mixed (shot) with yellowish white (cream).

[9] staccato (stuh•KAH•toh)—formed of short, crisp sounds or movements.

He loves *this house!*

This portrait of a man and woman on the porch of their home was taken by the African American photographer Ellie Lee Weems (1901–1983). ▶

"Hello," he said.

Mama got up and followed him through the front door. The girls knew better than to go in too.

Presently Mama's head emerged. Her eyes were lamps turned on.

"It's all right," she exclaimed. "He got it. It's all over. Everything is all right."

The door slammed shut. Mama's footsteps hurried away.

"I think," said Helen, rocking rapidly, "I think I'll give a party. I haven't given a party since I was eleven. I'd like some of my friends to just **casually**[10] see that we're homeowners."

---

[10] **casually** (KA•zhoo•uhl•lee)—in a relaxed manner.

Knoxville, Tennessee

by Nikki Giovanni

About the Author

Poet, essayist, and lecturer Nikki Giovanni was born Yolande Cornelia Giovanni, Jr., in 1943. She was educated at Fisk University, the University of Pennsylvania, and Columbia University. At age 27, she founded her own publishing company. Giovanni's work changes often, supporting her view that change is necessary for growth. Her early poetry served as a major voice in the civil rights movement of the 1960s. Later poems focused on family and her childhood home, Knoxville, Tennessee. Giovanni's recent work has a global outlook.

I always like summer
best
you can eat fresh corn
from daddy's garden
and okra
and greens
and cabbage
and lots of
barbecue

and buttermilk
and homemade ice-cream
at the church picnic
and listen to
gospel music
outside
at the church
homecoming
and go to the mountains with
your grandmother
and go barefooted
and be warm
all the time
not only when you go to bed
and sleep

I always like
summer best

◀ A Baltimore youth group
enjoys a picnic in this
photograph by Susie Fitzhugh.

Questions to Consider

Responding

1. Did you ever have to move from your **home**? How did it make you feel?

Analyzing

2. Why do you think the author of "Home" set her story at dusk?

3. Why do you think Mama and Helen act and talk as though losing the house might be okay?

4. In a poem, the speaker is the voice that talks to the reader. How do you know that the speaker of "Knoxville, Tennessee" is a child who loves his or her home?

Extending

5. What do you think of the statement that "people make a house a home"?

Activity

Writing About Setting

Create a setting chart that focuses on your home. Write column headings for various elements of setting. Write a list under each heading. For location, list places that you associate with your home or neighborhood. For season, list whatever distinct seasons you experience where you live. For time of day, write morning, afternoon, evening, and nighttime. For customs and lifestyle, list your daily activities and special events in your home and community that you have attended. Then pick one item from each column. Write a paragraph describing the setting made up of those elements.

Literature Connection

*The **setting** of a literary work is the time and place of the action. Sometimes the setting is clear and well-defined; at other times, it is left to the reader's imagination. Look at the following passage from "Home":*

> But she felt that the little line of white, somewhat ridged with smoked purple, and all that cream-shot saffron, would never drift across any western sky except that in back of this house. The rain would drum with as sweet a dullness nowhere but here.

1. What details of setting does the author provide here?

2. How do these details convey the characters' feeling for their home?

3. What feeling is expressed by the details of setting the author gives in "Knoxville, Tennessee"?

Ellis Island

by Joseph Bruchac

About the Author

Writer, poet, and storyteller Joseph Bruchac (BROO•shak)was born in 1942 in Saratoga Springs, New York. His father's family was Slovak and his mother was English and Native American. Bruchac embraced his Indian ancestry and became a scholar of Native American culture. He has written more than 50 books of poetry and stories. With his wife, he founded the Greenfield Review Press, which publishes multicultural literature. In 1999, Bruchac was honored with the Lifetime Achievement Award of the Native Writers Circle of the Americas.

About the Selections

In Native American cultures of times past, land was used by those who needed it. Many tribes defended their territories against other tribes, but individuals did not own land. Land belonged to the spirits and the animals. Europeans who settled in early America, however, had a long tradition of land ownership. The conflict between Native American and European **concepts of land ownership** caused many problems during the development of the United States. As you read "Ellis Island" and "The Time We Climbed Snake Mountain" (page 11), look for how the poets use comparison and contrast to highlight that conflict.

These moccasins were made by the Micmac, Native Americans who were allies of the Abenaki people to whom Joseph Bruchac traces his ancestry.

▼

Beyond the red brick of Ellis Island[1]
where the two Slovak children
who became my grandparents
waited the long days of **quarantine**,[2]
after leaving the sickness,
the old Empires of Europe,
a Circle Line ship slips easily
on its way to the island
of the tall woman, green
as dreams of forests and meadows
waiting for those who'd worked
a thousand years
yet never owned their own.

Like millions of others,
I too come to this island,
nine decades the answerer
of dreams.

Yet only one part of my blood loves
    that memory.
Another voice speaks
of native lands
within this nation.
Lands invaded
when the earth became owned.
Lands of those who followed
the changing Moon,
knowledge of the seasons
in their veins.

---

[1] Ellis Island—island near New York City that served as chief U.S. immigration station between 1892 and 1943.

[2] **quarantine** (KWAWR•uhn•teen)—being held in isolation on suspicion of carrying a contagious disease.

The Time We Climbed

Snake Mountain

by Leslie Marmon Silko

About the Author

Leslie Marmon Silko defines herself as a person of mixed ancestry—Laguna Pueblo, Mexican, and white. Born in 1948, she grew up on the Laguna Pueblo reservation hearing many traditional stories. She draws upon that heritage in her novels, short stories, essays, poetry, articles, and filmscripts. Her most celebrated novel is Ceremony *(1977). It is the story of a returning World War II veteran of Native American ancestry. In addition to writing, she teaches English at the University of Arizona in Tucson.*

Seeing good places
    for my hands
I grab the warm parts of the cliff
      and I feel the mountain as I climb.
Somewhere   around here
    yellow spotted snake is sleeping   on his rock
      in the sun.
So
  please, I tell them
    watch out,
don't step on the spotted yellow snake
      he lives here.
The mountain is his.

Responding

1. Did you ever have a disagreement with someone about sharing something you both wanted? How did you resolve the conflict?

Analyzing

2. In "Ellis Island," how are the speaker's European ancestors like his Native American ancestors?

3. In "The Time We Climbed Snake Mountain," how does the speaker refer to the snake?

4. Which **concept of land ownership**—Native American or European—does each poem favor?

Extending

5. Imagine you lived in early America. What would your opinion be in the conflict between the Native Americans and Europeans over land ownership?

*A **theme** is a message about life or human nature that is communicated by a literary work. The theme of a literary work is not the same as its subject. The subject is what the work is about, such as the natural world, romantic love, or old age. The theme is a statement of what the author is saying concerning this subject. Sometimes the theme is stated directly. In many cases, however, a reader must infer what the writer's message is.*

1. What common subject is shared by "Ellis Island" and "The Time We Climbed Snake Mountain"?

2. How would you express the theme of "Ellis Island"?

3. How would you express the theme of "The Time We Climbed Snake Mountain"?

4. How do the themes of these two poems differ?

Activities

Writing About a Special Place

Write a short poem about a place that is important to you. Use the following form. The first line contains one word and states the subject. The next line contains two words and describes the way the subject looks, sounds, tastes, smells, or feels. The third line contains three words and describes an action related to the subject. The fourth line contains four words and expresses a feeling about the subject. The fifth line contains one word and sums up the poem. After writing one poem, write a summary of its theme.

Telling a Story

Look through a collection of Native American stories. Find one with a theme about land. Read it at least five times. Practice telling it without looking at the text. Try different voices for different characters. Remember to speak slowly. Use pauses to create drama. Arrange to tell the story to an audience, such as your classmates, young children, or even your parents. Then discuss the story's meaning with your listeners.

THE ☆THER PIONEERS

BY ROBERTO FÉLIX SALAZAR

About the Author

Roberto Félix Salazar was born in 1921. He is a Mexican American and a native of Laredo, Texas. He wrote his most famous poem, "The Other Pioneers," in 1939. He wanted people to remember that the first pioneers in the Southwest had Spanish names—just as their American descendants do.

About the Selections

Before Texas became part of the United States in 1845, it was an independent republic. Before that, it was part of Mexico. In the Mexican Constitution of 1824, Mexican citizens in the future Texas were referred to as **Tejanos** (tay•HAH•nohs). This is because the area was once part of a Spanish province called Tejas. When people of non-Spanish ancestry became active in the future Texas, they referred to themselves as Texians. Later, they became Texans. Today, all the people of Texas may be called Texans. The term Tejano is still used to refer to the people of Mexican descent in Texas. As you read, "The Other Pioneers" and "Gold" (page 16), think about how the poets—both Tejanos—express their connection to their ancestors and the land.

HERE IS THE LAND

*for our sons
and the sons
of our sons.*

◀ Hispanic families like that
of Don Vincente Lugo
(1820–1889) were among
the early settlers of the
American Southwest.

Now I must write
Of those of mine who rode these plains
Long years before the Saxon[1] and the Irish came.
Of those who plowed the land and built the towns
And gave the towns soft-woven Spanish names.
Of those who moved across the Rio Grande
Toward the hiss of Texas snake and Indian yell.
Of men who from the earth made thick-walled homes
And from the earth raised churches to their God.
And of the wives who bore them sons
And smiled with knowing joy.

---

[1] Saxon (SAK•suhn)—person of English descent.

They saw the Texas sun rise golden-red with promised wealth
And saw the Texas sun sink golden yet, with wealth unspent.
"Here," they said. "Here to live and here to love."
"Here is the land for our sons and the sons of our sons."
And they sang the songs of ancient Spain
And they made new songs to fit new needs.
They cleared the brush and planted the corn
And saw green stalks turn black from lack of rain.
They roamed the plains behind the herds
And stood the Indian's cruel attacks.
There was dust and there was sweat.
And there were tears and the women prayed.

And the years moved on.
Those who were first placed in graves
Beside the broad mesquite[2] and the tall nopal.[3]
Gentle mothers left their graces and their arts
And **stalwart**[4] fathers pride and manly strength.
Salinas, de la Garza, Sánchez, García,
Uribe, González, Martinez, de León:[5]
Such were the names of the fathers.
Salinas, de la Garza, Sánchez, García,
Uribe, González, Martinez, de León:
Such are the names of the sons.

---

[2] mesquite (meh•SKEET)—thorny shrub of the Southwest and northern Mexico.

[3] nopal (NOH•puhl)—cactus with discs strung together; prickly pear cactus.

[4] **stalwart** (STAWL•wuhrt)—firm and determined.

[5] Salinas (sah•LEE•nahs), de la Garza (day lah GAHR•sah), Sánchez (SAHN•chays), García (gahr•SEE•ah), Uribe (oo•REE•bay), Gonzáles (gohn•SAH•lays), Martinez (mahr•TEE•nays), de León (day lay•OHN).

GOLD

BY PAT MORA

About the Author

Pat Mora's four grandparents migrated in the early 1900s from Mexico to El Paso, Texas, where she was born in 1942. In her poetry, short stories, and essays, she portrays the cultural richness and visual beauty of the Southwest. In 1997, Mora and her illustrator, Raul Colon, received the Tomás Rivera Mexican American Children's Book Award for Tomás and the Library Lady. *The award is given to authors and illustrators of books that present the lives of Mexican Americans in the Southwest. Mora is also active in efforts to create a national holiday that celebrates children, books, languages, and cultures.*

When Sun paints the desert
with its gold,
I climb the hills.
Wind runs round boulders, ruffles
my hair. I sit on my favorite rock,
lizards for company, a rabbit,
ears stiff in the shade
of a saguaro.[6]
In the wind, we're all
eye to eye.

---

[6] saguaro (suh•GWAHR•oh)—tall, branching cactus of the Southwest and northern Mexico.

Sparrow on saguaro watches
rabbit watch us in the gold
of sun setting.
Hawk sails on waves of light, sees
sparrow, rabbit, lizards, me,
our eyes shining,
watching red and purple
   sand rivers stream down the hill.

I stretch my arms wide as the sky
like hawk extends her wings
in all the gold light of this, home.

SUN PAINTS

the desert with its gold.

Saguaro cactuses in the Sonoran
Desert appear dark against the gold
of the setting sun. ▶

Questions to Consider

Responding

1. How would you express your feelings about your cultural heritage and about the nature of the land where you live?

Analyzing

2. In "The Other Pioneers," how would you describe the speaker's attitude toward the first **Tejanos?**

3. The speaker mentions the "Indian's cruel attacks" on the early Spanish settlers. How might the Indians' view of these early settlers have been like the Tejanos' view of later settlers?

4. In "Gold," how is the speaker's connection to the Southwest expressed?

Extending

5. What would you like people to know that they might not know now about your ancestors?

Literature Connection

The **mood** *of a literary work is a feeling that it conveys to readers. Writers use many literary devices to create mood, including setting, imagery, and dialogue. Look at the following lines from "The Other Pioneers":*

> They cleared the brush and planted
>   the corn
> And saw green stalks turn black from
>   lack of rain.

1. What device is the writer here using to create mood?

2. What words would you use to describe that mood?

3. How do the moods of "The Other Pioneers" and "Gold" differ?

Activities

Writing About Your Name

Names are like flags. They often announce your nationality or cultural heritage. Write a poem that celebrates your name. First write the letters of your name in a row down the left side of your page. Use the beginning letter on each line to start the first word of that line of your poem. Make your poem about your heritage, which may be reflected your name. If you like, include a reference to the land where your ancestors settled or the land from which they came.

Creating a Gallery

The Tejanos have a special connection to Texas and its landscapes. What special connection do you have to your state or the land on which you live? Create a gallery of images that show this special connection. Prepare comments about each image. Present your gallery to your classmates, your family, or your community. As an alternative, create a website with your images and comments.

Tears of Autumn

by Yoshiko Uchida

About the Author

Yoshiko Uchida (1922–1992) was born in California. During World War II, Uchida and her family were sent to an internment camp along with other Japanese Americans. (See page 363.) Uchida had been in college at the time. She was eventually allowed to leave the camp and return to her studies. She later went to Japan to collect Japanese folk tales. Uchida's experiences deepened her respect for Japanese culture. Her books deal with her experiences in the internment camp and the difficulties of being both Japanese and American.

About the Selections

By 1900, there were thousands of single Japanese and Korean men in the United States, but very few single Asian women. Families and friends back home began to arrange marriages, which was the custom in Asian countries. Couples exchanged letters and photographs to get to know each other. Then the *"picture brides"* (as they were called) crossed the Pacific Ocean to meet their new husbands. As you read "Tears of Autumn" and "Picture Bride" (page 28), think about the double challenge of leaving one's homeland and going to a new country to start a new relationship.

Hana Omiya stood at the railing of the small ship that shuddered toward America in a **turbulent**[1] November sea. She shivered as she pulled the folds of her silk kimono[2] close to her throat and tightened the wool shawl about her shoulders.

She was thin and small, her dark eyes shadowed in her pale face, her black hair piled high in a pompadour[3] that seemed too heavy for so slight a woman. She clung to the moist rail and breathed the damp salt air deep into her lungs. Her body seemed leaden and lifeless, as though it were simply the vehicle transporting her soul to a strange new life, and she longed with childlike intensity to be home again in Oka Village.

> Why did I ever leave Japan? she wondered bitterly.

She longed to see the bright persimmon dotting the barren trees beside the thatched roofs, to see the fields of golden rice stretching to the mountains where only last fall she had gathered plum white mushrooms, and to see once more the maple trees lacing their flaming colors through the green pine. If only she could see a familiar face, eat a meal without retching, walk on solid ground, and stretch out at night on a *tatami* mat[4] instead of in a hard narrow bunk. She thought now of seeking the warm shelter of her bunk but could not bear to face the relentless smell of fish that penetrated the lower decks.

Why did I ever leave Japan? she wondered bitterly. Why did I ever listen to my uncle? And yet she knew it was she herself who had begun the chain of events that placed her on this heaving ship. It was she who had first planted in her uncle's mind the thought that she would make a good wife for Taro Takeda, the lonely man who had gone to America to make his fortune in Oakland, California.

It all began one day when her uncle had come to visit her mother.

"I must find a nice young bride," he had said, startling Hana with this blunt talk of marriage in her presence. She blushed and was ready to leave the room when her uncle quickly

---

[1] **turbulent** (TUR•byuh•luhnt)—full of violent motion.

[2] kimono (kuh•MOH•nuh)—long, wide-sleeved, robelike Japanese dress.

[3] pompadour (PAHM•puh•dawr)—hairstyle formed by sweeping the hair up and back from the forehead into a roll.

[4] *tatami* (tah•TAH•mee) mat—woven straw floor mat, traditionally used in Japanese homes.

Photos such as this one were sent by the families of Japanese picture brides to men they planned to marry.

youngest daughter of what once had been a fine family. Her father, until his death fifteen years ago, had been the largest landholder of the village and one of its last samurai.[5] They had once had many servants and field hands, but now all that was changed. Their money was gone. Hana's three older sisters had made good marriages, and the eldest remained in their home with her husband to carry on the Omiya name and perpetuate the homestead. Her other sisters had married merchants in Osaka and Nagoya and were living comfortably.

Now that Hana was twenty-one, finding a proper husband for her had taken on an urgency that produced an embarrassing secretive air over the entire matter. Usually, her mother didn't speak of it until they were lying side by side on their quilts at night. Then, under the protective cover of darkness, she would suggest one name and then another, hoping that Hana would indicate an interest in one of them.

Her uncle spoke freely of Taro Takeda only because he was so sure Hana would never consider him. "He is a conscientious, hardworking man who has been in the United States for almost ten years. He is thirty-one,

added, "My good friend Takeda has a son in America. I must find someone willing to travel to that far land."

This last remark was intended to indicate to Hana and her mother that he didn't consider this a suitable prospect for Hana, who was the

---

[5] samurai (SAM•uh•ry)—Japanese army officer or member of the military class.

operates a small shop, and rents some rooms above the shop where he lives." Her uncle rubbed his chin thoughtfully. "He could provide well for a wife," he added.

"Ah," Hana's mother said softly. "You say he is successful in this business?" Hana's sister inquired.

> She wanted to escape the smothering strictures of life in her village.

"His father tells me he sells many things in his shop—clothing, stockings, needles, thread, and buttons— such things as that. He also sells bean paste, pickled radish, bean cake, and soy sauce. A wife of his would not go cold or hungry."

They all nodded, each of them picturing this merchant in varying degrees of success and **affluence**.[6] There were many Japanese emigrating to America these days, and Hana had heard of the picture brides who went with nothing more than an exchange of photographs to bind them to a strange man.

"Taro San[7] is lonely," her uncle continued. "I want to find for him a fine young woman who is strong and brave enough to cross the ocean alone."

"It would certainly be a different kind of life," Hana's sister ventured, and for a moment, Hana thought she glimpsed a longing ordinarily concealed behind her quiet, obedient face. In that same instant, Hana knew she wanted more for herself than her sisters had in their proper, arranged, and loveless marriages. She wanted to escape the smothering strictures[8] of life in her village. She certainly was not going to marry a farmer and spend her life working beside him planting, weeding, and harvesting in the rice paddies until her back became bent from too many years of stooping and her skin was turned to brown leather by the sun and wind. Neither did she particularly relish the idea of marrying a merchant in a big city as her two sisters had done. Since her mother objected to her going to Tokyo to seek employment as a teacher, perhaps she would consent to a flight to America for what seemed a proper and respectable marriage.

Almost before she realized what she was doing, she spoke to her uncle. "Oji San, perhaps I should go to America to make this lonely man a good wife."

---

[6] **affluence** (AF•loo•uhns)—wealth.

[7] San—Japanese term added to a person's name to show respect.

[8] strictures (STRIHK•chuhrs)—limits.

"You, Hana Chan?"[9] Her uncle observed her with startled curiosity. "You would go all alone to a foreign land so far away from your mother and family?"

"I would not allow it." Her mother spoke fiercely. Hana was her youngest and she had **lavished**[10] upon her the attention and latitude[11] that often befall the last child. How could she permit her to travel so far, even to marry the son of Takeda who was known to her brother?

But now, a notion that had seemed quite impossible a moment before was lodged in his receptive mind, and Hana's uncle grasped it with the pleasure that comes from an unexpected discovery.

"You know," he said looking at Hana, "it might be a very good life in America."

Hana felt a faint fluttering in her heart. Perhaps this lonely man in America was her means of escaping both the village and the encirclement of her family.

Her uncle spoke with increasing enthusiasm of sending Hana to become Taro's wife. And the husband of Hana's sister, who was head of their household, spoke with equal eagerness. Although he never said so,

Hana guessed he would be pleased to be rid of her, the spirited younger sister who stirred up his **placid**[12] life with what he considered radical ideas about life and the role of women. He often claimed that Hana had too much schooling for a girl. She had graduated from Women's High School in Kyoto, which gave her five more years of schooling than her older sister.

"It has **addled**[13] her brain—all that learning from those books," he said when he tired of arguing with Hana.

A man's word carried much weight for Hana's mother. Pressed by the two men, she consulted her other daughters and their husbands. She discussed the matter carefully with her brother and asked the village priest. Finally, she agreed to an exchange of family histories and an investigation was begun into Taro Takeda's family, his education, and his health, so they would be assured there was no insanity or tuberculosis or police records concealed in his family's past. Soon Hana's uncle was

---

[9] Chan—Japanese term added to a familiar female's name.
[10] **lavished**—given in abundance.
[11] latitude—freedom from normal limitations.
[12] **placid** (PLAS•ihd)—calm, quiet.
[13] **addled** (AD•ld)—confused.

devoting his energies entirely to serving as go-between for Hana's mother and Taro Takeda's father.

When at last an agreement to the marriage was almost reached, Taro wrote his first letter to Hana. It was brief and proper and gave no more clue to his character than the stiff formal portrait taken at his graduation from middle school. Hana's uncle had given her the picture with apologies from his parents, because it was the only photo they had of him and it was not a flattering likeness.

Hana hid the letter and photograph in the sleeve of her kimono and took them to the outhouse to study in private. Squinting in the dim light and trying to ignore the foul odor, she read and reread Taro's letter, trying to find the real man somewhere in the **sparse**[14] unbending prose.

By the time he sent her money for her steamship tickets, she had received ten more letters, but none revealed much more of the man than the first. In none did he disclose his loneliness or his need, but Hana understood this. In fact, she would

> **What would she say to Taro Takeda when they first met?**

have recoiled from a man who bared his intimate thoughts to her so soon. After all, they would have a lifetime together to get to know one another.

So it was that Hana had left her family and sailed alone to America with a small hope trembling inside of her. Tomorrow, at last, the ship would dock in San Francisco and she would meet face to face the man she was soon to marry. Hana was overcome with excitement at the thought of being in America, and terrified of the meeting about to take place. What would she say to Taro Takeda when they first met, and for all the days and years after?

Hana wondered about the flat above the shop. Perhaps it would be luxuriously furnished with the finest of brocades[15] and lacquers,[16] and perhaps there would be a servant, although he had not mentioned it. She worried whether she would be able to manage on the meager English she had learned at Women's High School. The overwhelming anxiety for the day to come and the violent rolling of the ship were more than Hana could bear.

---

[14] **sparse**—not abundant.
[15] brocades (broh•KAYDZ)—heavy fabrics with elegant, raised designs.
[16] lacquers (LAK•uhrz)—highly polished decorative wood items.

Shuddering in the face of the wind, she leaned over the railing and became violently and wretchedly ill.

By five the next morning, Hana was up and dressed in her finest purple silk kimono and coat. She could not eat the bean soup and rice that appeared for breakfast and took only a few bites of the yellow pickled radish. Her bags, which had scarcely been touched since she boarded the ship, were easily packed, for all they contained were her kimonos and some of her favorite books. The large willow basket, tightly secured by a rope, remained under the bunk, untouched since her uncle had placed it there.

She had not befriended the other women in her cabin, for they had lain in their bunks for most of the voyage, too sick to be company to anyone. Each morning Hana had fled the closeness of the sleeping quarters and spent most of the day huddled in a corner of the deck, listening to the lonely songs of some Russians also traveling to an alien land.

As the ship approached land, Hana hurried up to the deck to look out at the gray expanse of ocean and sky, eager for a first glimpse of her new homeland.

"We won't be docking until almost noon," one of the deckhands told her.

Hana nodded, "I can wait," she answered, but the last hours seemed the longest.

When she set foot on American soil at last, it was not in the city of San Francisco as she had expected, but on Angel Island,[17] where all third-class passengers were taken. She spent two miserable days and nights waiting, as the immigrants were questioned by officials, examined for trachoma[18] and tuberculosis, and tested for hookworm.[19] It was a bewildering, **degrading**[20] beginning, and Hana was sick with anxiety, wondering if she would ever be released.

On the third day, a Japanese messenger from San Francisco appeared with a letter for her from Taro. He had written it the day of her arrival, but it had not reached her for two days.

Taro welcomed her to America, and told her that the bearer of the letter would inform Taro when she was to be released so he could be at the pier to meet her.

---

[17] Angel Island—island in San Francisco Bay where an immigration station was established in 1910.

[18] trachoma (truh•KOH•muh)—contagious eye disease.

[19] hookworm—disease caused by hookworms, small worms that attach themselves to the intestines.

[20] **degrading** (dih•GRAY•dihng)—insulting.

The letter eased her anxiety for a while, but as soon as she was released and boarded the launch for San Francisco, new fears rose up to smother her with a feeling almost of dread.

The early morning mist had become a light chilling rain, and on the pier black umbrellas bobbed here and there, making the task of recognition even harder. Hana searched desperately for a face that resembled the photo she had studied so long and hard. Suppose he hadn't come. What would she do then?

this is the man J came to *marry*

A Japanese bride sits beside her husband in a wedding photograph. ▶

Hana took a deep breath, lifted her head and walked slowly from the launch. The moment she was on the pier, a man in a black coat, wearing a derby and carrying an umbrella, came quickly to her side. He was of slight build, not much taller than she, and his face was sallow and pale. He bowed stiffly and murmured, "You have had a long trip, Miss Omiya. I hope you are well."

Hana caught her breath. "You are Takeda San?" she asked.

He removed his hat and Hana was further startled to see that he was already turning bald.

"You are Takeda San?" she asked again. He looked older than thirty-one.

"I am afraid I no longer resemble the early photo my parents gave you. I am sorry."

Hana had not meant to begin like this. It was not going well.

"No, no," she said quickly. "It is just that I . . . that is, I am terribly nervous. . . ." Hana stopped abruptly, too flustered to go on.

"I understand," Taro said gently. "You will feel better when you meet my friends and have some tea. Mr. and Mrs. Toda are expecting you in Oakland. You will be staying with them until . . ." He couldn't bring himself to mention the marriage just yet and Hana was grateful he hadn't.

He quickly made arrangements to have her baggage sent to Oakland, then led her carefully along the rain-slick pier toward the streetcar that would take them to the ferry.

Hana shuddered at the sight of another boat, and as they climbed to its upper deck she felt a queasy tightening of her stomach.

"I hope it will not rock too much," she said anxiously. "Is it many hours to your city?"

> I am afraid I no longer resemble the early photo my parents gave you.

Taro laughed for the first time since their meeting, revealing the gold fillings of his teeth. "Oakland is just across the bay," he explained. "We will be there in twenty minutes."

Raising a hand to cover her mouth, Hana laughed with him and suddenly felt better. I am in America now, she thought, and this is the man I came to marry. Then she sat down carefully beside Taro, so no part of their clothing touched.

Picture Bride

by Cathy Song

About the Author

Born in Hawaii in 1955, Cathy Song grew up learning the Asian culture of her Korean and Chinese ancestors. After attending Wellesley College and Boston University, she returned to Hawaii. Song has won many awards for her poetry. Her first collection, Picture Bride, won the Yale Series of Young Poets Award in 1982. Her poetry is mainly about family relationships and her Asian heritage.

She was a year younger
than I,
twenty-three when she left Korea.
Did she simply close
the door of her father's house
and walk away? And
was it a long way
through the tailor shops of Pusan[20]
to the wharf where the boat
waited to take her to an island
whose name she had
only recently learned,
on whose shore
a man waited,
turning her photograph
to the light when the lanterns
in the camp outside
Waialua Sugar Mill[21] were lit
and the inside of his room
grew **luminous**[22]
from the wings of moths
migrating out of the cane stalks?

---

[20] Pusan—seaport in South Korea.
[21] Waialua Sugar Mill—sugar refinery in the Hawaiian Islands.
[22] **luminous** (LOO•muh•nuhs)—full of light.

What things did my grandmother
take with her? And when
she arrived to look into
the face of the stranger
who was her husband,
thirteen years older than she,

did she politely untie
the silk bow of her jacket,
her tent-shaped dress
filling with the dry wind
that blew from the surrounding fields
where the men were burning the cane?

What things
did my
grandmother take with her?

▲
Picture brides are shown on shipboard.

Responding

1. How would you feel about marrying someone you knew only through letters and photographs?

Analyzing

2. In "Tears of Autumn," what motivates Hana to leave her homeland and become a picture bride?

3. What do Taro's letters and his behavior toward Hana reveal about him?

4. Why do you think "Picture Bride" is composed of a series of questions?

5. Taken together, what effect do all these questions have?

6. How are the two **picture brides** alike? How are they different?

Extending

7. Why do you think arranged marriages are no longer common in today's Asian-American families?

Literature Connection

Characterization consists of all the techniques writers use to create and develop characters. There are four basic methods of developing a character: (1) physical description of the character; (2) presenting the character's thoughts, speech, and actions; (3) presenting the ways in which other characters think about, speak to, and interact with the character; (4) direct comments about the character's nature.

1. In "Tears of Autumn," how does the writer's physical description of Hana contribute to the development of her character?

2. How is the characterization of Hana developed using the other characters?

3. What are the principal ways in which the speaker in "Picture Bride" develops the character of her grandmother?

Activity

Writing About a Character

The first Japanese and Korean men came to the United States in the early 1900s. Most of them were young. Because of U.S. immigration laws, however, many of these men never married. Between 1924 and 1952, Asian immigration to the United States was not allowed. Write a brief narrative in which one of these early immigrants reflects on his long bachelorhood and its causes. Include other characters if you like. Use as many of the characterization techniques as you can. When your scene is complete, ask several classmates to read it. Have them describe the character(s) you created to check the success of your characterization.

THE Tropics IN NEW YORK

BY CLAUDE MCKAY

About the Author

African-American writer Claude McKay (1890–1948) was born in Jamaica. He moved to the United States at age 23. The racism McKay faced as a black immigrant led him to write about that problem and about black identity. Many of his poems, essays, and novels focused on life in New York's African-American community, Harlem, where he lived for many years. McKay became one of major figures of the Harlem Renaissance of the 1920s. He influenced many younger poets, including Langston Hughes. His autobiography, A Long Way from Home (1937), and a study of Harlem were his last works.

About the Selections

Claude McKay never forgot his Jamaican homeland, where his father grew cocoa, bananas, sugarcane, and coffee. He wrote passionately about it in poems and in his autobiography. Judith Ortiz Cofer has said that although she no longer lives among Puerto Ricans, "the obsession called the island has always been with me." As you read "The Tropics in New York" and "Exile" (page 33), consider how these immigrant writers express their **sense of exile**— their feeling of being separated from their homelands.

Bananas ripe and green, and ginger-root,
Cocoa in pods and alligator pears,[1]
And tangerines and mangoes and grapefruit,
Fit for the highest prize at parish[2] fairs,

Set in the window, bringing memories
Of fruit-trees laden[3] by low-singing rills,[4]
And dewy dawns, and **mystical**[5] blue skies
In **benediction**[6] over nun-like hills.

My eyes grew dim, and I could no more gaze;
A wave of longing through my body swept,
And, hungry for the old, familiar ways,
I turned aside and bowed my head and wept.

---

[1] alligator pears—avocados.

[2] parish—church district.

[3] laden—weighed down with a load.

[4] rills—little streams.

[5] **mystical** (MIHS•tih•kuhl)—of spiritual or religious importance.

[6] **benediction** (behn•ih•DIHK•shuhn)—prayer or blessing.

Colombian artist Ana Mercedes Hoyos (1942–   ) painted
La Palangana de Zeni ("The Bowl of Tropical Fruit"). ▶

Exile

BY JUDITH ORTIZ COFER

About the Author

Judith Ortiz Cofer was born in Puerto Rico in 1952, and moved to New Jersey as a child. Her writing explores the experiences of Hispanic-American immigrants. Cofer's first novel, The Line of the Sun *(1989), relates the story of a family caught between two cultures. Her collection of essays,* Silent Dancing: A Partial Remembrance of a Puerto Rican Childhood *(1990), has received numerous awards and honors. In addition to writing, Cofer teaches at the University of Georgia.*

I left my home behind me
but my past clings to my fingers
so that every word I write hears
the mark like a cancelled postage stamp
of my birthplace.
There was no angel to warn me
of the dangers of looking back.
Like Lot's wife, I would trade
my living blood for one last look[7]
at the house where each window held
a face framed as in a family album.

---

[7] no angel to warn me . . . Lot's wife . . . one last look—reference to the biblical story in which Lot's wife is turned into a pillar of salt. She had disobeyed the angels' order not to look back while fleeing the cities of Sodom and Gomorrah, which were being destroyed for their wickedness.

And the plaza lined with palms
where my friends and I strolled in our pink
and yellow and white Sunday dresses, dreaming
of husbands, houses, and orchards where
our children would play in the leisurely summer
of our future. Gladly would I spill
my remaining years like salt[8] upon the ground,
to gaze again on the fishermen of the bay
dragging their catch in nets glittering
like pirate gold, to the shore.
Nothing remains of that world, I hear,
but the skeletons of houses, all colors
bled from the fabric of those
who stayed behind
inhabiting the dead cities
like the shadows of Hiroshima.[9]

---

[8] spill my remaining years like salt—refers to the superstition that spilling salt brings bad luck, which reflects the age-old belief that salt is sacred.

[9] Hiroshima (heer•uh•SHEE•muh)—Japanese city destroyed on August 6, 1945, by U.S. forces with the first atomic bomb used in warfare.

I LEFT MY HOME

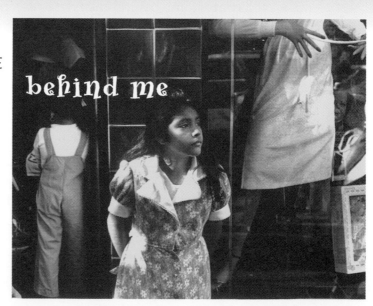

This young girl was photographed by David Grossman on a street in Los Angeles. ▶

Questions to Consider

Responding

1. Have you ever left someplace, certain that you would never see it again? How did you feel when you thought of it later?

Analyzing

2. In "The Tropics in New York," what stimulates the speaker's **sense of exile**?

3. In "Exile," what have been "the dangers of looking back" for the speaker?

4. Why do you think both poems include religious ideas and images?

Extending

5. What images of your homeland would you cherish in your memory if you ever moved to another country?

Literature Connection

The **tone** *of a literary work expresses the writer's attitude toward a subject. Words such as* angry, sad, *or* humorous *can be used to describe tone.*

1. How does the speaker in "The Tropics in New York" indicate his feelings about his homeland?

2. What attitude does the speaker in "Exile" have toward her homeland?

3. How are the tones of the two poems different?

Activities

Writing a Letter

Imagine that you have to leave your native country—probably forever—and move to another country. Write a letter to a friend you are leaving behind. Express how you feel about both your former homeland and your new country. Be sure to include plenty of specific details about both places.

Performing a Skit

With a partner, perform a short improvisational skit about two immigrants who meet and strike up a conversation. Set your skit anywhere—at a deli, a soccer game, a barbecue. Concentrate on what the characters say, not what they do. Have the characters discuss how and why they immigrated and their feelings about their new country. Have them also explain their sense of exile. Perform your skit before the class.

TSALI OF THE CHEROKEES

BY NORAH ROPER, AS TOLD TO ALICE MARRIOTT

About the Selection

*Since the 1600s, white settlers had pushed Native Americans westward as they took more and more Indian land. By the early 1800s, about 100,000 Native Americans still lived east of the Mississippi River. Among them were the Cherokee, who lived in parts of Alabama, Georgia, North Carolina, and Tennessee. Many whites wanted their land. In 1827, the discovery of gold on Cherokee land increased demands by whites that the Native Americans be moved. In 1830, the U.S. government passed a law to force the **removal of American Indian peoples** from their homelands to reservations west of the Mississippi. In 1838, federal troops rounded up about 16,000 Cherokees and forced them into camps. Some, like the Cherokee farmer Tsali and his family, refused to go. As you read "Tsali of the Cherokee," examine why these Cherokees decide to resist being moved.*

They knew that their tribal chiefs traveled back and forth to the white man's place called Washington more often than they used to do. They knew that when the chiefs came back from that place, there were quarrels in the tribal council.

Up in the hills and the back country, where the *Ani Keetoowah*—the true Cherokees—lived, word of the changes came more slowly than the changes themselves came to the valley Cherokees. Many of the hill people never left their farm lands, and those who did went only to the nearest trading post and back. Few travelers ever came into the uplands, where the mists of the Smokies[1] shut out the **encroaching**[2] world.

So, when the news came that some of the chiefs of the Cherokees had touched the pen, and put their names or their marks on a paper, and agreed by doing so that this was no longer Cherokee country, the *Ani Keetoowah* could not believe what they heard. Surely, they said to each other, this news must be false. No Cherokee—not even a mixed-blood— would sign away his own and his people's lands. But that was what the chiefs had done.

Then the word came that the chiefs were even more divided among themselves and that not all of them had touched the pen. Some were not willing to move away to the new lands across the Mississippi and settle in the hills around Fort Gibson, Oklahoma.

"Perhaps we should hang on," the *Ani Keetoowah* said to one another. "Perhaps we will not have to go away after all." They waited and hoped, although they knew in their hearts that hope is the cruelest curse on mankind.

One of the leaders of the *Ani Keetoowah* was Tsali. The white men had trouble pronouncing his name, so they called him "Charley" or "Dutch." Tsali was a full blood, and so were his wife and their family. They were of the oldest *Keetoowah* Cherokee blood and would never have let themselves be shamed by having half-breed relatives.

Tsali and his four sons worked two hillsides and the valley between them, in the southern part of the hill country. Tsali and his wife and their

---

[1] Smokies—Great Smoky Mountains in North Carolina and Tennessee, which are part of the Appalachian Mountain system.

[2] **encroaching** (ehn•KROHCH•ihng)—advancing gradually or sneakily to take possession of something belonging to another.

youngest son lived in a log house at the head of the hollow. The others had their own homes, spread out along the hillsides. They grew corn and beans, a few English peas, squashes and pumpkins, tobacco and cotton, and even a little sugar cane and indigo.[3] Tsali's wife kept chickens in a fenced run away from the house.

The women gathered wild hemp[4] and spun it; they spun the cotton, and the wool from their sheep. Then they wove the thread into cloth, and sometimes in winter when their few cattle and the sheep had been cared for and the chickens fed and there was not much else to do, the men helped at the looms,[5] which they had built themselves. The women did all the cutting and the making of garments for the whole family.

> **THEY HAD HARDLY SEEN WHITE MAN'S METAL MONEY IN THEIR LIVES.**

Tsali and his family were not worldly rich, in the way that the chiefs and some of the Cherokees of the valley towns were rich. They had hardly seen white man's metal money in their lives. But Tsali's people never lacked for food, or good clothing, or safe shelter.

The missionaries seldom came into the uplands then. Tsali took his sons and their wives, and his own wife, to the great dance ground where the seven *Keetoowah* villages gathered each month at the time of the full moon. There they danced their prayers in time to the beating of the women's terrapin-shell[6] leg rattles, around and around the mound of packed white ashes on top of which bloomed the eternal fire that was the life of all the Cherokees.

The occasional missionaries fussed over the children. They gave them white men's names, so that by Tsali's time everyone had an Indian name and an English one. The Cherokees listened to the missionaries politely, for the missionaries were great gossips, and the Cherokees heard their news and ignored the rest of their words.

"You will have to go soon," said one white preacher to Tsali. "There's no hope this time. The lands have all been sold, and the Georgia troopers are moving in. You'll have to go west."

---

[3] indigo (IHN•dih•goh)—plant used to make dark blue dye.
[4] hemp—plant from which rough cloth and rope are made.
[5] looms—devices on which thread is woven to make cloth.
[6] terrapin-shell—turtle-shell.

TSALI AND HIS FAMILY WERE NOT WORLDLY RICH

▲

A Cherokee family is shown near their home in North Carolina around 1890.

"We'll never leave," Tsali answered. "This is our land and we belong to it. Who could take it from us—who would want it? It's hard even for us to farm here, and we're used to hill farming. The white men wouldn't want to come here—they'll want the rich lands in the valleys, if the lowland people will give them up."

"They want these hills more than any other land," the missionary said. He sounded almost threatening. "Don't you see, you poor ignorant Indian? They are finding gold—gold, man, gold—downstream in the lower *Keetoowah* country. That means that the source of the gold is in the headwaters of the rivers that flow from here down into the valleys. I've seen gold dust in those streams myself."

"Gold?" asked Tsali. "You mean this yellow stuff?" And he took a buckskin pouch out of the pouch that hung from his sash, and opened it. At the sight of the yellow dust the pouch contained, the missionary seemed to go a little crazy.

"That's it!" he cried. "Where did you get it? How did you find it? You'll be rich if you can get more."

"We find it in the rivers, as you said," Tsali replied. "We gather what we need to take to the trader. I have this now because I am going down to the valley in a few days, to get my wife some ribbons to trim her new dress."

"Show me where you got it," the missionary begged. "We can all be rich. I'll protect you from the other white men, if you make me your partner."

"No, I think I'd better not," said Tsali thoughtfully. "My sons are my partners, as I was my father's. We do not need another partner, and, as long as we have our old squirrel guns, we do not need to be protected. Thank you, but you can go on. We are better off as we are."

The missionary coaxed and threatened, but Tsali stood firm. In the end, the white man went away, without any gold except a pinch that Tsali gave him, because the missionary seemed to value the yellow dust even more than the trader did.

Then it was time to go to the trading post. When Tsali came in the store, the trader said to him, "Well, Chief, glad to see you. I hear you're a rich man these days."

"I have always been a rich man," Tsali answered. "I have my family and we all have our good health. We have land to farm, houses to live in,

This beaded shoulder bag was made by a Cherokee woman around the time of the removal. ▶

food on our tables, and enough clothes. Most of all, we have the love in our hearts for each other and our friends. Indeed, you are right. We are very rich."

"That's one way of looking at it," said the trader, "but it isn't what I was thinking about. From what I hear, there's gold on your land. You've got a gold mine."

"A gold man?" repeated Tsali. "I never heard of a gold man."

"No!" shouted the trader. "A gold mine, I said. A place where you can go and pick up gold."

"Oh, that!" Tsali exclaimed. "Yes, we have some places like that on our land. Here's some of the yellow dust we find there."

And he opened the pouch to show the trader. The trader had seen pinches of Tsali's gold dust before, and taken it in trade, without saying much about it. Now he went as crazy as the missionary. "Don't tell anybody else about this, Charley," he whispered, leaning over the counter. "We'll just keep it to ourselves. I'll help you work it out, and I'll keep the other white men away. We'll all be rich."

"Thank you," said Tsali, "but I don't believe I want to be rich that way. I just want enough of this stuff to trade you for ribbons and sugar."

"Oh, all right," answered the trader **sulkily**,[7] "have it your own way. But don't blame me if you're sorry afterwards."

"I won't blame anybody," said Tsali, and bought his ribbon.

A month later, when the Georgia **militia**[8] came riding up the valley to Tsali's house, the missionary and the trader were with them. The men all stopped in front of the house, and Tsali's wife came out into the dogtrot, the open-ended passage that divided the two halves of the house and made a cool breezeway where the family sat in warm weather. She spoke to the men.

"Won't you come in and sit down?"

"Where's the old man?" the militia captain asked.

"Why, he's working out in the fields," said Amanda. "Sit down and have a cool drink of water while I send the boy for him."

"Send the boy quickly," the captain ordered. "We'll wait in our saddles and not trouble to get down."

"All right, if you'd rather not," Amanda said. "Do you mind telling me why you're here?"

---

[7] **sulkily** (SUHL•kih•lee)—in a sullen or resentful manner.
[8] **militia** (muh•LIHSH•uh)—army of ordinary citizens instead of professional soldiers.

"We're here to put you off this place," said the captain. "Haven't you heard? This isn't Cherokee land any more; the chiefs signed it over to the government, and now it's open for settlement. One or the other of these two gentlemen will probably claim it."

"They can't do that!" Amanda protested. "It's our land—nobody else's. The chiefs had no right to sign it away. My husband's father worked this place, and his father before him. This is our home. This is where we belong."

> IT'S OUR LAND—
> NOBODY ELSE'S.
> THE CHIEFS HAD
> NO RIGHT TO
> SIGN IT AWAY.

"No more," said the captain. "You belong in the removal camps down by the river, with the rest of the Indians. They're going to start shipping the Cherokees west tomorrow morning."

Amanda sat down on the bench in the dogtrot with her legs trembling under her. "All of us?" she asked.

"Every one of you."

"Let me call my son and send him for his daddy," Amanda said.

"Hurry up!"

Amanda went into the house, calling to the boy, who was just four-teen and had been standing, listening, behind the door. She gave him his father's old squirrel gun, and he sneaked his own blowgun and darts and slid out the back of the house. Amanda went back to the dogtrot and sat and waited. She sat there and waited, while the missionary, the trader, and the captain quarreled about which of their wives should cook in her kitchen. She let them quarrel and hoped her men were all right.

Tsali and his older sons were working the overhill corn field, when the boy came panting up and told them what had happened.

"Is your mother all right?" Tsali asked.

"She was when I left," the boy answered.

"We'll hide in the woods till they're gone," Tsali told his older sons. "If they find us, they'll have to kill us to put us off this land."

"What about the women?" the oldest son asked.

"They'll be all right," Tsali answered. "Your mother's a quick-thinking woman; she'll take care of them. If we can hide in the caves by the river till dark, we'll go back then and get them."

They slipped away into the woods, downhill to the river, taking the boy with them, although he offered to go back and tell the white men he couldn't find his father.

All afternoon Amanda waited. Her daughters-in-law saw the strange men and horses in front of the big house and came to join her. At dusk, the captain gave up and ordered his men to make camp in the front yard. "We'll wait here until the men come back," he said.

With the white men camped all around the house, the women went into the kitchen and barred all the doors. It was a long time before the campfires made from the fence pickets ceased to blaze and began to smolder. It was a longer time until the women heard it—a scratch on the back door, so soft and so light that it would have embarrassed a mouse. Amanda slid back the bar, and Tsali and his sons slipped into the darkened room. There was just enough moonlight for them to make out each other's shapes.

"We came to get you," Tsali said. "Come quickly. Leave everything except your knives. Don't wait a minute."

Amanda and her daughters-in-law always wore their knives at their belts, so they were ready. One at a time, Tsali last, the whole family crept out of their home and escaped into the woods.

In the morning, when the white men stretched and scratched and woke, the *Ani Keetoowah* were gone.

It was spring, and the weather was warm, but the rain fell and soaked the Cherokees. They had brought no food, and they dared not fire a gun. One of the daughters-in-law was pregnant, and her time was close.

Amanda was stiff and crippled with rheumatism.[9] They gathered wild greens, for it was too early for berries or plums, and the men and boy trapped small animals and birds in string snares the women made by pulling out their hair and twisting it.

THE CHEROKEES WERE TIRED AND COLD AND HUNGRY, BUT THEY WERE SILENT.

Day by day, for four weeks, the starving family listened to white men beating through the woods. The Cherokees were tired and cold and hungry, but they were silent. They even began to hope that in time the white men would go away and the Indians would be safe.

---

[9] rheumatism (ROO•muh•tihz•uhm)—painful stiffness and swelling of the muscles and joints.

The famous American artist George Catlin (1796–1872) sketched these Cherokee men in their Southeastern homeland before their forced removal to Oklahoma.

It was not to be. One trooper brought his dog, and the dog caught the human scent. So the dog, with his man behind him, came sniffing into the cave, and Tsali and his family were caught before the men could pick up their loaded guns.

The militiamen shouted, and other white men came thudding through the woods. They tied the Cherokee men's hands behind them and bound them all together along a rope. The militiamen pushed Tsali and his sons through the woods. The women followed, weeping.

At last they were back at their own house, but they would not have recognized it. The troopers had plundered the garden and trampled the plants they didn't eat. The door from the kitchen into the dogtrot hung **askew**,[10] and the door to the main room had been wrenched off its hinges. Clothes and bedding lay in filthy piles around the yard. What the militiamen could not use, they ruined.

"Oh, my garden!" cried Amanda, and, when she saw the scattered feathers, "Oh, my little hens!"

---

[10] **askew** (uh•SKYOO)—twisted to one side.

"What are you going to do with us?" Tsali demanded.

"Take you down to the river. The last boat is loading today. There's still time to get you on it and out of here."

"I—will—not—go," Tsali said quietly. "You—nor you—nor you— nobody can make me go."

"Our orders are to take all the Cherokees. If any resist, shoot them."

"Shoot me, then!" cried Tsali. The captain raised his rifle.

"Stop!" Amanda screamed. She stepped over beside her husband. "If you shoot, shoot us both," she ordered. "Our lives have been one life since we were no older than our boy here. I don't want to go on living without my husband. And I cannot leave our home any more than he can. Shoot us both."

The four sons stepped forward. "We will die with our parents," the oldest one said. "Take our wives to the boat, if that is the only place where they can be safe, but we stay here." He turned to his wife and the other young women.

"That is my order as your husband," Tsali's son said. "You must go away to the west and make new lives for yourselves while you are still young enough to do so." The wives sobbed and held out their arms, but the husbands turned their backs on the women. "We will stay with our parents," all the young men said.

The young boy, too, stood with his brothers, beside his father. "Let this boy go," Tsali said to the white men. "He is so young. A man grows, and plants his seed, and his seed goes on. This is my seed. I planted it. My older sons and I have had our chances. They will leave children, and their names will never be forgotten. But this boy is too young. His seed has not ripened for planting yet. Let him go, to care for his sisters, on the way to the west."

"Very well," said the captain. "He can't do much harm if he does live." He turned to two militiamen. "Take the boy and the young women away," he ordered. "Keep them going till they come to the boats, and load them on board."

The young women and the boy, stunned and silenced, were driven down the road before they could say goodbye, nor would the trooper let them look back. Behind them, as they started on the long main road, they heard the sound of the shots.

Questions to Consider

Responding

1. If you were being made to leave your home by force, how would you react?

Analyzing

2. Why do you think Tsali and his family decide to resist their **forced removal** from their homelands?

3. What is the difference between Tsali's view of being rich and the views of the missionary and trader?

4. How does the story support the author's statement that "hope is the cruelest curse on mankind?"

5. Why do you think the Cherokee would wish to preserve the legend of Tsali?

Extending

6. Proposals have been made for compensating Native Americans whose ancestors were victims of white injustice. What is your opinion of such proposals?

Literature Connection

In literature, conflict is the struggle between opposing forces. It may be external, as in a struggle between two or more characters or between characters and an outside force, such as nature. It also may be internal, as in a struggle within a character about an issue or action.

1. What external conflicts are faced by Tsali and his family?

2. What internal conflicts do you think they are facing?

Activities

Writing a News Article

Norah Roper's grandfather, Sequoyah, created a writing system for the Cherokee. Sequoyah's alphabet was used in the first Native American newspaper, the Cherokee Phoenix. *Imagine that you are a reporter for the* Cherokee Phoenix *in 1828, its first year of publication. Write a news article about Sequoyah and his alphabet. Include the five Ws: who, what, when, where, and why.*

Front page of the
Cherokee Phoenix. ▶

The CIRCUIT

BY FRANCISCO JIMÉNEZ

About the Author

Four-year-old Francisco Jiménez (hih•MAY•nays) crossed the border between Mexico and California with his family in the late 1940s. He began a life as a poor farm worker, moving from camp to camp to follow the harvest. In 1997, he published the story of that existence, The Circuit: Stories from the Life of a Migrant Child. Growing up, learning was the only stable thing in his life. Today Jiménez is a professor at Santa Clara University. He teaches Spanish because he loves his native language and culture.

About the Selection

Large-scale farm production in this country requires the work of seasonal farmhands. These **migrant workers** often migrate, or move, from farm to farm. Migrant work doesn't attract people with good job skills or an education. The pay is typically very low and the living conditions are usually poor. Many poor, uneducated immigrants who don't speak English well take the work. Nearly all migrant workers are Mexican Americans. As you read "The Circuit," pay attention to the hardships faced by migrant workers.

It was that time of year again. Ito, the strawberry **sharecropper**,[1] did not smile. It was natural. The peak of the strawberry season was over and the last few days the workers, most of them *braceros*,[2] were not picking as many boxes as they had during the months of June and July.

As the last days of August disappeared, so did the number of *braceros*. Sunday, only one—the best picker— came to work. I liked him. Sometimes we talked during our half–hour lunch break. That is how I found out he was from Jalisco, the same state in Mexico my family was from. That Sunday was the last time I saw him.

_____

> **Everything we owned was neatly packed in cardboard boxes.**

_____

When the sun had tired and sunk behind the mountains, Ito signaled us that it was time to go home. *"Ya esora,"*[3] he yelled in his broken Spanish. Those were the words I waited for twelve hours a day, every day, seven days a week, week after week. And the thought of not hearing them again saddened me.

As we drove home, Papá did not say a word. With both hands on the wheel, he stared at the dirt road. My older brother, Roberto, was also silent. He leaned his head back and closed his eyes. Once in a while he cleared from his throat the dust that blew in from outside.

Yes, it was that time of year. When I opened the front door to the shack, I stopped. Everything we owned was neatly packed in cardboard boxes. Suddenly I felt even more the weight of hours, days, and months of work. I sat down on a box. The thought of having to move to Fresno[4] and knowing what was in store for me there brought tears to my eyes.

That night I could not sleep. I lay in bed thinking about how much I hated this move.

A little before five o'clock in the morning, Papá woke everyone up. A few minutes later, the yelling and screaming of my little brothers and sisters, for whom the move was a great adventure, broke the silence of dawn. Shortly, the barking of the dogs accompanied them.

_____

[1] **sharecropper**—farmer who gives a part of the crops to the landlord instead of rent; tenant farmer.

[2] *braceros* (brah•SEHR•ohs)—Mexican migrant workers; Spanish for "laborers."

[3] *Ya esora* (yah ehs•OH•rah)—broken Spanish for "It's time" (Ya es hora).

[4] Fresno (FREHZ•noh)—city in central California.

▲

Bernard Hoffmann (1913–1979) was a well-known photographer for *Life* magazine. He photographed this Mexican migrant worker in 1951.

right to be proud of it. He spent a lot of time looking at other cars before buying this one. When he finally chose the "Carcanchita," he checked it thoroughly before driving it out of the car lot. He examined every inch of the car. He listened to the motor, tilting his head from side to side like a parrot, trying to detect any noises that spelled car trouble. After being satisfied with the looks and sounds of the car, Papá then insisted on knowing who the original owner was. He never did find out from the car salesman, but he bought the car anyway. Papá figured the original owner must have been an important man because behind the rear seat of the car he found a blue necktie.

Papá parked the car out in front and left the motor running. *"Listo,"*[6] he yelled. Without saying a word, Roberto and I began to carry the boxes out to the car. Roberto carried the two big boxes and I carried the smaller ones. Papá threw the mattress on top of the car roof and tied it with ropes to the front and rear bumpers.

While we packed the breakfast dishes, Papá went outside to start the "Carcanchita."[5] That was the name Papá gave his old '38 black Plymouth. He bought it in a used-car lot in Santa Rosa in the winter of 1949. Papá was very proud of his car. *"Mi Carcanchita,"* my little jalopy, he called it. He had a

---

[5] Carcanchita—(kahr•kahn•CHEE•tah).

[6] *Listo* (LEES•toh)—Spanish for "ready."

The sun kept beating down.

Another *Life* photographer, Michael Rougier, took this picture of migrant farm workers picking grapes in 1959. ▶

Everything was packed except Mamá's pot. It was an old large **galvanized**[7] pot she had picked up at an army surplus store in Santa María the year I was born. The pot was full of many dents and nicks, and the more dents and nicks it had the more Mamá liked it. *"Mi olla,"*[8] she used to say proudly.

I held the front door open as Mamá carefully carried out her pot by both handles, making sure not to spill the cooked beans. When she got to the car, Papá reached out to help her with it. Roberto opened the rear car door and Papá gently placed it on the floor

---

[7] **galvanized** (GAL•vuh•nyzd)—coated with zinc to prevent rusting.
[8] *Mi olla* (mee OH•yah)—Spanish for "My pot."

behind the front seat. All of us then climbed in. Papá sighed, wiped the sweat off his forehead with his sleeve, and said wearily: "*Es todo.*"[9]

As we drove away, I felt a lump in my throat. I turned around and looked at our little shack for the last time.

At sunset we drove into a labor camp near Fresno. Since Papá did not speak English, Mamá asked the camp foreman if he needed any more workers. "We don't need no more," said the foreman, scratching his head. "Check with Sullivan down the road. Can't miss him. He lives in a big white house with a fence around it."

When we got there, Mamá walked up to the house. She went through a white gate, past a row of rose bushes, up the stairs to the front door. She rang the doorbell. The porch light went on and a tall husky man came out. They exchanged a few words. After the man went in, Mamá clasped her hands and hurried back to the car. "We have work! Mr. Sullivan said we can stay there the whole season," she said, gasping and pointing to an old garage near the stables.

The garage was worn out by the years. It had no windows. The walls, eaten by termites, strained to support the roof full of holes. The loose dirt floor, populated by earthworms, looked like a gray road map.

That night, by the light of a kerosene lamp, we unpacked and cleaned our new home. Roberto swept away the loose dirt, leaving the hard ground. Papá plugged the holes in the walls with old newspapers and tin can tops. Mamá fed my little brothers and sisters. Papá and Roberto then brought in the mattress and placed it on the far corner of the garage. "Mamá, you and the little ones sleep on the mattress. Roberto, Panchito, and I will sleep outside under the trees," Papá said.

Early next morning Mr. Sullivan showed us where his crop was, and after breakfast, Papá, Roberto, and I headed for the vineyard to pick.

Around nine o'clock the temperature had risen to almost one hundred degrees. I was completely soaked in sweat and my mouth felt as if I had been chewing on a handkerchief. I walked over to the end of the row, picked up the jug of water we had brought, and began drinking. "Don't drink too much; you'll get sick,"

---

[9] *Es todo* (ehs TOH•doh)—Spanish for "That's everything" or "That's all."

Roberto shouted. No sooner had he said that than I felt sick to my stomach. I dropped to my knees and let the jug roll off my hands. I remained motionless with my eyes glued on the hot sandy ground. All I could hear was the **drone**[10] of insects. Slowly I began to recover. I poured water over my face and neck and watched the dirty water run down my arms to the ground.

I still felt a little dizzy when we took a break to eat lunch. It was past two o'clock and we sat underneath a large walnut tree that was on the side of the road. While we ate, Papá jotted down the number of boxes we had picked. Roberto drew designs on the ground with a stick. Suddenly I noticed Papá's face turn pale as he looked down the road. "Here comes the school bus," he whispered loudly in alarm. **Instinctively**,[11] Roberto and I ran and hid in the vineyards. We did not want to get in trouble for not going to school. The yellow bus stopped in front of Mr. Sullivan's house. Two neatly dressed boys about my age got off. They carried books under their arms. After they crossed the street, the bus drove away. Roberto and I came out from hiding and joined Papá. *"Tienen que tener cuidado,"*[12] he warned us.

After lunch we went back to work. The sun kept beating down. The buzzing insects, the wet sweat, and the hot dry dust made the afternoon seem to last forever. Finally the mountains around the valley reached out and swallowed the sun. Within an hour it was too dark to continue picking. The vines blanketed the grapes, making it difficult to see the bunches. *"Vámonos,"*[13] said Papá, signaling to us that it was time to quit work. Papá then took out a pencil and began to figure out how much we had earned our first day. He wrote down numbers, crossed some out, wrote down some more. *"Quince,"*[14] he murmured.

When we arrived home, we took a cold shower underneath a waterhose. We then sat down to eat dinner around some wooden crates that served as a table. Mamá had cooked a special meal for us. We had rice and tortillas with *"carne con chile,"*[15] my favorite dish.

---

[10] **drone**—humming sound.

[11] **Instinctively** (ihn•STIHNGK•tihv•lee)—done without thinking.

[12] *Tienen . . . cuidado*—(tyeh•NEHN keh teh•NEHR kwee•DAH•daw) Spanish for "You have to be careful."

[13] *Vámonos* (VAH•moh•nos)—Spanish for "Let's go."

[14] *Quince* (KEEN•seh)—Spanish for "fifteen."

[15] *tortillas* (tawr•TEE•yahs) with *carne con chile* (KAHR•neh kawn CHEE•leh)—cornmeal pancakes with a stew of meat and peppers.

The next morning I could hardly move. My body ached all over. I felt little control over my arms and legs. This feeling went on every morning for days until my muscles finally got used to the work.

It was Monday, the first week of November. The grape season was over and I could now go to school. I woke up early that morning and lay in bed, looking at the stars and **savoring**[16] the thought of not going to work and of starting sixth grade for the first time that year. Since I could not sleep, I decided to get up and join Papá and Roberto at breakfast. I sat at the table across from Roberto, but I kept my head down. I did not want to look up and face him. I knew he was sad. He was not going to school today. He was not going tomorrow, or next week or next month. He would not go until the cotton season was over, and that was sometime in February. I rubbed my hands together and watched the dry, acid stained skin fall to the floor in little rolls.

When Papá and Roberto left for work, I felt relief. I walked to the top of a small grade next to the shack and watched the "Carcanchita" disappear in the distance in a cloud of dust.

Two hours later, around eight o'clock, I stood by the side of the road waiting for school bus number twenty. When it arrived I climbed in. Everyone was busy either talking or yelling. I sat in an empty seat in the back.

When the bus stopped in front of the school, I felt very nervous. I looked out the bus window and saw boys and girls carrying books under their arms. I put my hands in my pant pockets and walked to the principal's office. When I entered I heard a woman's voice say: "May I help you?" I was startled. I had

> The grape season was over and I could now go to school.

not heard English for months. For a few seconds I remained speechless. I looked at the lady who waited for my answer. My first instinct was to answer her in Spanish, but I held back. Finally, after struggling for English words, I managed to tell her that I wanted to enroll in the sixth grade. After answering many questions, I was led to the classroom.

Mr. Lema, the sixth grade teacher, greeted me and assigned me a desk. He then introduced me to the class. I was so nervous and scared at that

---

[16] **savoring** (SAY•vuhr•ihng)—deeply enjoying.

moment when everyone's eyes were on me that I wished I were with Papá and Roberto picking cotton. After taking roll, Mr. Lema gave the class the assignment for the first hour. "The first thing we have to do this morning is finish reading the story we began yesterday," he said enthusiastically. He walked up to me, handed me an English book, and asked me to read. "We are on page 125," he said politely. When I heard this, I felt my blood rush to my head; I felt dizzy. "Would you like to read?" he asked hesitantly. I opened the book to page 125. My mouth was dry. My eyes began to water. I could not begin. "You can read later," Mr. Lema said understandingly.

For the rest of the reading period, I kept getting angrier and angrier at myself. I should have read, I thought to myself.

During recess I went into the restroom and opened my English book to page 125. I began to read in a low voice, pretending I was in class. There were many words I did not know. I closed the book and headed back to the classroom.

Mr. Lema was sitting at his desk correcting papers. When I entered he looked up at me and smiled. I felt better. I walked up to him and asked if he could help me with the new words. "Gladly," he said.

The rest of the month I spent my lunch hours working on English with Mr. Lema, my best friend at school.

One Friday during lunch hour, Mr. Lema asked me to take a walk with him to the music room. "Do you like music?" he asked me as we entered the building.

"Yes, I like Mexican corridos,"[17] I answered. He then picked up a trumpet, blew on it and handed it to me. The sound gave me goose bumps. I knew that sound. I had heard it in many Mexican corridos. "How would you like to learn how to play it?" he asked. He must have read my face because before I could answer, he added: "I'll teach you how to play it during our lunch hours."

That day I could hardly wait to get home to tell Papá and Mamá the great news. As I got off the bus, my little brothers and sisters ran up to meet me. They were yelling and screaming. I thought they were happy to see me, but when I opened the door to our shack, I saw that everything we owned was neatly packed in cardboard boxes.

[17] corridos (koh•REE•dohs)—Mexican songs that tell a story; ballads.

Responding

1. The narrator is the person who tells the story. In what ways is your life similar to the narrator's life and in what ways is it different?

Analyzing

2. A circuit is a circular path around an area. How are the events of this story like a circular path?

3. How do you think these **migrant workers** might identify their homeland?

4. When the author describes Sullivan's house and then the garage, what is the effect on you as a reader?

5. Why do you think the narrator loves school so much?

Extending

6. What do you think should be done to ensure a decent life for migrant workers?

Literature Connection

Imagery consists of words and phrases that appeal to the five senses. Writers use sensory details to help readers imagine how things look, feel, smell, sound, and taste.

1. In "The Circuit," how does the writer use imagery to describe what the narrator sees while working in the fields?

2. How does he use imagery to describe what the narrator hears?

3. What other kinds of imagery does the writer use to describe what the narrator experiences working in the fields?

Activity

Writing a Descriptive Essay

One piece of advice often given to writers is "show, don't tell." This means that it is more effective to describe what is happening, rather than to state what is happening. In "The Circuit," for example, the author doesn't state that the boy's life was hard. He shows the readers this through the use of imagery. Write a descriptive essay about a school experience you had. Include imagery to bring your readers into the experience.

THE WAR OF THE WALL

by Toni Cade Bambara

About the Author

Toni Cade Bambara (1939–1996) was born in New York City. Her education included study of mime, theater, dance, and film. Bambara was one of several African-American writers in the 1960s and 1970s who combined writing and political activism. She worked for community projects and literacy programs, and directed films and plays about social issues. She produced several collections of short stories and two novels. Her novel The Salt Eaters won the American Book Award in 1981.

About the Selection

Toni Cade Bambara believed that authors "are everyday people who write stories that come out of their **neighborhoods**." She wrote about African Americans who show family pride and a strong sense of community. Her stories also often include women who are community activists, as she was. Sometimes these activists meet resistance from the neighborhood people they want to help. In "The War of the Wall," an unknown woman arrives in an African-American neighborhood. She wants to improve at least one wall of that neighborhood. As you read the story, think about how the community reacts to the stranger and her actions.

Me and Lou had no time for courtesies. We were late for school. So we just flat out told the painter lady to quit messing with the wall. It was our wall, and she had no right coming into our neighborhood painting on it. Stirring in the paint bucket and not even looking at us, she mumbled something about Mr. Eubanks, the barber, giving her permission. That had nothing to do with it as far as we were concerned. We've been pitching pennies against that wall since we were little kids. Old folks have been dragging their chairs out to sit in the shade of the wall for years. Big kids have been playing handball against the wall since so-called integration[1] when the crazies 'cross town poured cement in our pool so we couldn't use it. I'd sprained my neck one time boosting my cousin Lou up to chisel Jimmy Lyons's name into the wall when we found out he was never coming home from the war in Vietnam to take us fishing.

"If you lean close," Lou said, leaning hipshot against her beat-up car, "you'll get a whiff of bubble gum and kids' sweat. And that'll tell you something—that this wall belongs to the kids of Taliaferro Street." I thought Lou sounded very convincing. But the painter lady paid us no mind. She just snapped the brim of her straw hat down and hauled her bucket up the ladder.

"You're not even from around here," I hollered up after her. The license plates on her old piece of car said "New York." Lou dragged me away because I was about to grab hold of that ladder and shake it. And then we'd really be late for school.

"YOU'RE NOT EVEN FROM AROUND HERE," I HOLLERED UP AFTER HER.

When we came from school, the wall was slick with white. The painter lady was running string across the wall and taping it here and there. Me and Lou leaned against the gumball machine outside the pool hall and watched. She had strings up and down and back and forth. Then she began chalking them with a hunk of blue chalk.

The Morris twins crossed the street, hanging back at the curb next to the beat-up car. The twin with the red ribbons was hugging a jug of cloudy lemonade. The one with yellow ribbons was holding a plate of dinner away

---

[1] integration—in this case, policies and laws enacted in the 1960s that forbid separation of races in public places.

from her dress. The painter lady began snapping the strings. The blue chalk dust measured off halves and quarters up and down and sideways too. Lou was about to say how hip it all was, but I dropped my book satchel on his toes to remind him we were at war.

Some good aromas were drifting our way from the plate leaking pot likker[2] onto the Morris girl's white socks. I could tell from where I stood that under the tinfoil was baked ham, collard greens, and candied yams. And knowing Mrs. Morris,

> ## THE PAINTER LADY WAS GIVING A SHOW.

who sometimes bakes for my mama's restaurant, a slab of buttered cornbread was probably up under there too, sopping up some of the pot likker. Me and Lou rolled our eyes, wishing somebody would send us some dinner. But the painter lady didn't even turn around. She was pulling the strings down and prying bits of tape loose.

Side Pocket came strolling out of the pool hall to see what Lou and me were studying so hard. He gave the painter lady the once-over, checking out her paint-spattered jeans, her chalky T-shirt, her floppy-brimmed straw hat. He hitched up his pants and glided over toward the painter lady, who kept right on with what she was doing.

"Whatcha got there, sweetheart?" he asked the twin with the plate.

"Suppah," she said all soft and countrylike.

"For her," the one with the jug added, jerking her chin toward the painter lady's back.

Still she didn't turn around. She was rearing back on her heels, her hands jammed into her back pockets, her face squinched up like the masterpiece she had in mind was taking shape on the wall by magic. We could have been gophers crawled up into a rotten hollow for all she cared. She didn't even say hello to anybody. Lou was muttering something about how great her concentration was. I butt him with my hip, and his elbow slid off the gum machine.

"Good evening," Side Pocket said in his best ain't-I-fine voice. But the painter lady was moving from the milk crate to the step stool to the ladder, moving up and down fast, scribbling all over the wall like a crazy person. We looked at Side Pocket. He looked at the twins. The twins looked at us. The painter lady was giving a show. It was like those old-timey

---

[2] pot likker—juices from cooked food.

music movies where the dancer taps on the tabletop and then starts jumping all over the furniture, kicking chairs over and not skipping a beat. She didn't even look where she was stepping. And for a minute there, hanging on the ladder to reach a far spot, she looked like she was going to tip right over.

"Ahh," Side Pocket cleared his throat and moved fast to catch the ladder. "These young ladies here have brought you some supper."

"Ma'am?" The twins stepped forward. Finally the painter turned around, her eyes "full of sky," as my grandmama would say. Then she stepped down like she was in a trance. She wiped her hands on her jeans as the Morris twins offered up the plate and the jug. She rolled back the tinfoil, then wagged her head as though something terrible was on the plate.

"Thank your mother very much," she said, sounding like her mouth was full of sky too. "I've brought my own dinner along." And then, without even excusing herself, she went back up the ladder, drawing on the wall in a wild way. Side Pocket whistled one of those

▲
This mural, titled *Tuzuri Watu* (Swahili, "We Are a Beautiful People"), was painted in 1987 in San Francisco by Brooke Fancher.

oh-brother breathy whistles and went back into the pool hall. The Morris twins shifted their weight from one foot to the other, then crossed the street and went home. Lou had to drag me away, I was so mad. We couldn't wait to get to the firehouse to tell my daddy all about this rude woman who'd stolen our wall.

All the way back to the block to help my mama out at the restaurant, me and Lou kept asking my daddy for ways to run the painter lady out of town. But my daddy was busy talking about the trip to the country and telling Lou he could come too because Grandmama can always use an extra pair of hands on the farm.

L ater that night, while me and Lou were in the back doing our chores, we found out that the painter lady was a liar. She came into the restaurant and leaned against the glass of the steam table, talking about how starved she was. I was scrubbing pots and Lou was chopping onions, but we could hear her through the service window. She was asking Mama was that a ham hock in the greens, and was that a neck bone in the pole beans, and were there any

vegetables cooked without meat, especially pork.

"I don't care who your spiritual leader is," Mama said in that way of hers. "If you eat in the community, sistuh, you gonna eat pig by-and-by, one way or t'other."

Me and Lou were cracking up in the kitchen, and several customers at the counter were clearing their throats, waiting for Mama to really fix her wagon for not speaking to the elders when she came in. The painter lady took a stool at the counter and went right on with her questions. Was there cheese in the baked macaroni, she wanted to know? Were there eggs in the salad? Was it honey or sugar in the iced tea? Mama was fixing Pop Johnson's plate. And every time the painter lady asked a fool question, Mama would dump another spoonful of rice on the pile. She was tapping her foot and heating up in a dangerous way. But Pop Johnson was happy as he could be. Me and Lou peeked through the service window, wondering what planet the painter lady came from. Who ever heard of baked macaroni without cheese, or potato salad without eggs?

"Do you have any bread made with unbleached flour?" the painter lady asked Mama. There was a long pause, as though everybody in the restaurant was holding their breath, wondering if Mama would dump the next spoonful on the painter lady's head. She didn't. But when she set Pop Johnson's plate down, it came down with a bang.

When Mama finally took her order, the starving lady all of a sudden couldn't make up her mind whether she wanted a vegetable plate or fish and a salad. She finally settled on the broiled trout and a tossed salad. But just when Mama reached for a plate to serve her, the painter lady leaned over the counter with her finger all up in the air.

"Excuse me," she said. "One more thing." Mama was holding the plate like a Frisbee, tapping that foot, one hand on her hip. "Can I get raw beets in that tossed salad?"

"You will get," Mama said, leaning her face close to the painter lady's, "whatever Lou back there tossed. Now sit down." And the painter lady sat back down on her stool and shut right up.

All the way to the country, me and Lou tried to get Mama to open fire on the painter lady. But Mama said that seeing as how she was from the North, you couldn't expect her to have any manners. Then Mama said she was sorry she'd been so impatient

with the woman because she seemed like a decent person and was simply trying to stick to a very strict diet. Me and Lou didn't want to hear that. Who did that lady think she was, coming into our neighborhood and taking over our wall?

"Wellllll," Mama **drawled**,[3] pulling into the filling station so Daddy could take the wheel, "It's hard on an artist, ya know. They can't always get people to look at their work. So she's just doing her work in the open, that's all."

Me and Lou definitely did not want to hear that. Why couldn't she set up an easel downtown or draw on the sidewalk in her own neighborhood? Mama told us to quit fussing so much; she was tired and wanted to rest. She climbed into the back seat and dropped down into the warm hollow Daddy had made in the pillow.

> ALL WEEKEND LONG, ME AND LOU TRIED TO SCHEME UP WAYS TO RECAPTURE OUR WALL.

All weekend long, me and Lou tried to **scheme**[4] up ways to recapture our wall. Daddy and Mama said

---

[3] **drawled**—spoke with drawn-out vowels.
[4] **scheme**—make plans, especially secret ones.

Bernard Williams painted this mural, titled *Feed Your Child the Truth*, in Chicago in 1994.
▼

I DEDICATE
THIS WALL OF RESPECT

they were sick of hearing about it. Grandmama turned up the TV to drown us out. On the late news was a story about the New York subways. When a train came roaring into the station all covered from top to bottom, windows too, with writings and drawings done with spray paint, me and Lou slapped five. Mama said it was too bad kids in New York had nothing better to do than spray paint all over the trains. Daddy said that

in the cities, even grown-ups wrote all over the trains and buildings too. Daddy called it "graffiti." Grandmama called it a shame.

We couldn't wait to get out of school on Monday. We couldn't find any black spray paint anywhere. But in a junky hardware store downtown we found a can of white epoxy[5] paint, the kind you touch up old refrigerators

---

[5] epoxy (ih•PAHK•see)—plastic resin used in glues and paints.

with when they get splotchy and peely. We spent our whole allowance on it. And because it was too late to use our bus passes, we had to walk all the way home lugging our book satchels and gym shoes, and the bag with the epoxy.

When we reached the corner of Taliaferro and Fifth, it looked like a block party or something. Half the neighborhood was gathered on the sidewalk in front of the wall. I looked at Lou, he looked at me. We both looked at the bag with the epoxy and wondered how we were going to work our scheme. The painter lady's car was nowhere in sight. But there were too many people standing around to do anything. Side Pocket and his buddies were leaning on their cue sticks, hunching each other. Daddy was there with a lineman[6] he catches a ride with on Mondays. Mrs. Morris had her arms flung around the shoulders of the twins on either side of her. Mama was talking with some of her customers, many of them with napkins still at the throat. Mr. Eubanks came out of the barbershop, followed by a man in a striped poncho, half his face shaved, the other half full of foam.

"She really did it, didn't she?" Mr. Eubanks huffed out his chest. Lots of folks answered right quick that she surely did when they saw the straight razor in his hand.

Mama **beckoned**[7] us over. And then we saw it. The wall. Reds, greens, figures outlined in black. Swirls of purple and orange. Storms of blues and yellows. It was something. I recognized some of the faces right off. There was Martin Luther King, Jr. And there was a man with glasses on and his mouth open like he was laying down a heavy rap. Daddy came up alongside and reminded us that that was Minister Malcolm X. The serious woman with a rifle I knew was Harriet Tubman because my grandmama has pictures of her all over the house. And I knew Mrs. Fannie Lou Hamer[8] 'cause a signed photograph of her hangs in the restaurant next to the calendar.

Then I let my eyes follow what looked like a vine. It trailed past a man with a horn, a woman with a big white flower in her hair, a handsome dude in a tuxedo seated at a piano, and a man with a goatee holding a

---

[6] **lineman**—person who installs or maintains telephone or electric power lines.

[7] **beckoned**—invited or summoned with a gesture such as a wave or nod.

[8] Mrs. Fannie Lou Hamer—(1917–1977) African-American civil rights leader.

book. When I looked more closely, I realized that what had looked like flowers were really faces. One face with yellow petals looked just like Frieda Morris. One with red petals looked just like Hattie Morris. I could hardly believe my eyes.

"Notice," Side Pocket said, stepping close to the wall with his cue stick like a classroom pointer. "These are the flags of **liberation**,"[9] he said in a voice I'd never heard him use before. We all stepped closer while he pointed and spoke. "Red, black and green," he said, his pointer falling on the leaflike flags of the vine. "Our liberation flag. And here Ghana, there Tanzania. Guinea-Bissau, Angola, Mozambique."[10] Side Pocket sounded very tall, as though he'd been waiting all his life to give this lesson.

Mama tapped us on the shoulder and pointed to a high section of the wall. There was a fierce-looking man with his arms crossed against his chest guarding a bunch of children. His muscles bulged, and he looked a lot like my daddy. One kid was looking at a row of books. Lou hunched me 'cause the kid looked like me. The one that looked like Lou was spinning a globe on the tip of his finger like a basketball. There were other kids

there with microscopes and compasses. And the more I looked, the more it looked like the fierce man was not so much guarding the kids as defending their right to do what they were doing.

Then Lou gasped and dropped the paint bag and ran forward, running his hands over a rainbow. He had to tiptoe and stretch to do it, it was so high. I couldn't breathe either. The painter lady had found the chisel marks and had painted Jimmy Lyons's name in a rainbow.

"Read the **inscription**,[11] honey," Mrs. Morris said, urging little Frieda forward. She didn't have to urge much. Frieda marched right up, bent down, and in a loud voice that made everybody quit oohing and ahhing and listen, she read,

To the People of Taliaferro Street
I Dedicate This Wall of Respect
Painted in Memory of My Cousin
Jimmy Lyons

---

[9] **liberation** (lihb•uh•RAY•shuhn)—state of freedom achieved after a struggle.

[10] **Ghana . . . Mozambique**—African countries that were former European colonies and achieved independence in the 1950s, '60s, and '70s.

[11] **inscription** (ihn•SKRIHP•shuhn)—short message written or carved on a surface.

Questions to Consider

Responding

1. Have you ever misjudged someone's actions and ideas? How did you feel later when you discovered you were wrong about that person?

Analyzing

2. Why do the narrator and Lou feel protective about the wall?

3. How do the interactions of the characters tell you whether they are part of the **neighborhood** or not?

4. What effect do you think the mural will have on the life of the neighborhood?

Extending

5. How would you react if someone apparently very different from you and your neighbors moved into your neighborhood and tried to change something there?

Literature Connection

A story's plot is the series of related events that make up the story. The plot includes all the action, everything that happens in the story. Typically, a plot begins with exposition that introduces the characters and the conflict they face. Complications arise as the characters try to resolve the conflict. Eventually, the plot reaches a climax, the point of greatest interest or suspense. In the resolution that follows, loose ends are tied up and the story is brought to a close.

1. What is the conflict in "The War of the Wall"?

2. What complications develop as the narrator and Lou attempt to resolve the conflict?

3. Where does the climax occur?

4. How is the conflict resolved?

Activities

Writing a Parable

Toni Cade Bambara said she often wrote to "lift up a few useable truths." Stories that teach a truth or a lesson are called parables. Most of Bambara's stories were set in the streets she knew, with characters based on people she knew. Write a parable that takes place in your neighborhood. Use the people and situations you know as the basis of your story. Aim to "lift up a few useable truths" for your readers. You may want to start by identifying the central conflict in the story. Then determine what the characters learn by dealing with that conflict.

Researching Public Art

Beginning in the 1960s, public art in the form of murals has been used to protest against social injustices such as racism, and to promote positive ideas such as neighborhood pride. Using the Internet and library resource books, research community murals. Summarize your findings and gather images of several murals. Then present your information in a bulletin board display or as a website on the topic. If you like, focus on one muralist, on the murals in one city, or on murals that reflect the concerns of one cultural group.

Part Two

Traditions

Every ethnic group has its traditions, which might be preserved in legends and folktales, in customs, in art, or simply in the memories of individuals who pass on these traditions to new generations.

◀ Costumed dancers make their grand entry at one of the Native American gatherings known as powwows.

The Negro Speaks of Rivers

by Langston Hughes

About the Author

Langston Hughes (1902–1967) was born in Joplin, Missouri, and traveled widely as a young man. He finally made his home in Harlem. He attended Columbia University and received his degree from Lincoln University in Pennsylvania. Hughes was the first African American to support himself entirely from his writing. He wrote novels, short stories, plays, song lyrics, essays, and radio scripts, but is best known for his poetry. Wherever Hughes went, he wrote poetry in jazz clubs, letting the rhythm of the music emerge in his writing.

About the Selections

The term **roots** has a dual meaning. If you ask someone, "Where are your roots," that person will probably tell you the place of his or her birth and childhood. If you ask someone, "What are your roots," that person will probably tell you about the land and culture of his or her ancestors; to find your roots means "to discover your ancestry." As you read "The Negro Speaks of Rivers" and "Ancestors" (page 70), decide what each poet has to say about the importance of roots.

I've known rivers:
I've known rivers ancient as the world and older than the flow of human
   blood in human veins.

My soul has grown deep like the rivers.

I bathed in the Euphrates when dawns were young.
I built my hut near the Congo and it lulled me to sleep.
I looked upon the Nile[1] and raised the pyramids above it.
I heard the singing of the Mississippi when Abe Lincoln went down to New
   Orleans,[2] and I've seen its muddy bosom turn all golden in the sunset.

I've known rivers:
Ancient, dusky rivers.

My soul has grown deep like the rivers.

---

[1] Euphrates (yoo•FRAY•teez) . . . Congo . . . Nile—great rivers of Asia and Africa.
[2] Abe Lincoln . . . New Orleans—Abraham Lincoln traveled down the Mississippi to New Orleans on a flatboat in 1828.
His opposition to slavery was said to have begun from his first sight of it on this journey.

my soul
has grown deep

◀ A mounted king is shown with his attendants in this
bronze plaque made by the Benin people of West Africa.

Ancestors

By Dudley Randall

About the Author

Born in Washington, D.C., in 1914, African-American poet Dudley Randall moved to Detroit at age seven. His first published poem appeared in the Detroit Free Press when he was thirteen. He earned degrees from two Michigan universities and worked as a librarian before founding Detroit Broadside Press in 1965. Randall's publishing company helped make several African-American poets famous. He was named Detroit's poet laureate in 1981. One of his most celebrated poems is "Ballad of Birmingham," which is about the 1963 Alabama church bombing that killed four young girls.

Why are our ancestors
always kings or princes
and never the common people?

Was the Old Country a democracy
where every man was a king?
Or did the slavecatchers
take only the **aristocracy**[3]
and leave the fieldhands
laborers
streetcleaners
garbage collectors
dishwashers

---

[3] **aristocracy** (ar•ih•STAHK•ruh•see)—nobility; ruling class.

cooks
and maids
behind?

My own ancestor
(research reveals)
was a swineherd
who tended the pigs
in the Royal Pigstye
and slept in the mud
among the hogs.

Yet I'm as proud of him
as of any king or prince
dreamed up in fantasies
of bygone glory.

This young woman is costumed as a queen at a Gullah festival. The Gullah are a people of African descent who live in the Sea Islands and coastal regions of South Carolina, Georgia, and northern Florida. ▶

Responding

1. Why do you think African Americans might see a particular importance in finding their **roots**?

Analyzing

2. According to the speaker in "The Negro Speaks of Rivers," where are the roots of African Americans?

3. With whom is the speaker identifying in the line "I looked upon the Nile and raised the pyramids above it"?

4. How does the repetition of the phrases "I've known rivers" and "My soul has grown deep like the rivers" affect the feeling created by this poem?

5. What is the speaker in "Ancestors" saying about why people search for roots?

Extending

6. What do you consider to be your roots?

The **tone** *of a literary work expresses the writer's attitude toward a subject. Words such as* angry, sad, *or* humorous *can be used to describe tone.*

1. What common subject is shared by "The Negro Speaks of Rivers" and "Ancestors"?

2. What words would you use to describe the tone of "The Negro Speaks of Rivers"?

3. What words would you use to describe the tone of "Ancestors"?

Writing an Essay

The television miniseries "Roots: The Saga of an American Family" aired in 1977 to a record number of viewers. The miniseries was based on Alex Haley's Pulitzer Prize-winning novel, which traced seven generations of African Americans back to their African ancestry. The book and miniseries started a new interest in genealogy, the tracing of ancestry, particularly among African Americans. Using the Reader's Guide to Periodical Literature, *read articles written at the time the series came out. Then write an essay summarizing why the book and miniseries were so popular at that time.*

◀ Kunta Kinte (played by LeVar Burton), a West African kidnapped by slave traders, is shown in this scene from *Roots*.

High Horse's Courting

BY BLACK ELK AND JOHN NEIHARDT

About the Author

Black Elk (1863–1950) was a holy man of the Oglala Sioux (oh•GLAH•lah soo), a Native American people of the northern Great Plains. During his lifetime, the nomadic way of life of the Plains Indians ended as they were forced onto reservations. Black Elk was able to preserve accounts of his visionary experiences, of Sioux culture, and of their struggle against white domination. He told his life story to the poet John G. Neihardt (1881–1973). Black Elk's son and Neihardt's daughters helped to translate and record Black Elk's words. Neihardt used the translation as the basis of the book Black Elk Speaks, which was first published in 1932. "High Horse's Courting" is from that book.

About the Selection

*The traditional beliefs and practices that govern the way people enter into marriage are called **courtship customs**. Historically, most cultures had courtship customs that outlined strict patterns of behavior for potential marriage partners. In most modern societies, there are few socially directed forms of conduct to help guide people toward matrimony. As you read "High Horse's Courting," be aware of the habits and expectations of the Sioux regarding marriage.*

You know, in the old days, it was not so very easy to get a girl when you wanted to be married. Sometimes it was hard work for a young man and he had to stand a great deal. Say I am a young man and I have seen a young girl who looks so beautiful to me that I feel all sick when I think about her. I can not just go and tell her about it and then get married if she is willing. I have to be a very sneaky fellow to talk to her at all, and after I have managed to talk to her, that is only the beginning.

Probably for a long time I have been feeling sick about a certain girl because I love her so much, but she will not even look at me, and her parents keep a good watch over her. But I keep feeling worse and worse all the time; so maybe I sneak up to her tepee[1] in the dark and wait until she comes out. Maybe I just wait there all night and don't get any sleep at all and she does not come out. Then I feel sicker than ever about her.

Maybe I hide in the brush by a spring where she sometimes goes to get water, and when she comes by, if nobody is looking, then I jump out and hold her and just make her listen to me. If she likes me too, I can tell that from the way she acts, for she is very bashful and maybe will not say a word or even look at me the first time. So I let her go, and then maybe I sneak around until I can see her father alone, and I tell him how many horses I can give him for his beautiful girl, and by now I am feeling so sick that maybe I would give him all the horses in the world if I had them.

Well, this young man I am telling about was called High Horse, and there was a girl in the village who looked so beautiful to him that he was just sick all over from thinking about her so much and he was getting sicker all the time. The girl was very shy, and her parents thought a great deal of her because they were not young any more and this was the only child they had. So they watched her all day long, and they fixed it so that she would be safe at night too when they were asleep. They thought so much of her that they had made a rawhide bed for her to sleep in, and after they knew that High Horse was sneaking around after her, they took rawhide thongs[2] and tied the girl in bed at night so that nobody could steal her when they were asleep, but they were not sure but that their girl might really want to be stolen.

---

[1] tepee (TEE•pee)—cone-shaped tent of animal hide traditionally used by Plains Indian peoples.

[2] thongs—narrow leather strips used for binding.

Well, after High Horse had been sneaking around a good while and hiding and waiting for the girl and getting sicker all the time, he finally caught her alone and made her talk to him. Then he found out that she liked him maybe a little. Of course this did not make him feel well. It made him sicker than ever, but now he felt as brave as a bison bull, and so he went right to her father and said he loved the girl so much that he would give two good horses for her— one of them young and the other one not so very old.

But the old man just waved his hand, meaning for High Horse to go away and quit talking foolishness like that.

High Horse was feeling sicker than ever about it; but there was another young fellow who said he would loan High Horse two ponies and when he got some more horses, why, he could just give them back for the ones he had borrowed.

Then High Horse went back to the old man and said he would give four horses for the girl—two of them young and the other two not hardly old at all. But the old man just waved his hand and would not say anything.

So High Horse sneaked around until he could talk to the girl again, and he asked her to run away with him. He told her he thought he would just fall over and die if she did not. But she said she would not do that; she wanted to be bought like a fine woman. You see she thought a great deal of herself too.

A Lakota warrior approaches a young woman in this painting done in the late 1800s. Both carry umbrellas, a Plains Indian fashion at the time. Indian artists used the pages of ledgers such as this one to create their paintings. ▶

The girl was very shy.

That made High Horse feel so very sick that he could not eat a bit, and he went around with his head hanging down as though he might just fall down and die any time.

Red Deer was another young fellow, and he and High Horse were great comrades, always doing things together. Red Deer saw how High Horse was acting, and he said:

"Cousin, what is the matter? Are you sick in the belly? You look as though you were going to die."

Then High Horse told Red Deer how it was, and said he thought he could not stay alive much longer if he could not marry the girl pretty quick.

———
Then High Horse crawled under the tepee with a knife.
———

Red Deer thought awhile about it, and then he said: "Cousin, I have a plan, and if you are man enough to do as I tell you, then everything will be all right. She will not run away with you; her old man will not take four horses; and four horses are all you can get. You must steal her and run away with her. Then afterwhile you can come back and the old man cannot do anything because she will be your woman. Probably she wants you to steal her anyway."

So they planned what High Horse had to do, and he said he loved the girl so much that he was man enough to do anything Red Deer or anybody else could think up.

So this is what they did.

That night late they sneaked up to the girl's tepee and waited until it sounded inside as though the old man and the old woman and the girl were sound asleep. Then High Horse crawled under the tepee with a knife. He had to cut the rawhide thongs first, and then Red Deer, who was pulling up the stakes around that side of the tepee, was going to help drag the girl outside and gag her. After that, High Horse could put her across his pony in front of him and hurry out of there and be happy all the rest of his life.

When High Horse had crawled inside, he felt so nervous that he could hear his heart drumming, and it seemed so loud he felt sure it would 'waken the old folks. But it did not, and afterwhile he began cutting the thongs. Every time he cut one it made a pop and nearly scared him to death. But he was getting along all right and all the thongs were cut down as far as the girl's thighs, when he became so nervous that his knife slipped and stuck the girl. She gave a big, loud yell. Then the old folks jumped up and yelled too. By this time High Horse was outside, and he and Red Deer were running away like antelope. The old man and some other people chased the young men but they got away in the dark and nobody knew who it was.

Well, if you ever wanted a beautiful girl you will know how sick High Horse was now. It was very bad the way he felt, and it looked as though he would starve even if he did not drop over dead sometime.

Red Deer kept thinking about this, and after a few days he went to High Horse and said: "Cousin, take courage! I have another plan, and I am sure, if you are man enough, we can steal her this time." And High Horse said: "I am man enough to do anything anybody can think up, if I can only get that girl."

So this is what they did.

They went away from the village alone, and Red Deer made High Horse strip naked. Then he painted High Horse solid white all over, and after that he painted black stripes all over the white and put black rings around High Horse's eyes. High Horse looked terrible. He looked so terrible that when Red Deer was through painting and took a good look at what he had done, it scared even him a little.

"Now," Red Deer said, "if you get caught again, everybody will be so scared they will think you are a bad spirit and will be afraid to chase you."

So when the night was getting old and everybody was sound asleep, they sneaked back to the girl's tepee. High Horse crawled in with his knife, as before, and Red Deer waited outside, ready to drag the girl out and gag her when High Horse had all the thongs cut.

High Horse crept up by the girl's bed and began cutting at the thongs. But he kept thinking, "If they see me they will shoot me because I look so terrible." The girl was restless and kept squirming around in bed, and when a thong was cut, it popped. So High Horse worked very slowly and carefully.

But he must have made some noise, for suddenly the old woman awoke and said to her old man: "Old Man, wake up! There is somebody in this tepee!" But the old man was sleepy and didn't want to be bothered. He said: "Of course there is somebody in this tepee. Go to sleep and don't bother me." Then he snored some more.

But High Horse was so scared by now that he lay very still and as flat to the ground as he could. Now, you see, he had not been sleeping very well for a long time because he was so sick about the girl. And while he was lying there waiting for the old woman to snore, he just forgot everything, even how beautiful the girl was. Red Deer who was lying outside ready to do his part, wondered and wondered what had happened in there, but he did not dare call out to High Horse.

Afterwhile the day began to break and Red Deer had to leave with the two ponies he had staked there for his comrade and girl, or somebody would see him.

So he left.

Now when it was getting light in the tepee, the girl awoke and the first thing she saw was a terrible animal, all white with black stripes on it, lying asleep beside her bed. So she screamed, and then the old woman screamed and the old man yelled. High Horse jumped up, scared almost to death, and he nearly knocked the tepee down getting out of there.

People were coming running from all over the village with guns and bows and axes, and everybody was yelling.

By now High Horse was running so fast that he hardly touched the ground

---

By now High Horse was running so fast that he hardly touched the ground at all.

---

at all, and he looked so terrible that the people fled from him and let him run. Some braves wanted to shoot at him, but the others said he might be some sacred being and it would bring bad trouble to kill him.

High Horse made for the river that was near, and in among the brush he found a hollow tree and dived into it. Afterwhile some braves came there and he could hear them saying that it was some bad spirit that had come out of the water and gone back in again.

That morning the people were ordered to break camp and move away from there. So they did, while High Horse was hiding in his hollow tree.

Now Red Deer had been watching all this from his own tepee and trying to look as though he were as much surprised and scared as all the others. So when the camp moved, he sneaked back to where he had seen his comrade disappear. When he was down there in the brush, he called, and High Horse answered, because he knew his friend's voice. They washed off the paint from High Horse and sat down on the river bank to talk about their troubles.

High Horse said he never would go back to the village as long as he lived and he did not care what happened to him now. He said he was going to go on the war-path all by himself. Red Deer said: "No, Cousin, you are not going on the war-path alone, because I am going with you."

The two sides of this beaded pipe bag show a Plains Indian courting scene. A man offers a woman various gifts, including six horses. ▼

So Red Deer got everything ready, and at night they started out on the war-path all alone. After several days they came to a Crow[3] camp just about sundown, and when it was dark they sneaked up to where the Crow horses were grazing, killed the horse guard, who was not thinking about enemies because he thought all the Lakotas[4] were far away, and drove off about a hundred horses.

They got a big start because all the Crow horses stampeded and it was probably morning before the Crow warriors could catch any horses to ride. Red Deer and High Horse fled with their herd three days and three nights before they reached the village of their people. Then they drove the whole herd right into the village and up in front of the girl's tepee. The old man was there, and High Horse called out to him and asked if he thought maybe that would be enough horses for his girl. The old man did not wave him away that time. It was not the horses that he wanted. What he wanted was a son who was a real man and good for something.

So High Horse got his girl after all, and I think he deserved her.

---

[3] Crow—Native American people of the northern Great Plains.

[4] Lakotas (luh•KOH•tuhz)—division of the Sioux people that includes the Oglalas.

Questions to Consider

Responding

1. Did you ever feel about someone in the way High Horse does? What did you do about it?

Analyzing

2. How are the traditional **courtship customs** in this story similar and different from courtship customs in modern America?

3. How did the killing of the Crow horse guard affect your feelings as you read that part of this story?

4. How is High Horse a "fool for love"?

5. How does the end of the story use a surprising contrast to create humor?

Extending

6. How do you think courtship should be approached?

Activity

Creating a Comic Strip

Create a comic strip version of "High Horse's Courting." Feel free to exaggerate the desperation and misery of High Horse, the beauty of the girl, and the overprotective actions of the girl's parents. Avoid stereotypical portrayals of Native Americans. Instead, do research on the Oglala Sioux, High Horse's tribe, and show them in their native costume and landscape. Let the situations create the humor.

Literature Connection

Humor is a quality that provokes laughter or amusement. Writers create humor through exaggeration, mockery, surprising contrasts, amusing descriptions, and witty and wise conversation between characters. Look at the following passage from "High Horse's Courting." High Horse's friend has painted him to look frightening if he is caught trying to steal the girl he loves. But he frightens the girl so much that she screams.

High Horse jumped up, scared almost to death, and he nearly knocked the tepee down getting out of there.

People were coming running from all over the village with guns and bows and axes, and everybody was yelling.

By now High Horse was running so fast that he hardly touched the ground at all, and he looked so terrible that the people fled from him and let him run.

1. How is description used to create humor?

2. How is exaggeration used to create humor here?

MARÍA SABIDA

BY JUDITH ORTIZ COFER

About the Author

Judith Ortiz Cofer was born in Puerto Rico in 1952, and moved to New Jersey as a child. Her writing explores the experiences of Hispanic-American immigrants. Cofer's first novel, The Line of the Sun (1989), relates the story of a family caught between two cultures. Her collection of essays, Silent Dancing: A Partial Remembrance of a Puerto Rican Childhood (1990), has received numerous awards and honors. In addition to writing, Cofer teaches at the University of Georgia.

About the Selection

The **trickster** character is part of the traditional folk tales of many cultures. Sometimes clever, sometimes foolish, sometimes heroic, and usually mischievous, the trickster is always entertaining. Many trickster characters are animals that have humanlike ideas and actions. The trickster character is popular because he or she reflects life as it actually is—full of the unexpected.

Once upon a time there lived a girl who was so smart that she was known throughout Puerto Rico as María Sabida.[1] María Sabida came into the world with her eyes open. They say that at the moment of her birth she spoke to the attending midwife and told her what herbs to use to make a special *guarapo*, a tea that would put her mother back on her feet immediately. They say that the two women would have thought the infant was possessed[2] if María Sabida had not convinced them with her descriptions of life in heaven that she was touched by God and not spawned[3] by the Devil.

> **María Sabida came into the world with her eyes open.**

María Sabida grew up in the days when the King of Spain owned Puerto Rico, but had forgotten to send law and justice to this little island lost on the map of the world. And so thieves and murderers roamed the land terrorizing the poor people. By the time María Sabida was of marriageable age, one such *ladrón*[4] had taken over the district where she lived.

For years people had been subjected to abuse from this evil man and his henchmen.[5] He robbed them of their cattle and then made them buy their own cows back from him. He would take their best chickens and produce when he came into town on Saturday afternoons riding with his men through the stalls set up by farmers. Overturning their tables, he would yell, "Put it on my account." But of course he never paid for anything he took. One year several little children disappeared while walking to the river, and although the townspeople searched and searched, no trace of them was ever found. That is when María Sabida entered the picture. She was fifteen then, and a beautiful girl with the courage of a man, they say.

She watched the chief *ladrón* the next time he rampaged through the pueblo.[6] She saw that he was a young man: red-skinned, and tough as leather. *Cuero y sangre, nada más*, she said to herself, a man of flesh and blood. And so she prepared herself either to conquer or to kill this man.

---

[1] Sabida (sah•BEE•dah)—Spanish for "wise."
[2] possessed—controlled by a spirit.
[3] spawned—produced, brought forth.
[4] *ladrón* (lah•DROHN)—Spanish for "thief."
[5] henchmen—followers.
[6] pueblo (PWEHB•loh)—town.

She never felt afraid or lost.

This girl on horseback was painted by the contemporary Chicana artist Maya Gonzalez. ▶

María Sabida followed the horses' trail deep into the woods. Though she left the town far behind she never felt afraid or lost. María Sabida could read the sun, the moon, and the stars for direction. When she got hungry, she knew which fruits were good to eat, which roots and leaves were poisonous, and how to follow the footprints of animals to a waterhole. At nightfall, María Sabida came to the edge of a clearing where a large house, almost like a fortress, stood in the forest.

"No woman has ever set foot in that house," she thought, "no *casa*[7] is this, but a man-place." It was a house built for violence, with no windows on the ground level, but there were turrets on the roof where men could stand guard with guns. She waited until it was nearly dark and approached the house through the kitchen side. She found it by smell.

In the kitchen which she knew would have to have a door or window for ventilation, she saw an old man stirring a huge pot. Out of the pot stuck little arms and legs. Angered by the sight, María Sabida entered the kitchen, pushed the old man aside, and picking up the pot threw its horrible contents out of the window.

"Witch, witch, what have you done with my master's stew!" yelled the old

---

[7] *casa* (KAH•sah)—Spanish for "home."

man. "He will kill us both when he gets home and finds his dinner spoiled."

"Get, you filthy *viejo*."[8] María Sabida grabbed the old man's beard and pulled him to his feet. "Your master will have the best dinner of his life if you follow my instructions."

María Sabida then proceeded to make the most delicious *asopao*[9] the old man had ever tasted, but she would answer no questions about herself, except to say that she was his master's fiancée.

> Who are you, and why have you poisoned me?

When the meal was done, María Sabida stretched and yawned and said that she would go upstairs and rest until her *prometido*[10] came home. Then she went upstairs and waited.

The men came home and ate ravenously of the food María Sabida had cooked. When the chief *ladrón* had praised the old man for a fine meal, the cook admitted that it had been *la prometida* who had made the tasty chicken stew.

"My what?" the leader roared, "I have no *prometida*." And he and his men ran upstairs. But there were many floors, and by the time they were halfway to the room where María Sabida waited, many of the men had dropped down unconscious and the others had slowed down to a crawl until they too were overcome with irresistible sleepiness. Only the chief *ladrón* made it to where María Sabida awaited him holding a paddle that she had found among his weapons. Fighting to keep his eyes open, he asked her, "Who are you, and why have you poisoned me?"

"I am your future wife, María Sabida, and you are not poisoned, I added a special sleeping powder that tastes like oregano[11] to your *asopao*. You will not die."

"Witch!" yelled the chief *ladrón*, "I will kill you. Don't you know who I am?" And reaching for her, he fell on his knees, whereupon María Sabida beat him with the paddle until he lay curled like a child on the floor. Each time he tried to attack her, she beat him some more. When she was satisfied that he was **vanquished**,[12] María Sabida left the house and went back to town.

A week later, the chief *ladrón* rode into town with his men again. By then everyone knew what María Sabida had done and they were afraid of what

---

[8] *viejo* (bee•AY•hoh)— Spanish for "old man."

[9] *asopao* (ah•soh•PAH•oh)— Spanish for "rice soup."

[10] *prometido* (proh•may•TEE•doh)—Spanish for "fiancé," or "man promised for marriage."

[11] oregano (uh•REHG•uh•noh)—herb used as a seasoning.

[12] **vanquished**—defeated.

these evil men would do in retribution. "Why did you not just kill him when you had a chance, *muchacha*?"[13] many of the townswomen had asked María Sabida. But she had just answered mysteriously, "It is better to conquer than to kill." The townspeople then barricaded themselves behind closed doors when they heard the pounding of the thieves' horses approaching. But the gang did not stop until they arrived at María Sabida's house. There the men, instead of guns, brought out musical instruments: a *cuatro*, a *güiro*, *maracas*,[14] and a harmonica. Then they played a lovely melody.

"María Sabida, María Sabida, my strong and wise María," called out the leader, sitting tall on his horse under María Sabida's window, "come out and listen to a song I've written for you— I call it *The Ballad of María Sabida*."

María Sabida then appeared on her balcony wearing a wedding dress. The chief *ladrón* sang his song to her: a lively tune about a woman who had the courage of a man and the wisdom of a judge, and who had conquered the heart of the best bandido on the island of Puerto Rico. He had a strong voice and all the people cowering[15] in their locked houses heard his tribute to María Sabida and crossed themselves at the miracle she had wrought.

One by one they all came out and soon María Sabida's front yard was full of people singing and dancing. The *ladrónes* had come prepared with casks of wine, bottles of rum, and a wedding cake made by the old cook from the tender meat of coconuts. The leader of the thieves and María Sabida were married on that day. But all had not yet been settled between them. That evening, as she rode behind him on his horse, she felt the dagger concealed beneath his clothes. She knew then that she had not fully won the battle for this man's heart.

On her wedding night María Sabida suspected that her husband wanted to kill her. After their dinner, which the man had insisted on cooking himself, they went upstairs. María Sabida asked for a little time alone to prepare herself. He said he would take a walk but would return very soon. When she heard him leave the house, María Sabida went down to the kitchen and took several gallons of honey from the pantry. She went back to the

---

[13] *muchacha* (moo•CHAH•chah)—Spanish for "young woman."

[14] *cuatro* (KWAH•troh) . . . *güiro* (GWEE•roh) . . . *maracas* (mah•RAH•kahs)—Spanish names for a small guitar and two types of rhythm instruments made from gourds.

[15] cowering—cringing in fear.

▲
Portrait of a Man with a Mexican Blanket Over his Shoulder
was painted by British artist Mark Gertler (1891–1939).

bedroom and there she fashioned a life-sized doll out of her clothes and poured the honey into it. She then blew out the candle, covered the figure with a sheet and hid herself under the bed.

After a short time, she heard her husband climbing the stairs. He tiptoed into the dark room thinking her asleep in their marriage bed. Peeking out from under the bed, María Sabida saw the glint of the knife her husband pulled out from inside his shirt. Like a fierce panther he leapt onto the bed

and stabbed the doll's body over and over with his dagger. Honey splattered his face and fell on his lips. Shocked, the man jumped off the bed and licked his lips.

"How sweet is my wife's blood. How sweet is María Sabida in death— how sour in life and how sweet in death. If I had known she was so sweet, I would not have murdered her." And so declaring, he kneeled down on the floor beside the bed and prayed to María Sabida's soul for forgiveness.

At that moment María Sabida came out of her hiding place. "Husband, I have tricked you once more, I am not dead." In his joy, the man threw down his knife and embraced María Sabida, swearing that he would never kill or steal again. And he kept his word, becoming in later years an honest farmer. Many years later he was elected mayor of the same town he had once terrorized with his gang of *ladrónes*.

María Sabida made a real *casa* out of his thieves' den, and they had many children together, all of whom could speak at birth. But, they say, María Sabida always slept with one eye open, and that is why she lived to be one hundred years old and wiser than any other woman on the island of Puerto Rico, and her name was known even in Spain.

Questions to Consider

Responding

1. What do you think would be the advantages and disadvantages of being unusually clever?

Analyzing

2. The name María Sabida means "Wise Mary." How is that fitting for this character?

3. How does the fact that the **trickster** in this story is a young woman affect what happens?

4. Which of María's actions support her husband's discovery that she is sweet?

Extending

5. Why do you think the trickster is a common character in many traditional folk tales?

Literature Connection

A character's **motivation** *is the reason he or she acts, feels, or thinks a certain way. Motivation is a driving force in a story's development because it makes characters do what they do.*

1. What is María's motivation for wanting to marry the chief bandit?

2. How and why does the bandit's motivation for marrying María change?

Activity

Creating a Map

Working with a partner, research tricksters around the world. Include tricksters such as Raven, Coyote, Brer Rabbit, Anansi, Nasreddin Hodja, Reynard, Puss in Boots, Hermes, Loki, Maui, and Mah Low Jing (the Monkey King). Then create a trickster map. Draw an image of each trickster. Pin the images on a copy of a world map in the regions where they are best known. Post the map on a bulletin board. On note cards, write a brief description of each trickster. Place the notecards around the map. Then connect the images to the note cards with a piece of yarn or string.

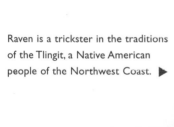

Raven is a trickster in the traditions of the Tlingit, a Native American people of the Northwest Coast. ▶

Miss Butterfly

By Toshio Mori

About the Author

Toshio Mori (1910–1980) wrote the first collection of Japanese-American fiction to be published. Mori's collection of short stories was originally supposed to appear in 1941, but was not published until 1949 because of anti-Japanese feeling during and after World War II. The stories in his Yokohama, California describe a Japanese-American community before the war. Mori's writing career faded in the post-war years. In 1970, several young Asian-American writers came across a copy of his book, located him, and helped him restart his literary career. Mori had a novel and another collection of short stories published in the late 1970s.

About the Selection

*The **traditional dress**, or typical costume, of a culture can provide several different kinds of information. It may indicate the social class, marriage status, and age group of the wearer. It may also tell about the climate and folk art of the native country. Changes in traditional dress may offer information about the history of the culture. In most modern cities, young people have given up wearing traditional dress in favor of Western fashion, especially in America. They may still, however, wear traditional garments for social or religious events tied to their culture. As you read "Miss Butterly," note what traditional Japanese dress represents to different characters in the story.*

The doorbell rang and Sachi ran **nimbly**[1] to the door. "Yuki!" she called to her younger sister. "I think they're here!"

"I'll be out in a moment," Yuki answered from the bedroom.

Sachi opened the door and found an old man standing on the porch. "Oh hello, Hamada-*san*,"[2] she said, her face plainly revealing disappointment.

"Good evening, Sachi-*chan*,"[3] greeted Hamada-*san*, entering the hall. "Is your father home?"

Sachi looked up and down the street and then closed the door. "Yes, Hamada-*san*. He's in the living room. Go right in."

The old man looked admiringly at her, pausing for a word with her. "My, you are growing prettier every day. Is Yuki-*chan* home too?"

She smiled and nodded. "We're going to the dance tonight with our boy friends," she added eagerly.

Hamada-*san's* face fell but brightened quickly. "Do you still have those Japanese records—the festival music, I mean?"

"Yes," Sachi replied, looking puzzled. "We still have them."

"And is your phonograph in good condition?" he asked.

She nodded impatiently, anxious to return to her dressing.

"Good!" cried the old man, clapping his hand. "Please come into the living room. I wish to have a talk with you and your father."

"But I will be late for the dance!" she protested. "I must dress now."

Hamada-*san* looked pleadingly at her. "Please, Sachi-*chan*. Please, this is my special request."

The old man led her into the living room where her father sat reading the Japanese daily. "Saiki-*san*, how are you?"

Saiki-*san* dropped his paper and took off his glasses. "Good evening, Hamada-*san*. Anything new?"

Hamada-*san* dropped into the easy chair, leaning forward eagerly. "Saiki-*san*, I have one special request to make of your daughters tonight. It will bring me much happiness, and I shall forget that I am a lonely man for a short while. Please ask Sachi-*chan* and Yuki-*chan* to do it for an old man's sake."

"What is it you want?" asked Saiki-*san*.

---

[1] **nimbly**—quickly; lightly.

[2] *–san*—Japanese term added to a person's name to show respect.

[3] *–chan*—Japanese term added to a familiar female's name.

"You may recall my repeated request in the past. I want to see the cherry blossom, the *taiko* bridge,[4] and hear the Japanese paper houses hum when the wind blows. I want to dream of the pine-studded hills, the crystal-clear lakes, Fujiyama, Miyajima,[5] and New Year festivals . . . the old Japan. My mouth waters with the flavors of the island fruits, rice cakes, and fish. My heart runs away with the color of the kimonos,[6] the plaintive[7] songs, and the loss of my many ancestors. Do you get it?"

Sachi groaned and waved her hands protestingly.

"So you wish them to perform Japanese folk dances," Saiki-*san* said, smilingly.

Hamada-*san* beamed and eagerly added, "Odori[8]—that's what I mean. Please, Sachi-*chan*, wear your beautiful kimono tonight and perform one dance for me. Just one, that is all I ask. I want to capture my lost memories and dream. Dance for an old man and let him enter his old world for several minutes."

> Make Hamada-san happy tonight. Wear your kimono and dance.

"No, I won't," she said **emphatically**,[9] standing impatiently by the door. "I won't."

"Daughter, what are you saying?" Saiki-*san* said. "Make Hamada-*san* happy tonight. Wear your kimono and dance."

"One dance, Sachi-*chan*," begged the old man, humbly bowing. "For your father's old friend. He is poor and cannot reward you. Otherwise, he would shower you with gifts."

"I don't want anything," said Sachi, and looking at her father added, "I hate to wear kimono."

Hamada-*san* looked horrified. "Ah, Sachi-*chan*!" he cried. "Please do not say that. Don't you Nisei[10] girls realize the truth? When you wear your bright, colorful kimono you are the most beautiful women in the world. Your eyes brighten up, your figure becomes **symmetrical**,[11] your gestures move naturally. Don't you see, Sachi-*chan*?"

---

[4] *taiko* (TY•koh) bridge—ornamental Japanese bridge shaped like a drum ("taiko").

[5] Fujiyama, Miyajima (foo•jee•YAH•muh, mee•yah•JEE•muh)—Mount Fujiyama is a volcano sacred to the Japanese; Miyajima is a historic and scenic Japanese island.

[6] kimonos (kuh•MOH•nuhs)—long, wide-sleeved, robelike Japanese dresses.

[7] plaintive—sad.

[8] Odori (oh•DOH•ree)—Japanese folk dance.

[9] **emphatically**—forcefully; definitely.

[10] Nisei (NEE•say)—person born in America of parents who emigrated from Japan.

[11] **symmetrical** (sih•MEHT•rih•kuhl)—balanced.

Sachi stood speechless, hesitating whether to laugh or smile.

"Sachi, why don't you like to wear kimono?" her father asked.

"It takes so much time, and I feel clumsy and stiff," she replied.

Hamada-*san* smiled and shook his head. "You don't look it when you wear it. You are merely saving that for an excuse. I don't believe it."

She looked at her watch and cried, "I've lost five minutes already."

"What time does the dance begin?" Saiki-*san* asked her.

"At eight sharp," Sachi answered eagerly. "Papa, may I go now?"

"Saiki-*san*! Please remember your old-time friend," cried Hamada-*san*.

From the bedroom came the younger sister in her glittering white

These Japanese girls perform traditional dances as part of a spring festival in the city of Kyoto.

evening gown. "I heard what you said about Nisei girls, Hamada-*san*," Yuki said, smiling. "Sachi, let's do one odori for him. It won't take but ten minutes, dressing and all, and it'll make him happy. I have your gown and the rest of your things out, all ready for you to slip them on."

Sachi thought for a moment. "All right. I'll do it," she said suddenly. "Papa, please select the record and be ready when we come out."

Beautiful, beautiful! The whole world should see you now.

"I'll do that," Hamada-san said, beaming. "Saiki-*san*, just sit and relax."

Eagerly he began sorting out the record albums. The girls rushed into the bedroom. After much deliberation the old man selected two records and went to the phonograph.

"This is my favorite," Hamada-*san* said to his friend, holding up one record. "This is about a day in autumn in Japan. The wind blows and the leaves fall. The sky is clear and the air is beginning to cool. The chants of the insects are dying out and late harvest is about over. The flowers shrivel and the last of the leaves **flaunt**[12] their brilliant colors in the wind, and the day awaits the icy blast of winter."

The girls' father sat silently, lit his pipe, and blew smoke. He watched his old friend **poring**[13] over the words of another record and wished he had some kind of an answer for him.

"It's a beautiful piece," Hamada-*san* informed, indicating the first record. "Especially when dancers perform skillfully as Sachi-*chan* and Yuki-*chan*."

The two girls hurriedly skipped into the room. They wore their best kimono, a colorful design on silk, enhancing their youthful beauty.

"Are you ready with the music, Hamada-*san*?" asked Yuki. "We're all set."

At that sight of the girls in kimono Hamada-*san* sat up, his eyes wide with open admiration. "Beautiful, beautiful! The whole world should see you now."

Sachi laughed it off, and Yuki smiled happily. They went over to the phonograph and inspected the record. Satisfied with the selection they rushed Hamada-*san* to a seat.

---

[12] **flaunt**—show off.

[13] **poring**—reading or studying carefully.

"Sit down and enjoy yourself," Sachi said. "We'll watch the record. Hamada-*san*, there will be positively one performance tonight."

"Two?" the old man asked timidly.

"Positively one," Sachi repeated.

*T*he music began, and the girls waited alertly for their cue. Hamada-*san* poked Saiki-*san* in the ribs as the two girls performed. He clapped his hands, keeping time with the music. His eyes, round with excitement, twinkled. His body swayed this way and that way. Then he forgot his friend, the time and place. Long after the music stopped and the girls paused by the phonograph, Hamada-*san* sat fixedly.

"Good night, Hamada-*san*," called the girls at the door.

"Wait!" cried Hamada-san springing to his feet. "Sachi-*chan*, Yuki-*chan*, one more! The parasol[14] dance! Please, just one more. Please!"

The girls looked at each other, hesitating. Hamada-*san* ran to the phonograph and started the record going. "Hurry, girls. Get your parasols!" he cried.

The high notes of a *samisen*[15] and the mixed instruments cut the air.

The girls ran to get their parasols. Hamada-*san* beamed and clapped his hands in tune with the music. Saiki-*san* sat comfortably in his chair, his eyes closed, and sucked his pipe.

The girls returned and instantly snapped into the dance. Their parasols opened and twirling, they leaped over imaginary puddles and worried about their slippers. They looked up at the sky, their hands out to see if the rain was falling. Their faces bright with smiles they twirled their parasols with happy abandonment.[16] The sun is out once again, and they forget the puddles, the mud, and discomfort. Their bodies, minds, and hearts join to greet the sunny day, their somber aliveness increasing to gay abandon.

Once more Hamada-*san* sat motionlessly, unheeding the end of the music and the dance. Sachi stopped the phonograph.

"Wonderful! Wonderful!" cried Hamada-*san*, becoming alive. "I shall never forget this performance."

"Yuki, how much time have we?" asked Sachi hurriedly.

"Exactly ten minutes," Yuki said. "Let's hurry."

---

[14] parasol—paper umbrella to keep out the sun.

[15] *samisen* (SAM•ih•sehn)—Japanese stringed instrument with a very long neck.

[16] abandonment—unbounded enthusiasm.

The girls dashed into their room.

"Wasn't it wonderful, Saiki-*san*? Wasn't it?" asked Hamada-*san*.

"Yes, they were pretty good," replied Saiki-*san*.

When the girls returned to the room their father was reading the paper. Hamada-*san* sat silently by himself in the corner, his eyes staring in the distance.

"How do we look, Papa?" Sachi asked, the two girls showing off their new evening gowns.

"Swell," Saiki-*san* said, looking up.

"What do you think of them, Hamada-*san*?" Yuki asked the old man. "Hamada-*san*!"

"Please don't ask me such a question, Yuki-*chan*. Not tonight," Hamada-*san* said sadly.

Sachi looked puzzled. "What's happened to you, Hamada-*san*? Are you ill?"

"Nothing is the matter with me. I'm all right," he said, cheering up with an effort. Then he added, "Sachi-*chan* and Yuki-*chan*, please be careful with your kimono. Don't let the moths get into them."

"We'll be very careful with them," Sachi promised.

"And don't you forget the odori. Keep brushing up."

The girls nodded obediently. Outside a horn blared.

"Oh, they're here!" cried Sachi, running to the window.

"Isn't it exciting?" Yuki cried, moving to her sister's side. "We're going to have a good band tonight."

The girls waved their hands, and the horn tooted again. "Good night, Hamada-*san*. Good night, Papa," they said.

"What is this dance? What kind?" the old man asked his friend, watching the girls skip out of the house.

"A social dance. Popular American pastime," answered Saiki-*san*, without looking up from his paper.

In the living room Saiki-*san* smoked **incessantly**[17] and the place became stuffy. He continued to read the paper. Hamada-*san* sat mutely in the corner, his eyes smarting with smoke. He could have gone outside for a bit of fresh air but did not move. His eyes took in the phonograph, the record albums, the spots where the girls danced, and the room that was now empty. In the silence he heard the clock in the hall ticking.

---

[17] **incessantly**—constantly.

Responding

1. How do you react when older people want you to share their likes and dislikes?

Analyzing

2. How does the way Hamada and Sachi speak tell you that they think differently about the world?

3. What does the Japanese **traditional dress** of the kimono represent to different characters in the story?

4. What is wrong with Hamada after he watches the girls dance?

5. What is the significance of the last sentence in this story?

Extending

6. How much of cultural tradition do you think younger generations should try to preserve?

Activities

Researching Costume

Using the Internet and library resources, research the traditional dress of one of the following Asian cultures: Japan, China, Korea, Thailand, or India. Present a report to your classmates that compares the traditional dress of the country you chose with modern or Western fashion, compare both the Asian country and that nation's segment of Asian-American culture.

A Korean-American girl wears traditional dress at an ethnic celebration. ▶

Literature Connection

In literature, conflict is the struggle between opposing forces. It may be external, as in a struggle between two or more characters or between characters and an outside force such as nature. It also may be internal, as in a struggle within a character about an issue or action.

1. In "Miss Butterfly," at which point in the story do you first sense conflict between generations in this family?

2. What internal conflict do you think Sachi resolved when she finally wore the kimono and performed the dances?

Legacies

by Nikki Giovanni

About the Author

Poet, essayist, and lecturer Nikki Giovanni was born Yolande Cornelia Giovanni, Jr., in 1943. She was educated at Fisk University, the University of Pennsylvania, and Columbia University. At age 27, she founded her own publishing company. Giovanni's work changes often, supporting her view that change is necessary for growth. Her early poetry served as a major voice in the civil rights movement of the 1960s. Later poems focused on family and her childhood home, Knoxville, Tennessee. Giovanni's recent work has a global outlook.

About the Selections

The **role of grandparents** is different in different cultures. In some cultures, grandparents exercise a central, dominating role; in other cultures, their position is more marginal. The role of grandparents also changes over time. In recent years, as more and more women work outside the home, many grandparents are exercising a much larger role in raising their grandchildren. As you read "Legacies" and "Lineage" (page 98), examine the roles these African-American grandmothers have in their grandchildren's lives.

---

title legacies (LEHG•uh•sees)—items or conditions passed down from an ancestor.

her grandmother called her from the playground
"yes, ma'am"
"i want chu to learn how to make rolls" said the old
woman proudly
but the little girl didn't want
to learn how because she knew
even if she couldn't say it that
that would mean when the old one died she would be less
dependent on her spirit so
she said
"i don't want to know how to make no rolls"
with her lips poked out
and the old woman wiped her hands on
her apron saying "lord
these children"
and neither of them ever
said what they meant
and i guess nobody ever does

This portrait of a Louisiana woman and her
great-grandchild was taken by photographer
Susie Fitzhugh. ▶

Lineage

by Margaret Walker

About the Author

In 1966, after 40 years of research and writing, Margaret Walker (1915–1998) published Jubilee, the story of a slave's daughter. The book is based on the life of her maternal great-grandmother as told to Walker by her maternal grandmother. Walker also wrote other novels, short stories, essays, speeches, and poems. She was the first African American to win the Yale Series of Younger Poets award, for her poem, "For My People." Walker received degrees from Northwestern University and the University of Iowa. She taught at Jackson State University, where she founded an institute of black studies.

▲
Robert Gwathmey (1903–1988) painted
Portrait of a Farmer's Wife in 1951.

My grandmothers were strong.
They followed plows and bent to toil.
They moved through fields sowing seed.
They touched earth and grain grew.
They were full of sturdiness and singing.
My grandmothers were strong.

My grandmothers are full of memories
Smelling of soap and onions and wet clay
With veins rolling roughly over quick hands
They have many clean words to say.
My grandmothers were strong.
Why am I not as they?

---

title lineage (LIHN•ee•ihj)—line of inheritance; ancestry.

Questions to Consider

Responding

1. What is the **role of grandparents** in your family?

Analyzing

2. In "Legacies," what do you think the poet means by the phrase, "dependent on her spirit"?

3. What do you think the girl and her grandmother in "Legacies" would say to each other if they said what they meant?

4. In "Lineage," what makes the grandmothers so strong?

Extending

5. What do you think the role of grandparents will be by the time you have grandchildren?

Literature Connection

A **theme** is a message about life or human nature that is communicated by a literary work. The theme of a literary work is not the same as its subject. The subject is what the work is about, such as the natural world, romantic love, or old age. The theme is a statement of what the author is saying concerning this subject. Sometimes the theme is stated directly. In many cases, however, a reader must infer what the writer's message is.

1. What is the subject of both of these poems?

2. How would you express the theme of "Legacies"?

3. How would you express the theme of "Lineage"?

4. How do the themes of these poems differ?

Activities

Writing a Letter

Make a list of the actions and character traits you admire about your grandmother or another older woman in your family. Add your memories of particular conversations or events you shared with her to the list. Then, using your list, write a personal letter to that special woman, telling her what you might not have been able to say in person. Send her the letter. Remember that your theme should be appreciation of who she is, not simply thanks for what she has done for you.

Creating a Photo Essay

Working with another classmate, create a photo essay about grandparents today. Make sure the photographs you select display people from a variety of cultures and the different roles which grandparents serve in contemporary families.

The Medicine Bag

by Virginia Driving Hawk Sneve

About the Author

Virginia Driving Hawk Sneve (SNAY•vee) was born in 1933 and raised on the Rosebud Reservation in South Dakota. She is a member of the Lakota Sioux (luh•KOH•tuh soo), a Native American people of the northern Great Plains. Sneve went to college at South Dakota State University, then taught in public and reservation schools in South Dakota. Many of her books for children and adults are inspired by folk stories and Lakota history she learned from her grandmothers. Sneve has won several awards, including the Spirit of Crazy Horse Award in 1996 and a National Humanities Medal in 2000.

About the Selection

In many cultures, particularly Native American ones, spiritual healers and others carried **medicine bags**. A medicine bag is a small pouch (usually of leather) that holds objects that are meaningful to the wearer. The objects might represent a particular power or desire, such as protection or happiness. Traditionally, the objects are from the natural world, such as a stone, an herb, or an animal tooth. One person might have several medicine bags, each for a different purpose. As you read "The Medicine Bag," try to understand what value such traditions might have in the modern world.

My kid sister Cheryl and I always bragged about our Sioux grandpa, Joe Iron Shell. Our friends, who had always lived in the city and only knew about Indians from movies and TV, were impressed by our stories. Maybe we exaggerated and made Grandpa and the reservation sound glamorous, but when we'd return home to Iowa after our yearly summer visit to Grandpa, we always had some exciting tale to tell.

We always had some **authentic**[1] Sioux article to show our listeners. One year Cheryl had new moccasins[2] that Grandpa had made. On another visit he gave me a small, round, flat rawhide drum that was decorated with a painting of a warrior riding a horse. He taught me a real Sioux chant to sing while I beat the drum with a leather-covered stick that had a feather on the end. Man, that really made an impression.

We never showed our friends Grandpa's picture. Not that we were ashamed of him, but because we knew that the glamorous tales we told didn't go with the real thing. Our friends would have laughed at the picture because Grandpa wasn't tall and stately like TV Indians. His hair wasn't in braids but hung in stringy, gray strands on his neck, and he was old. He was our great-grandfather, and he didn't live in a tepee,[3] but all by himself in a part log, part tar-paper shack on the Rosebud Reservation in South Dakota. So when Grandpa came to visit us, I was so ashamed and embarrassed I could've died.

> Grandpa wasn't tall and stately like TV Indians.

There are a lot of yippy poodles and other fancy little dogs in our neighborhood, but they usually barked singly at the mailman from the safety of their own yards. Now it sounded as if a whole pack of mutts were barking together in one place.

I got up and walked to the curb to see what the commotion was. About a block away I saw a crowd of little kids yelling, with the dogs yipping and growling around someone who was walking down the middle of the street.

I watched the group as it slowly came closer and saw that in the center of the strange **procession**[4] was a man

---

[1] **authentic**—real; genuine.

[2] moccasins—soft leather slippers traditionally worn by Native Americans.

[3] tepee (TEE•pee)—cone-shaped tent of animal hide traditionally used by Plains Indian peoples.

[4] **procession** (pruh•sesh•uhn)—group of people or things or moving forward, often in ceremony.

wearing a tall black hat. He'd pause now and then to peer at something in his hand and then at the houses on either side of the street. I felt cold and hot at the same time as I recognized the man. "Oh, no!" I whispered. "It's Grandpa!"

I stood on the curb, unable to move even though I wanted to run and hide. Then I got mad when I saw how the yippy dogs were growling and nipping at the old man's baggy pant legs and how wearily he poked them away with his cane. "Stupid mutts," I said as I ran to rescue Grandpa.

When I kicked and hollered at the dogs to get away, they put their tails between their legs and scattered. The kids ran to the curb, where they watched me and the old man.

"Grandpa," I said, and felt pretty dumb when my voice cracked. I reached for his beat-up old tin suit-case, which was tied shut with a rope. But he set it down right in the street and shook my hand.

"*Hau, Takoza*, Grandchild," he greeted me formally in Sioux.

All I could do was stand there with the whole neighborhood watching and shake the hand of the leather-brown old man. I saw how his gray hair straggled from under his big black hat, which had a drooping feather in its crown. His rumpled black suit hung like a sack over his stooped frame. As he shook my hand, his coat fell open to expose a bright-red satin shirt with a beaded bolo tie[5] under the collar. His get-up wasn't out of place on the reservation, but it sure was here, and I wanted to sink right through the pavement.

"Hi," I muttered with my head down. I tried to pull my hand away when I felt his bony hand trembling, and looked up to see fatigue in his face. I felt like crying. I couldn't think of anything to say, so I picked up Grandpa's suitcase, took his arm, and guided him up the driveway to our house.

Mom was standing on the steps. I don't know how long she'd been watching, but her hand was over her mouth and she looked as if she couldn't believe what she saw. Then she ran to us.

"Grandpa," she gasped. "How in the world did you get here?"

> "Grandpa," she gasped. "How in the world did you get here?"

---

[5] bolo tie—tie of leather or cloth string held together with a sliding device.

She checked her move to embrace Grandpa, and I remembered that such a display of affection is unseemly[6] to the Sioux and would embarrass him.

"*Hau*, Marie," he said as he shook Mom's hand. She smiled and took his other arm.

As we supported him up the steps, the door banged open and Cheryl came bursting out of the house. She was all smiles and was so obviously glad to see Grandpa that I was ashamed of how I felt.

"Grandpa!" she yelled happily. "You came to see us!"

Grandpa smiled and Mom and I let go of him as he stretched out his arms to my ten-year-old sister, who was still young enough to be hugged.

"*Wicincala*, little girl," he greeted her and then collapsed.

He had fainted. Mom and I carried him into her sewing room, where we had a spare bed.

---

[6] unseemly—improper.

Photographer Don Doll, S.J., took this portrait of a 102-year-old Lakota man, James Holy Eagle, in 1991. ▶

After we had Grandpa on the bed, Mom stood there helplessly patting his shoulder.

"Shouldn't we call the doctor, Mom?" I suggested, since she didn't seem to know what to do.

"Yes," she agreed, with a sigh. "You make Grandpa comfortable, Martin."

I reluctantly moved to the bed. I knew Grandpa wouldn't want to have Mom undress him, but I didn't want to, either. He was so skinny and frail that his coat slipped off easily. When I loosened his tie and opened his shirt collar, I felt a small leather pouch that hung from a thong around his neck. I left it alone and moved to remove his boots. The scuffed old cowboy boots were tight, and he moaned as I put pressure on his legs to jerk them off.

I put the boots on the floor and saw why they fit so tight. Each one was stuffed with money. I looked at the bills that lined the boots and started to ask about them, but Grandpa's eyes were closed again.

Mom came back with a basin of water. "The doctor thinks Grandpa is suffering from heat exhaustion," she explained as she bathed Grandpa's face. Mom gave a big sigh, *"Oh hinh,* Martin. How do you suppose he got here?"

▲

In 1904, the photographer Edward S. Curtis (1868–1952) began a huge project of recording the lives of Native Americans. These medicine bags, photographed by Curtis, belonged to the Piegans, a Blackfoot people of the northern Great Plains.

We found out after the doctor's visit. Grandpa was angrily sitting up in bed while Mom tried to feed him some soup.

"Tonight you let Marie feed you, Grandpa," spoke my dad, who had gotten home from work just as the doctor was leaving. "You're not really sick," he said as he gently pushed Grandpa back against the pillows. "The doctor said you just got too tired and hot after your long trip."

Grandpa relaxed, and between sips of soup, he told us of his journey. Soon after our visit to him, Grandpa decided that he would like to see where his only living descendants lived and what our home was like. Besides, he admitted sheepishly, he was lonesome after we left.

I knew everybody felt as guilty as I did—especially Mom. Mom was all Grandpa had left. So even after she married my dad, who's a white man and teaches in the college in our city, and after Cheryl and I were born, Mom made sure that every summer we spent a week with Grandpa.

I never thought that Grandpa would be lonely after our visits, and none of us noticed how old and weak he had become. But Grandpa knew, and so he came to us. He had ridden on buses for two and a half days. When he arrived in the city, tired and stiff from sitting for so long, he set out, walking, to find us.

He had stopped to rest on the steps of some building downtown, and a policeman found him. The cop, according to Grandpa, was a good man who took him to the bus stop and waited until the bus came and told the driver to let Grandpa out at Bell View Drive. After Grandpa got off the bus, he started walking again. But he couldn't see the house numbers on the other side when he walked on the sidewalk, so he walked in the middle of the street. That's when all the little kids and dogs followed him.

I knew everybody felt as bad as I did. Yet I was proud of this eighty-six-year-old man, who had never been away from the reservation, having the courage to travel so far alone.

"You found the money in my boots?" he asked Mom.

"Martin did," she answered, and roused herself to scold. "Grandpa, you shouldn't have carried so much money. What if someone had stolen it from you?"

Grandpa laughed. "I would've known if anyone tried to take the boots off my feet. The money is what I've saved for a long time—a hundred dollars—for my funeral. But you take it now to buy groceries so that I won't be a burden to you while I am here."

"That won't be necessary, Grandpa," Dad said. "We are honored to have you with us, and you will never be a burden. I am only sorry that we never thought to bring you home with us this summer and spare you the discomfort of a long trip."

Grandpa was pleased. "Thank you," he answered. "But do not feel bad that you didn't bring me with you, for I would not have come then. It was not time." He said this in such a way that no one could argue with him. To Grandpa and the Sioux, he once told me, a thing would be done when it was the right time to do it, and that's the way it was.

> I have come because it is soon time for Martin to have the medicine bag.

"Also," Grandpa went on, looking at me, "I have come because it is soon time for Martin to have the medicine bag."

We all knew what that meant. Grandpa thought he was going to die, and he had to follow the tradition of his family to pass the medicine bag, along with its history, to the oldest male child.

"Even though the boy," he said still looking at me, "bears a white man's name, the medicine bag will be his."

I didn't know what to say. I had the same hot and cold feeling that I had when I first saw Grandpa in the street. The medicine bag was the dirty leather pouch I had found around his neck. "I could never wear such a thing," I almost said aloud. I thought of having my friends see it in gym class or at the swimming pool and could imagine the smart things they would say. But I just swallowed hard and took a step toward the bed. I knew I would have to take it.

But Grandpa was tired. "Not now, Martin," he said, waving his hand in dismissal, "It is not time. Now I will sleep."

So that's how Grandpa came to be with us for two months. My friends kept asking to come see the old man, but I put them off. I told myself that I didn't want them laughing at Grandpa. But even as I made excuses, I knew it wasn't Grandpa that I was afraid they'd laugh at.

Nothing bothered Cheryl about bringing her friends to see Grandpa. Every day after school started, there'd be a crew of giggling little girls or round-eyed little boys crowded around the old man on the patio, where he'd gotten in the habit of sitting every afternoon.

Grandpa would smile in his gentle way and patiently answer their questions, or he'd tell them stories of brave warriors, ghosts, animals; and the kids listened in awed silence. Those little guys thought Grandpa was great.

Finally, one day after school, my friends came home with me because nothing I said stopped them. "We're going to see the great Indian of Bell View Drive," said Hank, who was supposed to be my best friend. "My brother has seen him three times so he oughta be well enough to see us."

When we got to my house, Grandpa was sitting on the patio. He had on his red shirt, but today he also wore a fringed leather vest that was decorated with beads. Instead of his usual cowboy boots, he had solidly beaded moccasins on his feet that stuck out of his black trousers. Of course, he had his old black hat on— he was seldom without it. But it had been brushed and the feather in the beaded headband was proudly erect, its tip a brighter white. His hair lay in silver strands over the red shirt collar.

I stared just as my friends did, and I heard one of them murmur, "Wow!"

Grandpa looked up, and, when his eyes met mine, they twinkled as if he were laughing inside. He nodded to me, and my face got all hot. I could tell that he had known all along I was afraid he'd embarrass me in front of my friends.

"*Hau, hoksilas*, boys," he greeted and held out his hand.

My buddies passed in a single file and shook his hand as I introduced them. They were so polite I almost laughed. "How, there, Grandpa," and even a "How-do-you-do, sir."

"You look fine, Grandpa," I said as the guys sat on the lawn chairs or on the patio floor.

"*Hanh*, yes," he agreed. "When I woke up this morning, it seemed the right time to dress in the good clothes. I knew that my grandson would be bringing his friends."

> We're going to see the great Indian of Bell View Drive.

"You guys want some lemonade or something?" I offered. No one answered. They were listening to Grandpa as he started telling how he'd killed the deer from which his vest was made.

Grandpa did most of the talking while my friends were there. I was so proud of him and amazed at how respectfully quiet my buddies were. Mom had to chase them home at supper time. As they left, they shook Grandpa's hand again and said to me,

"Martin, he's really great!"

"Yeah, man! Don't blame you for keeping him to yourself."

"Can we come back?"

But after they left, Mom said, "No more visitors for a while, Martin. Grandpa won't admit it, but his strength hasn't returned. He likes having company, but it tires him."

That evening Grandpa called me to his room before he went to sleep.

"Tomorrow," he said, "when you come home, it will be time to give you the medicine bag."

> There was a strong need for guidance from Wakantanka, the Great Spirit.

I felt a hard squeeze from where my heart is supposed to be and was scared, but I answered, "OK, Grandpa."

All night I had weird dreams about thunder and lightning on a high hill. From a distance I heard the slow beat of a drum. When I woke up in the morning, I felt as if I hadn't slept at all. At school it seemed as if the day would never end and, when it finally did, I ran home.

Grandpa was in his room, sitting on the bed. The shades were down, and the place was dim and cool. I sat on the floor in front of Grandpa, but he didn't even look at me. After what seemed a long time, he spoke.

"I sent your mother and sister away. What you will hear today is only for a man's ears. What you will receive is only for a man's hands." He fell silent and I felt shivers down my back.

"My father in his early manhood," Grandpa began, "made a vision quest[7] to find a spirit guide for his life. You cannot understand how it was in that time, when the great Teton Sioux[8] were first made to stay on the reservation. There was a strong need for guidance from *Wakantanka*,[9] the Great Spirit. But too many of the young men were filled with despair and hatred. They thought it was hopeless to search for a vision when the glorious life was gone and only the hated confines of a reservation lay ahead. But my father held to the old ways.

"He carefully prepared for his quest with a purifying sweat bath, and then he went alone to a high **butte**[10] top to fast and pray. After three days he received his sacred dream—in which

---

[7] vision quest—individual's search for a spiritual sign or message. A vision quest formed part of young people's coming-of-age in many Native American cultures.

[8] Teton Sioux—largest and westernmost of the Sioux peoples.

[9] *Wakantanka* (wah•kuhn•TANK•eh)—most important spirit in the Sioux religion, regarded as the creator of the world.

[10] **butte** (byoot)—steep hill with a flat top standing alone on a plain.

he found, after long searching, the white man's iron. He did not understand his vision of finding something belonging to the white people, for in that time they were the enemy. When he came down from the butte to cleanse himself at the stream below, he found the remains of a campfire and the broken shell of an iron kettle. This was a sign that reinforced his dream. He took a piece of the iron for his medicine bag, which he had made of elk skin years before, to prepare for his quest.

"He returned to his village, where he told his dream to the wise old men of the tribe. They gave him the name *Iron Shell*, but neither did they understand the meaning of the dream. This first Iron Shell kept the piece of iron with him at all times and believed it gave him protection from the evils of those unhappy days.

"Then a terrible thing happened to Iron Shell. He and several other young men were taken from their homes by the soldiers and sent far away to a white man's boarding school. He was angry and lonesome for his parents and the young girl he had wed before he was taken away. At first Iron Shell resisted the teacher's attempts to change him, and he did not try to learn. One day it was his turn to work in the school's blacksmith shop. As he walked into the place, he knew that his medicine had brought him there to learn and work with the white man's iron.

"Iron Shell became a blacksmith and worked at the trade when he returned to the reservation. All of his life he treasured the medicine bag. When he was old and I was a man, he gave it to me, for no one made the vision quest anymore."

◀ This trunk made of painted rawhide was used by the Lakota to carry clothing.

the courage to travel
so far alone

Grandpa quit talking, and I stared in disbelief as he covered his face with his hands. His shoulders were shaking with quiet sobs, and I looked away until he began to speak again.

"I kept the bag until my son, your mother's father, was a man and had to leave us to fight in the war across the ocean. I gave him the bag, for I believed it would protect him in battle, but he did not take it with him. He was afraid that he would lose it. He died in a faraway place."

> Never open it again until you pass it on to your son.

Again Grandpa was still and I felt his grief around me.

"My son," he went on after clearing his throat, "had only a daughter, and it is not proper for her to know of these things."

He unbuttoned his shirt, pulled out the leather pouch, and lifted it over his head. He held it in his hand, turning it over and over as if memorizing how it looked.

"In the bag," he said as he opened it and removed two objects, "is the broken shell of the iron kettle, a pebble from the butte, and a piece of the sacred sage."[11] He held the pouch upside down and dust drifted down.

"After the bag is yours you must put a piece of prairie sage within and never open it again until you pass it on to your son." He replaced the pebble and the piece of iron, and tied the bag.

I stood up, somehow knowing I should. Grandpa slowly rose from the bed and stood upright in front of me holding the bag before my face. I closed my eyes and waited for him to slip it over my head. But he spoke.

"No, you need not wear it." He placed the soft leather bag in my right hand and closed my other hand over it. "It would not be right to wear it in this time and place where no one will understand. Put it safely away until you are again on the reservation. Wear it then, when you replace the sacred sage."

Grandpa turned and sat again on the bed. Wearily he leaned his head against the pillow. "Go," he said, "I will sleep now."

"Thank you, Grandpa," I said softly and left with the bag in my hands.

That night Mom and Dad took Grandpa to the hospital. Two weeks later I stood alone on the lonely prairie of the reservation and put the sacred sage in my medicine bag.

---

[11] sage—plant with grayish-green leaves belonging to the mint family of plants.

Questions to Consider

Responding

1. What special items do you treasure and why?

Analyzing

2. How is the Sioux idea that things are done when it is "the right time" supported by the events of the story?

3. Why do you think the author included Martin's dream? What does the dream hint at?

4. How does the **medicine bag** represent the generations of the narrator's family?

5. How might Martin describe his Grandpa at the end of the story?

6. How does this story reflect both the old ways and the new ways of the Teton Sioux?

Extending

7. What place do you see in the modern world for such traditions as the medicine bag?

Literature Connection

A conversation between characters in a literary work is called dialogue. *In poetry, novels, and short stories, dialogue is usually set off with quotation marks to indicate a speaker's exact words. (In a play, dialogue follows a character's name and is not placed within quotation marks.) Dialogue is a very effective way of revealing character.*

1. In "The Medicine Bag," what does the writer's use of dialogue reveal about Grandpa's character?

2. What does dialogue reveal about the attitudes of the different family members toward Grandpa?

3. Why do you think the writer uses dialogue to create the scene in which Grandpa passes the medicine bag on to Martin?

Activities

Writing About a Family Tradition

Does your family have an object that has been handed down through the generations (an heirloom)? If so, ask your parents or grandparents to describe its history and importance. Then write a transcript of the conversation about the heirloom, using dialogue to show who said what. Insert a copy of the transcript in a special envelope that can be given to whomever inherits the object.

These traditional Russian nesting dolls represent succeeding generations.
▼

Koreans

Have a Reason Not to Smile

by K. Connie Kang

About the Author

Home Was the Land of Morning Calm *(1995)* is the first novel of K. Connie Kang. Kang, a writer for the Los Angeles Times, *is the first Korean American to break into mainstream journalism in the United States. Her novel blends stories about her family with Korean history* since 1900. Kang was born in Korea, escaped to Japan during the Korean War, and then came to America for college. She soon returned to Korea, where she was a professor and journalist. Eventually, Kang married an American journalist and immigrated to the United States.

About the Selection

Over 2,500 years ago, a Chinese thinker named Kung-Fu-tzu ("Master Kung") developed a system of ideas about how a good person should behave. Kung—known to Westerners as Confucius (kuhn•FYOO•shuhs)—deeply influenced the development of Asian society and culture. Confucian teachings tell people how to act in different situations with rulers, parents, spouses, siblings, and friends. Major **Confucian values** are kindness, helping family and friends, conservative spending, harmony, and respect for elders. As you read "Koreans Have a Reason Not to Smile," pay attention to the way the values of the Confucian tradition affect Korean Americans.

One of the two black-led boycotts of Korean grocers in Brooklyn[1] ended last week, but the original, eight-month boycott continues. It is no longer a community affair, but a national concern.

As an Asian-American, I was jolted at the beginning of the boycott, which allegedly began with an assault on a customer by a store employee, by a comment from a black resident: "The Koreans are a very rude people. They don't understand you have to smile."

Would she have reacted differently had she known smiling at strangers just isn't part of the Korean culture? Would it have made a difference had she known Koreans are just as "unfriendly" to their own because they equate being **solicitous**[2] to being insincere? The Korean **demeanor**[3] is the absence of a demeanor. Koreans have a name for it: *mu-pyo-jung*. It means "lack of expression."

Koreans who travel or live abroad are often concerned that this trait causes misunderstanding. Before the 1988 Seoul Olympics, South Korean officials launched a television and radio campaign urging citizens to greet visitors with a friendly smile.

Some tried but found it difficult. As one housewife told me: "It's hard to smile at strangers when you're not used to it. It seems so phony."

Though it may be difficult for most Americans to tell Koreans apart from Japanese and Chinese, who have been in this country much longer, the contrast between Koreans and their Asian neighbors is striking. Having suffered invasions and a long period of colonization by Japan in this century, Koreans have had to fight for their lives to retain their language and culture. Koreans are feisty. They certainly don't fit the **subservient**[4] or **docile**[5] Asian stereotype.

> Koreans have had to fight for their lives to retain their language and culture.

---

[1] two black-led boycotts . . . in Brooklyn—In 1990, African Americans led two boycotts against Korean-owned groceries in Brooklyn, New York. The African Americans claimed that the Koreans did not treat their black customers with respect.

[2] **solicitous** (suh•LIH•sih•tuhs)—overly attentive and anxious to please.

[3] **demeanor** (dih•MEE•ner)—way a person behaves.

[4] **subservient** (suhb•SUR•vee•uhnt)—behaving like a servant or excessively submissive.

[5] **docile** (DOHS•uhl)—ready and willing to take direction or supervision.

It's hard to smile at strangers

▲
A crowd on a Brooklyn street listens to a speaker during the African-American boycott of Korean businesses.

And Koreans live by *cheong*—a concept that has no Western translation. *Cheong* is love, respect, affinity and loyalty rolled into one. Cheong comes only with time, and only betrayal can end it. For a people who live by this ethos,[6] a mechanical smile is hard to produce.

In America's inner cities, newcomers from Korea do business where no one else will, and where frustration levels are high. Koreans, crippled by the language barrier and the downward mobility that accompanies it, display their worst traits to customers, increasing the frustration. Culturally

[6] ethos—characteristic attitudes or values of a group.

and socially, the newcomers are ill equipped to run businesses in America's inner cities. But because they, like other Asian immigrants, are denied mainstream jobs, they pool their resources and start mom-and-pop stores.

Inner-city African-Americans wonder how these newcomers, who can hardly speak English, have the money to run their own businesses when they themselves can't even get a small loan from a bank. They have little hope of escaping the poverty cycle, yet they see new arrivals living in better neighborhoods and driving better cars.

What they don't see are the 16-hour days and the deep sacrifices made for their children. They don't see the contributions of family and friends, and the informal money-lending system called *kye* that Koreans use instead of banks.

All immigrants go through an "American passage" that requires cultural insight on both sides. Koreans, like other Asians who live in the U.S. mustn't forget that they are indebted to blacks for the social gains won by their civil rights struggle.

Asian-Americans must also remember that while the Confucian culture has taught us how to be good parents, sons and daughters and how to behave with people we know, it has not prepared us for living in a democracy. The Confucian ethos lacks the social conscience that makes democracy work. It isn't enough that we educate our children; we need to think of other people's children too.

One of the boycotted grocers told me this had been a painful but valuable experience: "We Koreans must learn to participate in this society," he said. "When this is over, I'm going to reach out. I want to give part-time work to black youths."

By working together, maybe we can do privately what institutions can't. With Asian-American drive and African-American political experience, we can make it work not only in New York but in Los Angeles, San Francisco, Oakland and Chicago.

Questions to Consider

Responding

1. How do you feel about the American practice of smiling at strangers?

Analyzing

2. Which specific **Confucian values** do you see represented by the Korean Americans, as described by Kang?

3. How might Confucian values and the values of a democracy work together to resolve conflicts between Asian Americans and African Americans?

4. What are the similarities and differences between what Kang is asking Asian Americans to do and what she is asking African Americans to do?

Extending

5. How would you mediate a dispute in which one culture group's traditional beliefs had brought it into conflict with another group?

Literature Connection

A *fact* is a statement that can be proven. An opinion is a statement that reflects a person's belief and cannot be proven. Most nonfiction contains both facts and opinions. Look at the following passage from "Koreans Have a Reason Not to Smile":

One of the two black-led boycotts of Korean grocers in Brooklyn ended last week, but the original, eight-month boycott continues. It is no longer a community affair, but a national concern.

1. Which part of this passage contains a fact?

2. Which part contains an opinion?

Activities

Writing an Editorial

Write an editorial about this quote by former president John F. Kennedy: "We are not afraid to entrust the American people with unpleasant facts, foreign ideas, alien philosophies, and competitive values. For a nation that is afraid to let its people judge the truth and falsehood in an open market is a nation that is afraid of its people." Take any position you like. You may wish to break each part of the quote down before taking it as a whole. Be sure to support your opinions with facts and include examples that your audience will understand. End your editorial by asking your readers to take a specific action.

Performing a Skit

Locate a book with Confucius's teachings. Work with two other students to pick at least three statements of ideas that you believe are worthy to remember and apply. Then present a short skit for each statement that demonstrates its application in the modern world. After performing each skit, ask your audience to summarize what they think the skit taught. Then write the Confucian idea on the blackboard.

Linking Cultures
Festivals

One way in which the members of ethnic groups celebrate their sense of community and their traditions is through festivals. Some of these festivals have their origins in historical events; others are traditional religious or cultural observances. All these festivals provide an opportunity for joyous self-awareness and ethnic pride.

▲
Elaborately dressed marchers participate in a Caribbean Day Parade in Brooklyn, New York.

◀ These marchers are part of an Hispanic celebration.

Mexican Americans carrying an image of the Lady of
Guadalupe lead a ceremony marking the Day of the
Dead, November 2. This festival is an ancient observance
when families both remember their dead and celebrate
the continuity of life.

▲
Native Americans of New Mexico perform a cloud dance.

◀ These Hmong girls are wearing the traditional dress of their people, who come from Laos in Southeast Asia.

▲

Japanese-American women in traditional dress participate in a festival.

The annual Puerto Rican Day Parade in New York celebrates the outstanding contributions of the Puerto Rican people to the city's history. ▶

◀ Korean-American girls wear traditional dress to show ethnic pride at a celebration.

▲
Marchers carry traditional dragon figures to mark Chinese New Year in New York City's Chinatown.

◀ A group of children in Brooklyn, New York, enjoy a Chinese New Year celebration.

▲
African Americans in Ohio hold an annual Jubilation to mark the end of slavery.

Marchers parade in observance of Philippine Independence Day, June 12, which marks the anniversary of the day in 1898 when rebel leader Emilio Aguinaldo declared the independence of the Philippines from Spain. ▶

A griot, a traditional African storyteller, performs for the crowd at a Gullah festival in South Carolina. The Gullah are members of an African-American community of the Sea Islands off the southeast coast of the United States. These islands became a rich storehouse of African-American traditions, because the people living there in isolation retained a purer version of the culture brought over from Africa.

Formally dressed young Mexican Americans in San Antonio celebrate Cinco de Mayo ("Fifth of May"), a Mexican patriotic holiday.
▼

▲
A young Pakistani-American girl wears traditional Pakistani dress at a celebration.

Part Three

Growing Up

The experience of growing up has universal qualities—the sense of wonder, the struggle to measure up. But the character of childhood can also be affected by membership in an ethnic group.

◀ This African-American child jumping rope was photographed by Susie Fitzhugh in Baltimore.

The Secret LION

BY ALBERTO ALVARO RÍOS

About the Author

Born in 1952 to Mexican and British parents, Alberto Alvaro Ríos was raised in Nogales, Arizona, near the Mexican border. His poems and short stories reflect his mixed heritage as well as the region of his youth. His first book of short stories, The Iguana Killers (1984), has been praised for the way it gets into the minds of young boys facing the challenges of growing up in a bilingual and bicultural setting. A winner of numerous awards, Ríos directs the creative writing program at Arizona State University.

About the Selection

Although the **concept of childhood** differs across cultures, in most contemporary societies childhood is a formal phase of social and physical development. The bridge to adulthood appears in the teenage years, but is not legally crossed until age 16 or 18. Historians believe that children over age seven were treated as miniature adults until the 1700s. The modern concept of childhood stresses the innocence of children, the obligation to protect them from harm, and the need to prepare them for adulthood. In general, children are viewed as having a different nature from adults. Culture determines many of the changes that occur from childhood to adulthood. As you read "The Secret Lion," think about how the narrator views childhood, and his childhood, in particular.

I was twelve and in junior high school and something happened that we didn't have a name for, but it was there nonetheless like a lion, and roaring, roaring that way the biggest things do. Everything changed. Just like that. Like the rug, the one that gets pulled— or better, like the tablecloth those magicians pull where the stuff on the table stays the same but the gasp! from the audience makes the staying-the-same part not matter. Like that.

What happened was there were teachers now, not just one teacher, teacher-erz, and we felt personally abandoned somehow. When a person had all these teachers now, he didn't get taken care of the same way, even though six was more than one. Arithmetic went out the door when we walked in. And we saw girls now, but they weren't the same girls we used to know because we couldn't talk to them anymore, not the same way we used to, certainly not to Sandy, even though she was my neighbor, too. Not even to her. She just played the piano all the time. And there were words, oh there were words in junior high school, and we wanted to know what they were, and how a person did them—that's what school was supposed to be for. Only,

in junior high school, school wasn't school, everything was backwardlike. If you went up to a teacher and said the word to try and find out what it meant you got in trouble for saying it. So we didn't. And we figured it must have been that way about other stuff, too, so we never said anything about anything—we weren't stupid.

But my friend Sergio and I, we solved junior high school. We would come home from school on the bus, put our books away, change shoes, and go across the highway to the **arroyo**.[1] It was the one place we were not supposed to go. So we did. This was, after all, what junior high had at least shown us. It was our river, though, our personal Mississippi, our friend from long back, and it was full of stories and all the branch forts we had built in it when we were still the Vikings of America,[2] with our own symbol, which we had carved every-where, even in the sand, which let the water take it. That was good, we had decided; whoever was at the end of this river would know about us.

At the very very top of our growing lungs, what we would do down there was shout every dirty word we could

---

[1] **arroyo** (uh•ROY•oh)—dry creek bed.

[2] Vikings of America—Scandinavian people of the Middle Ages who established settlements in North America around 1000.

think of, in every combination we could come up with, and we would yell about girls, and all the things we wanted to do with them, as loud as we could—we didn't know what we wanted to do with them, just things—and we would yell about teachers, and how we loved some of them, like Miss Crevelone, and how we wanted to **dissect**[3] some of them, making signs of the cross, like priests, and we would yell this stuff over and over because it felt good, we couldn't explain why, it just felt good and for the first time in our lives there was nobody to tell us we couldn't. So we did.

> "Whatisit?" We didn't know. We just knew it was great.

One Thursday we were walking along shouting this way, and the railroad, the Southern Pacific, which ran above and along the far side of the arroyo, had dropped a grinding ball down there, which was, we found out later, a cannonball thing used in mining. A bunch of them were put in a big vat which turned around and crushed the ore. One had been dropped, or thrown—what do caboose[4] men do when they get bored—but it got down there regardless and as we were walking along yelling about one girl or another, a particular Claudia, we found it, one of these things, looked at it, picked it up, and got very very excited, and held it and passed it back and forth, and we were saying, "Guythisis, this is, geeGuythis. . .": we had this perception about nature then, that nature is imperfect and that round things are perfect: we said "GuyGodthis is perfect, thisisthis is perfect, it's round, round and heavy, it'sit's the best thing we'veeverseen. Whatisit?" We didn't know. We just knew it was great. We just, whatever, we played with it, held it some more.

And then we had to decide what to do with it. We knew, because of a lot of things, that if we were going to take this and show it to anybody, this discovery, this best thing, was going to be taken away from us. That's the way it works with little kids, like all the polished quartz, the tons of it we had collected piece by piece over the years. Junior high kids too. If we took it home, my mother, we knew, was going to look at it and say, "Throw that dirty thing in the, get rid of it." Simple like, like that. "But ma it's the best thing I" "Getridofit." Simple.

---

[3] **dissect**—cut apart.

[4] caboose—last car on a freight train, having kitchen and sleeping facilities for the train crew.

So we didn't. Take it home. Instead, we came up with the answer. We dug a hole and we buried it. And we marked it secretly. Lots of secret signs. And came back the next week to dig it up and, we didn't know, pass it around some more or something, but we didn't find it. We dug up that whole bank, and we never found it again. We tried.

Sergio and I talked about that ball or whatever it was when we couldn't find it. All we used were small words, neat, good. Kid words. What we were really saying, but didn't know the words, was how much that ball was like that place, that whole arroyo: couldn't tell anybody about it, didn't understand what it was, didn't have a name for it. It just felt good. It was just perfect in the way it was that place, that whole going to that place, that whole junior high school lion. It was just iron-heavy, it had no name, it felt good or not, we couldn't take it home to show our mothers, and once we buried it, it was gone forever.

The ball was gone, like the first reasons we had come to that arroyo years earlier, like the first time we had seen the arroyo, it was gone like everything else that had been taken away. This was not our first lesson. We stopped going to the arroyo after not finding the thing, the same way we had stopped going there years earlier and headed for the mountains. Nature seemed to keep pushing us around one way or another, teaching us the same thing every place we ended up. Nature's gang was tough that way, teaching us stuff.

When we were young we moved away from town, me and my family. Sergio's was already out there. Out in the wilds. Or at least the new place seemed like the wilds since everything looks bigger the smaller a man is. I was five, I guess, and we had moved three miles north of Nogales, where we had lived, three miles north of the Mexican border. We looked across the highway in one direction and there was the arroyo; hills stood up in the other direction. Mountains, for a small man.

When the first summer came the very first place we went to was of course the one place we weren't supposed to go, the arroyo. We went down in there and found water running, summer rainwater mostly, and we went swimming. But every third or fourth or fifth day, the sewage treatment plant that was, we found out, upstream, would release whatever it

Dennis Stock photographed this New Mexico boy examining desert plants in 1969. ▶

was that it released, and we would never know exactly what day that was, and a person really couldn't tell right off by looking at the water, not every time, not so a person could get out in time. So, we went swimming that summer and some days we had a lot of fun. Some days we didn't. We found a thousand ways to explain what happened on those other days, constructing elaborate stories about neighborhood dogs, and hadn't she, my mother, miscalculated her step before, too? But she knew something was up because we'd come running into the house those days, wanting to take a shower, even—if this can be imagined—in the middle of the day.

That was the first time we stopped going to the arroyo. It taught us to look the other way. We decided, as the second side of summer came, we wanted to go into the mountains. They were still mountains then. We

went running in one summer Thursday morning, my friend Sergio and I, into my mother's kitchen, and said, well, what'zin, what'zin those hills over there—we used her word so she'd understand us—and she said nothingdon'tworryaboutit. So we went out, and we weren't dumb, we thought with our eyes to each other, ohhoshe'stryingtokeep somethingfromus. We knew adults.

We had read the books, after all; we knew about bridges and castles and wildtreacherousraging alligator-mouth rivers. We wanted them. So we were going to go out and get them. We went back that morning into that kitchen and we said, "We're going out there, we're going into the hills, we're going away for three days, don't worry." She said, "All right."

"You know," I said to Sergio, "if we're going to go away for three days, well, we ought to at least pack a lunch."

But we were two young boys with no patience for what we thought at the time was mom-stuff: making sa-and-wiches. My mother didn't offer. So we got our little kid knapsacks that my mother had sewn for us, and into them we put the jar of mustard. A loaf of bread. Knivesforksplates, bottles of Coke, a can opener. This was lunch for the two of us. And we were weighed down, humped over to be strong enough to carry this stuff. But we started walking, anyway, into the hills. We were going to eat berries and stuff otherwise. "Goodbye." My mom said that.

After the first hill we were dead. But we walked. My mother could still see us. And we kept walking. We walked until we got to where the sun is straight overhead, noon. That place. Where that is doesn't matter; it's time to eat. The truth is we weren't anywhere close to that place. We just agreed that the sun was overhead and that it was time to eat, and by tilting our heads a little we could make that the truth.

"We really ought to start looking for a place to eat."

"Yeah. Let's look for a good place to eat." We went back and forth saying that for fifteen minutes, making it lunch time because that's what we always said back and forth before lunch times at home. "Yeah, I'm hungry all right." I nodded my head. "Yeah, I'm hungry all right too. I'm hungry." He nodded his head. I nodded my head back. After a good deal more nodding, we were ready, just as we came over a little hill. We hadn't found the mountains yet. This was a little hill.

And on the other side of this hill we found heaven.

It was just what we thought it would be.

Perfect. Heaven was green, like nothing else in Arizona. And it wasn't a cemetery or like that because we had seen cemeteries and they had gravestones and stuff and this didn't. This was perfect, had trees, lots of trees, had birds, like we had never seen before. It was like *The Wizard of Oz*, like when they got to Oz and everything was so green, so emerald, they had to wear those glasses,[5] and we ran just like them, laughing, laughing that way we did that moment, and we went running down to this clearing in it all, hitting each other that good way we did.

> **Heaven was green, like nothing else in Arizona.**

---

[5] *The Wizard of Oz* . . . glasses—In L. Frank Baum's fantasy *The Wizard of Oz*, the inhabitants of Oz wear green-tinted glasses to protect their eyes from the brightness of the "emerald city."

We got down there, we kept laughing, we kept hitting each other, we unpacked our stuff, and we started acting "rich." We knew all about how to do that, like blowing on our nails, then rubbing them on our chests for the shine. We made our sandwiches, opened our Cokes, got out the rest of the stuff, the salt and pepper shakers. I found this particular hole and I put my Coke right into it, a perfect fit, and I called it my Coke-holder. I got down next to it on my back, because everyone knows that rich people eat lying down, and I got my sandwich in one hand and put my other arm around the Coke in its holder. When I wanted a drink, I lifted my neck a little, put out my lips, and tipped my Coke a little with the crook of my elbow. Ah.

We were there, lying down, eating our sandwiches, laughing, throwing bread at each other and out for the birds. This was heaven. We were laughing and we couldn't believe it. My mother was keeping something from us, ah ha, but we had found her out. We even found water over at the side of the clearing to wash our plates with—we had brought plates. Sergio started washing his plates when he was done, and I was being rich with my Coke, and this day in summer was right.

When suddenly these two men came, from around a corner of trees and the tallest grass we had ever seen. They had bags on their backs, leather bags, bags and sticks.

We didn't know what clubs were, but I learned later, like I learned about the grinding balls. The two men yelled at us. Most specifically, one wanted me to take my Coke out of my Coke-holder so he could sink his golf ball into it.

Something got taken away from us that moment. Heaven. We grew up a little bit, and couldn't go backward. We learned. No one had ever told us about golf. They had told us about heaven. And it went away. We got golf in exchange.

We went back to the arroyo for the rest of that summer, and tried to have fun the best we could. We learned to be ready for finding the grinding ball. We loved it, and when we buried it we knew what would happen. The truth is, we didn't look so hard for it. We were two boys and twelve summers then, and not stupid. Things get taken away.

We buried it because it was perfect. We didn't tell my mother, but together it was all we talked about, till we forgot. It was the lion.

Responding

1. Have you ever found a special place or object that represented something important to you? How did this experience affect your life?

Analyzing

2. When the narrator and Sergio discover the grinding ball, how does the author express their excitement?

3. Why do you think the narrator's mother allowed the narrator and his friend to go to the hills/mountains but not to the arroyo?

4. How would you sum up the **concept of childhood** that this story expresses?

Extending

5. How might the idea that "things get taken away" apply to life beyond childhood?

A *symbol* is a person, a place, an object, or an action that stands for something beyond itself. A flag, for example, may symbolize a country; or a bird might symbolize freedom.

1. What things in "The Secret Lion" do you think are intended to be symbolic?

2. What do they symbolize?

3. How is the symbolism of the grinding ball like that of the golf course?

4. How might the narrator's changing experiences at the arroyo symbolize the changes of childhood?

Writing an Essay

Write a personal essay about a special place or object from your past. Explain how the place or object symbolizes your childhood. Use dialogue, anecdotes (stories that serve as examples of a point you are making), and sensory details to bring your essay to life. Use your natural style of speaking in your writing as much as possible.

Drenched in Light

by Zora Neale Hurston

About the Author

Although she was born in Alabama, Zora Neale Hurston (1891–1960) claimed Eatonville, Florida as her hometown. She lived there for most of her childhood, and it shaped much of her writing. Hurston studied in the North, but returned to Florida to collect and publish Southern folklore. She was known as a major figure of the Harlem Renaissance, an African-American cultural movement of the 1920s. However, she did not have commercial success during her lifetime. In the 1970s, her novel Their Eyes Were Watching God *(1937) was rediscovered. Today she has become a popular literary figure.*

About the Selection

*A **dialect** is a form of language that is spoken in a particular place or by a particular group of people. The dialects of a language may differ from one another in pronunciation, vocabulary, and grammar. Within one language, there is typically a standard dialect that is used by the mass media and in public institutions such as courts and schools. A growing child may first speak dialect at home and later learn a more standard form of the language. As you read "Drenched in Light," see how the author uses the child Isis Watt's dialect to make her a vivid character.*

You Isie Watts! Git 'own offen dat gate post an' rake up dis yahd!"

The little brown figure perched upon the gate post looked yearningly up the gleaming shell road that led to Orlando, and down the road that led to Sanford and shrugged her thin shoulders. This heaped kindling on Grandma Potts' already burning ire.

"Lawd a-mussy!" she screamed, enraged—"Heah Joel, gimme dat wash stick. Ah'll show dat limb of Satan[1] she kain't shake huhseff at me. If she ain't down by de time Ah gets dere, Ah'll break huh down in de lines."[2]

"Aw Gran'ma, Ah see Mist' George and Jim Robinson comin' and Ah wanted to wave at 'em," the child said **petulantly**.[3]

"You jes wave dat rake at dis heah yahd, madame, else Ah'll take you down a button hole lower. You'se too 'oomanish jumpin' up in everybody's face dat pass."

This struck the child in a very sore spot for nothing pleased her so much as to sit atop of the gate post and hail the passing vehicles on their way South to Orlando, or North to Sanford. That white shell road was her great attraction. She raced up and down the stretch of it that lay before her gate like a round eyed puppy hailing gleefully all travelers. Everybody in the country, white and colored, knew little Isis Watts, the joyful. The Robinson brothers, white cattlemen, were particularly fond of her and always extended a stirrup for her to climb up behind one of them for a short ride, or let her try to crack the long bull whips and yee whoo at the cows.

Grandma Potts went inside and Isis literally waved the rake at the "chaws" of ribbon cane[4] that lay so bountifully about the yard in company with the knots and peelings, with a thick sprinkling of peanut hulls.

The herd of cattle in their envelope of gray dust came alongside and Isis dashed out to the nearest stirrup and was lifted up.

> Everybody in the country, white and colored, knew little Isis Watts, the joyful.

---

[1] limb of Satan—mischievous child.

[2] lines—dialect for "loins," the area between the ribs and hips.

[3] **petulantly** (PECH•uh•luhnt•lee)—with unreasonable ill-temper.

[4] "chaws" of ribbon cane—strips of sugar cane for chewing.

American artist Robert Henri painted this portrait, *Eva Green*, in 1907.

"Hello theah, Snidlits, I was wonderin' wheah you was," said Jim Robinson as she snuggled down behind him in the saddle. They were almost out of the danger zone when Grandma emerged.

"You Isie-e!" she bawled.

The child slid down on the opposite side from the house and executed a flank[5] movement through the corn patch that brought her into the yard from behind the privy.

"You lil' hasion[6] you! Wheah you been?"

"Out in de back yahd," Isis lied and did a cart wheel and a few fancy steps on her way to the front again.

"If you doan git tuh dat yahd, Ah make a mommuk[7] of you!" Isis observed that Grandma was cutting a fancy assortment of switches from peach, guana, and cherry trees.

She finished the yard by raking everything under the edge of the porch and began a romp with the dogs, those lean, floppy eared 'coon hounds that all country folks keep. But Grandma vetoed this also.

"Isie, you set 'own on dat porch! Uh great big 'leben yeah ole gal racin' an' rompin' lak dat—set 'own!"

Isis impatiently flung herself upon the steps.

"Git up offa dem steps, you aggravatin' limb, 'fore Ah git dem hick'ries tuh you, an' set yo' seff on a cheah."

Isis petulantly arose and sat down as violently as possible in a chair, but slid down until she all but sat upon her shoulder blades.

"Now look atcher," Grandma screamed, "Put yo' knees together, an' git up offen yo' backbone! Lawd, you

---

5 flank—side.

6 hasion—perhaps dialect for "heathen."

7 mommuk—dialect word meaning "piece."

know dis hellion is gwine make me stomp huh insides out."

Isis sat bolt upright as if she wore a ramrod[8] down her back and began to whistle. Now there are certain things that Grandma Potts felt no one of this female persuasion should do—one was to sit with the knees separated, "settin' **brazen**"[9] she called it; another was whistling, another playing with boys, neither must a lady cross her legs.

Up she jumped from her seat to get the switches.

"So youse whistlin' in mah face, huh!" She glared till her eyes were beady[10] and Isis bolted for safety. But the noon hour brought John Watts, the widowed father, and this excused the child from sitting for criticism.

Being the only girl in the family, of course she must wash the dishes, which she did in intervals between frolics[11] with the dogs. She even gave Jake, the puppy, a swim in the dish-pan by holding him suspended above the water that reeked of "pot likker"—just high enough so that his feet would be immersed. The **deluded**[12] puppy swam and swam without ever crossing the pan, much to his annoyance. Hearing Grandma

she hurriedly dropped him on the floor, which he tracked up with feet wet with dishwater.

Grandma took her patching and settled down in the front room to sew. She did this every afternoon, and invariably slept in the big red rocker with her head lolled back over the back, the sewing falling from her hand.

Isis had crawled under the center table with its red plush cover with little round balls for fringe. She was lying on her back imagining herself various personages. She wore trading robes, golden slippers with blue bottoms. She rode white horses with flaring pink nostrils to the horizon, for she still believed that to be land's end. She was picturing herself gazing over the edge of the world into the abyss when the spool of cotton fell from Grandma's lap and rolled away under the whatnot.[13] Isis drew back from her contemplation of the nothingness at the horizon and glanced up at the sleeping woman. Her head had fallen far back. She breathed with a regular "snark" intake and soft "poosah"

---

[8] ramrod—rod to clean guns, referring to a straight posture.

[9] **brazen** (BRAY•zuhn)—very bold.

[10] beady—like small, round, shiny beads.

[11] frolics—playing.

[12] **deluded** (dih•LOOD•ehd)—deceived.

[13] whatnot—shelf displaying decorative objects.

exhaust. But Isis was a visual minded child. She heard the snores only sub-consciously but she saw straggling beard on Grandma's chin, trembling a little with every "snark" and "poosah." They were long gray hairs curled here and there against the dark brown skin. Isis was moved with pity for her mother's mother.

> **No ladies don't weah no whiskers if they kin help it.**

"Poah Gran-ma needs a shave," she murmured, and set about it. Just then Joel, next older than Isis, entered with a can of bait.

"Come on Isie, les' we all go fishin'. The perch is bitin' fine in Blue Sink."

"Sh-sh—" cautioned his sister, "Ah got to shave Gran'ma."

"Who say so?" Joel asked, surprised.

"Nobody doan hafta tell me. Look at her chin. No ladies don't weah no whiskers if they kin help it. But Gran'ma gittin' ole an' she doan know how to shave like me."

The conference adjourned to the back porch lest Grandma wake.

"Aw, Isie, you doan know nothin' 'bout shavin' a-tall—but a *man* lak *me*—"

"Ah do so know."

"You don't not. Ah'm goin' shave her mahseff."

"Naw, you won't neither, Smarty. Ah saw her first an' thought it all up first," Isis declared, and ran to the calico covered box on the wall above the wash basin and seized her father's razor. Joel was quick and seized the mug and brush.

"Now!" Isis cried defiantly, "Ah got the razor."

"Goody, goody, goody, pussy cat, Ah got th' brush an' you can't shave 'thout lather—see! Ah know mo' than you," Joel retorted.

"Aw, who don't know dat?" Isis pretended to scorn. But seeing her progress blocked for lack of lather she compromised.

"Ah know! Les' we all shave her. You lather an' Ah shave."

This was agreeable to Joel. He made mountains of lather and anointed his own chin, and the chin of Isis and the dogs, splashed the walls and at last was persuaded to lather Grandma's chin. Not that he was loath[14] but he wanted his new plaything to last as long as possible.

---

[14] loath (lohth)—unwilling or reluctant.

Isis stood on one side of the chair with the razor clutched cleaver fashion. The niceties[15] of razor-handling had passed over her head. The thing with her was to *hold* the razor—sufficient in itself.

Joel splashed on the lather in great gobs and Grandma awoke.

For one bewildered moment she stared at the grinning boy with the brush and mug but sensing another presence, she turned to behold the business face of Isis and the razor-clutching hand. Her jaw dropped and Grandma, forgetting years and rheumatism,[16] bolted from the chair and fled the house, screaming.

"She's gone to tell papa, Isie. You didn't have no business wid his razor and he's gonna lick yo hide," Joel cried, running to replace mug and brush.

"You too, chuckle-head, you, too," retorted Isis. "You was playin' wid his brush and put it all over the dogs—Ah seen you put it on Ned an' Beulah." Isis shaved some slivers from the door jamb with the razor and replaced it in the box. Joel took his bait and pole and hurried to Blue Sink. Isis crawled under the house to brood over the whipping she knew would come. She had meant well.

But sounding brass and tinkling cymbal[17] drew her forth. The local lodge of the Grand United Order of Odd Fellows led by a braying, thudding band, was marching in full regalia down the road. She had forgotten the barbecue and log-rolling to be held today for the benefit of the new hall.

Music to Isis meant motion. In a minute razor and whipping forgotten, she was doing a fair imitation of the Spanish dancer she had seen in a medicine show some time before. Isis' feet were gifted—she could dance most anything she saw.

> **Isis crawled under the house to brood over the whipping she knew would come.**

Up, up went her spirits, her brown little feet doing all sorts of intricate things and her body in rhythm, hand curving above her head. But the music was growing faint. Grandma nowhere in sight. She stole out of the gate, running and dancing after the band.

---

[15] niceties (NY•suh•teez)—fine points, small details.

[16] rheumatism (ROO•muh•tihz•uhm)—painful stiffness and swelling of the muscles and joints.

[17] sounding brass and tinkling cymbal—music; an allusion to a verse in Paul's First Letter to the Corinthians in the New Testament.

Then she stopped. She couldn't dance at the carnival. Her dress was torn and dirty. She picked a long stemmed daisy and, thrust it behind her ear. But the dress, no better. Oh, an idea! In the battered round topped trunk in the bedroom!

She raced back to the house, then, happier, raced down the white dusty road to the picnic grove, gorgeously clad. People laughed good naturedly at her, the band played and Isis danced because she couldn't help it. A crowd of children gather admiringly about her as she wheeled lightly about, hand on hip, flower between her teeth with the red and white fringe of the tablecloth—Grandma's new red tablecloth that she wore in lieu of a Spanish shawl—trailing in the dust. It was too ample for her meager form, but she wore it like a gypsy. Her brown feet twinkled in and out of the fringe. Some grown people joined the children about her. The Grand Exalted Ruler rose to speak; the band was hushed, but Isis danced on, the crowd clapping their hands for her. No one listened to the Exalted one, for little by little the multitude had surrounded the brown dancer.

An automobile drove up to the crowd and halted. Two white men and a lady got out and pushed into the crowd, suppressing mirth discreetly behind gloved hands. Isis looked up and waved them a magnificent hail and went on dancing until—

Before Dawn is a mosaic created by African-American artist Romare Bearden in 1989. ▶

Grandma had returned to the house and missed Isis and straightway sought her at the festivities expecting to find her in her soiled dress, shoeless, gaping at the crowd, but what she saw drove her frantic. Here was her granddaughter dancing before a gaping crowd in her brand new red tablecloth, and reeking of lemon extract, for Isis had added the final touch to her costume. She *must* have perfume.

Isis saw Grandma and bolted. She heard her cry: "Mah Gawd, mah brand new tablecloth Ah jus' bought f'um O'landah!" as she fled through the crowd and on into the woods.

She followed the little creek until she came to the ford in a rutty wagon road that led to Apopka and laid down on the cool grass at the roadside. The April sun was quite hot.

Misery, misery and woe settled down upon her and the child wept. She knew another whipping was in store for her.

"Oh, Ah wish Ah could die, then Gran'ma an' papa would be sorry they beat me so much. Ah b'leeve Ah'll run away an' never go home no mo'. Ah'm goin' drown mahseff in th' creek!" Her woe grew attractive.

Isis got up and waded into the water. She routed out a tiny 'gator and a huge bull frog. She splashed and sang, enjoying herself immensely. The purr of a motor struck her ear and she saw a large, powerful car jolting along the rutty road toward her. It stopped at the water's edge.

> **Isis saw Grandma and bolted.**

"Well, I declare, it's our little gypsy," exclaimed the man at the wheel. "What are you doing here, now?"

"Ah'm killin' mahseff," Isis declared dramatically. "Cause Gran'ma beats me too much."

There was a hearty burst of laughter from the machine.

"You'll last sometime the way you are going about it. Is this the way to Maitland? We want to go to the Park Hotel."

Isis saw no longer any reason to die. She came up out of the water, holding up the dripping fringe of the tablecloth.

"Naw, indeedy. You go to Maitlan' by the shell road—it goes by mah house—an' turn off at Lake Sebelia to the clay road that takes you right to the do'."

"Well," went on the driver, smiling furtively. "Could you quit dying long enough to go with us?"

"Yessuh," she said thoughtfully, "Ah wanta go wid you."

The door of the car swung open. She was invited to a seat beside the driver. She had often dreamed of riding in one of these heavenly chariots but never thought she would, actually.

"Jump in then, Madame Tragedy, and show us. We lost ourselves after we left your barbecue."

During the drive Isis explained to the kind lady who smelt faintly of violets and to the **indifferent**[18] men that she was really a princess. She told them about her trips to the horizon, about the trailing gowns, the gold shoes with blue bottoms—she insisted on the blue bottoms—the white charger, the time when she was

> **This is where the child lives. I hate to give her up though.**

Hercules and had slain numerous dragons and sundry[19] giants. At last the car approached her gate over which stood the umbrella Chinaberry tree. The car was abreast of the gate and had all but passed when Grandma spied her glorious tablecloth lying back against the upholstery of the Packard.

"You Isie-e!" she bawled, "You lil' wretch you! Come heah *dis instunt*."

"That's me," the child confessed, **mortified**,[20] to the lady on the rear seat.

"Oh, Sewell, stop the car. This is where the child lives. I hate to give her up though."

"Do you wanta keep me?" Isis brightened.

"Oh, I wish I could, you shining little morsel. Wait, I'll try to save you a whipping this time."

She dismounted with the **gaudy**[21] lemon flavored culprit and advanced to the gate where Grandma stood glowering, switches in hand.

"You're gointuh ketchit f'um yo' haid to yo' heels m'lady. Jes' come in heah."

---

[18] **indifferent**—lacking concern or interest.
[19] **sundry**—various.
[20] **mortified** (MOHR•tuh•fyd)—ashamed.
[21] **gaudy**—showy in a tasteless or vulgar way.

◄ Frances Benjamin Johnston (1864–1952) was one of the first American women to become well-known as a photographer. She photographed these African-American children in rural Virginia around 1890.

"Why, good afternoon," she accosted[22] the furious grandparent. "You're not going to whip this poor little thing, are you?" the lady asked in **conciliatory**[23] tones.

"Yes, Ma'am. She's de wustest lil' limb dat ever drawed bref. Jes' look at mah new tablecloth, dat ain't never been washed. She done traipsed all over de woods, uh dancin' an' uh prancin' in it. She done took a razor to me t'day an' Lawd knows whut mo'."

Isis clung to the white hand fearfully.

"Ah wuzn't gointer hurt Gran'ma, miss—Ah wuz jus' gointer shave her whiskers fuh huh 'cause she's old an' can't."

The white hand closed tightly over the little brown one that was quite soiled. She could understand a voluntary act of love even though it miscarried.

"Now, Mrs. er—er—I didn't get the name—how much did your tablecloth cost?"

---

[22] accosted—greeted.

[23] **conciliatory.**(kuhn•SIHL•ee•uh•TAWR•ee)—in a way as to overcome another's distrust.

"One whole big silvah dollar down at O'landah—ain't had it a week yit."

"Now here's five dollars to get another one. The little thing loves laughter. I want her to go on to the hotel and dance in that tablecloth for me. I can stand a little light today—"

"Oh, yessum, yessum." Grandma cut in, "Everything's alright, sho' she kin go, yessum."

> **I want brightness and this Isis is joy itself, why she's drenched in light!**

The lady went on: "I want brightness and this Isis is joy itself, why she's drenched in light!"

Isis for the first time in her life, felt herself appreciated and danced up and down in an ecstasy of joy for a minute.

"Now, behave yo'seff, Isie, ovah at de hotel wid de white folks," Grandma cautioned, pride in her voice, though she strove to hide it. "Lawd, ma'am, dat gal keeps me so frackshus, Ah doan know mah haid f'um mah feet. Ah orter comb huh haid, too, befo' she go wid you all."

"No, no, don't bother. I like her as she is. I don't think she'd like it either, being combed and scrubbed. Come on, Isis."

Feeling that Grandma had been somewhat **squelched**[24] did not detract from Isis' spirit at all. She pranced over to the waiting motor and this time seated herself on the rear seat between the sweet, smiling lady and the rather aloof man in gray.

"Ah'm gointer stay wid you all," she said with a great deal of warmth, and snuggled up to her benefactress. "Want me tuh sing a song fuh you?"

"There, Helen, you've been adopted," said the man with a short, harsh laugh.

"Oh, I hope so, Harry." She put her arm about the red draped figure at her side and drew it close until she felt the warm puffs of the child's breath against her side. She looked hungrily ahead of her and spoke into space rather than to anyone in the car. "I want a little of her sunshine to soak into my soul. I need it."

---

[24] **squelched**—crushed, put down, or silenced.

Questions to Consider

Responding

1. As a child, how did you handle the problem of balancing what you wanted to do and what adults wanted you to do?

Analyzing

2. Why do you think Isis aggravates her grandmother so much?

3. How does the author use **dialect** to make Isis and the other characters come to life?

4. Why do you think Grandma lets Isis go to the hotel with the white folks?

5. Why do you think the white woman, Helen, is so taken with Isis, while the white men seem far less interested in her?

Extending

6. According to this story, what seem to be the good and bad things about growing up?

Literature Connection

A conversation between characters in a literary work is called dialogue. *In poetry, novels, and short stories, dialogue is usually set off with quotation marks to indicate a speaker's exact words. (In a play, dialogue follows a character's name and is not placed within quotation marks.) Dialogue is a very effective way of revealing character.*

1. How is the dialogue between Isis and the white folks different from the dialogue between her and her Grandma and brother?

2. What does the dialogue between Grandma and the white lady suggest about how they see their social standing to each other?

Activities

Writing Dialogue

With your parents' permission, tape-record a casual conversation among members of your family at the dinner table or while involved in some family task or entertainment. Then transcribe the recording (write what was said). Try to reproduce the actual speech patterns of your family. Use some of the dialogue you recorded in a short story featuring your family. Share the story with them, and get their feedback on your interpretation of their dialect.

Performing Dialect

Locate a literary selection that uses dialect. Perform a reading of the selection (either a portion or the whole) for your classmates. Have them first read the selection. After your performance, invite comments about how the oral recital affected their understanding and appreciation of the selection.

flash cards

by Rita Dove

About the Author

Born in Akron, Ohio, in 1952, Rita Dove was educated at Miami University in Ohio, the University of Iowa, and in Germany. She has written drama, short stories, and a novel, but is best known as a poet. Dove's poetry collection about her grandparents, Thomas and Beulah *(1986), won the Pulitzer Prize. In 1995, she became the youngest person and the first African American to become Poet Laureate of the United States. Today, she teaches and writes a column on poetry for the* Washington Post—*part of her goal to bring poetry into people's everyday lives.*

About the Selections

The **work ethic** *is a set of values based on the moral virtues of hard work and careful attention to one's duties. In American tradition, the work ethic is often traced back to the English Puritans who settled New England. However, the work ethic has also been emphasized by Americans from many other cultural backgrounds. Children learn the work ethic as part of growing up. As you read "Flash Cards" and "Mother to Son" (page 150), examine how each poem presents the values of the work ethic.*

In math I was the whiz kid, keeper
of oranges and apples. *What you don't understand,
master,* my father said; the faster
I answered, the faster they came.

I could see one bud on the teacher's geranium,
one clear bee sputtering[1] at the wet pane.
The tulip trees always dragged after heavy rain
so I tucked my head as my boots slapped home.

My father put up his feet after work
and relaxed with a highball and *The Life of Lincoln*.
After supper we drilled and I climbed the dark

before sleep, before a thin voice hissed
numbers as I spun on a wheel. I had to guess.
Ten, I kept saying, *I'm only ten.*

---

[1] sputtering—making short bursts of popping sounds by excited or confused movement.

◀ A girl grapples with math problems in this photograph by Peter Hrizdak.

In math
I was the
whiz kid

Mother to Son

by Langston Hughes

About the Author

Langston Hughes (1902–1967) was born in Joplin, Missouri, and traveled widely as a young man. He finally made his home in Harlem. He attended Columbia University and received his degree from Lincoln University in Pennsylvania. Hughes was the first African American to support himself entirely from his writing. He wrote novels, short stories, plays, song lyrics, essays, and radio scripts, but is best known for his poetry. Wherever Hughes went, he wrote poetry in jazz clubs, letting the rhythm of the music emerge in his writing.

Well, son, I'll tell you:
Life for me ain't been no crystal stair.
It's had tacks in it,
And splinters,
And boards torn up,
And places with no carpet on the floor—
Bare.
But all the time
I'se been a-climbin' on,
And reachin' landin's,
And turnin' corners,
And sometimes goin' in the dark
Where there ain't been no light.
So, boy, don't you turn back.
Don't you set down on the steps
'Cause you finds it's kinder hard.
Don't you fall now—
For I'se still goin', honey,
I'se still climbin',
And life for me ain't been no crystal stair.

Responding

1. How do you feel about the advice these parents give their children?

Analyzing

2. What does the speaker in "Flash Cards" mean by the phrase, "keeper of oranges and apples"?

3. To what is climbing a stair compared in "Mother to Son"?

4. In this poem, what do you suppose might have been the tacks, splinters, torn-up boards, and bare boards in the mother's climb?

5. What is each of these poems saying about children and the **work ethic**?

Extending

6. If someone asked for advice on how to succeed, what would you tell him or her?

An author's or narrator's voice is his or her distinctive style or manner of expression. It may reveal much about the author or narrator's personality. Look at the following passage from "Mother to Son":

Don't you fall now—
For I'se still goin', honey,
I'se still climbin',
And life for me ain't been no
    crystal stair.

1. What words would you use to describe the voice of this speaker?

2. How does the voice of the speaker in "Flash Cards" differ from that of the speaker in "Mother to Son"?

Gathering Advice

Working with some classmates, use quotation dictionaries to gather together some famous observations on what success in life is and how to achieve it. Discuss the various definitions of success and advice on how to get it. Decide which ones seem the best and which ones seem the worst. Letter the best on a piece of posterboard labeled "Do's" and the worst on another labeled "Don'ts." Then decorate the posters and display them both in your classroom.

AT LAST I KILL A BUFFALO

BY LUTHER STANDING BEAR

About the Author

Luther Standing Bear (1868–1939) was a chief of the Ogalala Lakota Sioux. He was raised as a traditional Sioux on the Pine Ridge Reservation in South Dakota. Standing Bear became one of the first Native Americans to attend the Carlisle Indian School in Pennsylvania. He toured with the Buffalo Bill Wild West Show and later worked as an actor. He fought to improve conditions on the reservations by writing books about the Sioux, including two autobiographies.

About the Selection

The American buffalo was particularly important to the Native Americans of the Great Plains. Historically, buffalo provided most of the Plains Indians' necessities: meat, hides for clothing and tents, sinew for thread and bow strings, bone for tools, and hooves for glue. The **significance of the buffalo** *was spiritual as well. The Plains tribes considered the buffalo a sacred animal. Some performed special songs and dances to bring the buffalo herds close for hunting. In addition, as a Plains Indian boy was growing up, his first buffalo hunt was a major step toward adulthood. In "At Last I Kill a Buffalo," note how the author expresses the significance of the buffalo in his own childhood and in the life of his people.*

At last the day came when my father allowed me to go on a buffalo hunt with him. And what a proud boy I was!

Ever since I could remember my father had been teaching me the things that I should know and preparing me to be a good hunter. I had learned to make bows and to string them and to make arrows and tip them with feathers. I knew how to ride my pony no matter how fast he would go, and I felt that I was brave and did not fear danger. All these things I had learned for just this day when Father would allow me to go with him on a buffalo hunt. It was the event for which every Sioux boy eagerly waited. To ride side by side with the best hunters of the tribe, to hear the terrible noise of the great herds as they ran, and then to help to bring home the kill was the most thrilling day of any Indian boy's life. The only other event which could equal it would be the day I went for the first time on the warpath to meet the enemy and protect my tribe.

On the following early morning we were to start, so the evening was spent in preparation. Although the tepees[1] were full of activity, there was no noise or confusion outside. Always the evening before a buffalo hunt and when everyone was usually in his tepee, an old man went around the circle of tepees calling, "I-ni-la, i-ni-la," not loudly, but so everyone could hear. The old man was saying, "Keep quiet, keep quiet." We all knew that the scouts had come in and reported buffalo near and that we must all keep the camp in stillness. It was not necessary for the old man to go into each tepee and explain to the men that tomorrow there would be a big hunt, as the buffalo were coming. He did not order the men to prepare their weapons, and neither did he order the mothers to keep children from crying. The one word, "I-ni-la," was sufficient to bring quiet to the whole camp. That night there would be no calling or shouting from tepee to tepee, and no child would cry aloud. Even the horses and dogs obeyed the command for quiet, and all night not a horse neighed and not a dog barked. The very presence of quiet was everywhere. Such is the orderliness of a Sioux camp that men, women, children, and animals seem to have a common understanding and sympathy. It is no mystery but natural that the Indian and his animals understand each other very well both with words and without words. There are

---

[1] tepees (TEE•peez)—cone-shaped tents of animal hide, traditionally used by Plains Indian peoples.

words, however, that the Indian uses that are understood by both his horses and dogs. When on a hunt, if one of the warriors speaks the word "A-a-ah" rather quickly and sharply, every man, horse, and dog will stop instantly and listen. Not a move will be made by an animal until the men move or speak further. As long as the hunters listen, the animals will listen also.

The night preceding a buffalo hunt was always an exciting night, even though it was quiet in camp. There would be much talk in the tepees around the fires. There would be sharpening of arrows and of knives. New bowstrings would be made, and quivers[2] would be filled with arrows.

It was in the fall of the year, and the evenings were cool as Father and I sat by the fire and talked over the hunt. I was only eight years of age, and I know that Father did not expect me to get a buffalo at all, but only to try perhaps for a small calf should I be able to get close enough to one. Nevertheless, I was greatly excited as I sat and watched Father working in his easy, firm way.

I was wearing my buffalo-skin robe, the hair next to my body. Mother had made me a rawhide belt, and this, wrapped around my waist, held my blanket on when I threw it off my shoulders. In the early morning I would wear it, for it would be cold. When it came time to shoot, I should not want my blanket, but the belt would hold it in place.

You can picture me, I think, as I sat in the glow of the campfire, my little brown body bare to the waist, watching, and listening intently to my father. My hair hung down my back, and I wore moccasins and breechcloth[3] of buckskin. To my belt was fastened a rawhide holster for my knife, for when I was eight years of age we had plenty of knives. I was proud to own a knife, and this night I remember I kept it on all night. Neither did I lay aside my bow, but went to sleep with it in my hand, thinking, I suppose, to be all the nearer ready in the morning when the start was made.

Father sharpened my steel points for me and also sharpened my knife. The whetstone[4] was a long stone which was kept in a buckskin bag, and sometimes this stone went all

---

[2] quivers—portable case for holding arrows.

[3] breechcloth—cloth used to cover the area between the waist and thighs.

[4] whetstone—hard stone used to sharpen metal blades.

over the camp; every tepee did not have one, so we shared this **commodity**[5] with one another. I had as I remember about ten arrows, so when Father was through sharpening them I put them in my rawhide quiver. I had a rawhide quirt,[6] too, which I would wear fastened to my waist. As Father worked, he knew I was watching him closely and listening whenever he spoke. By the time all preparations had been made, he had told me just how I was to act when I started out in the morning with the hunters.

We went to bed, my father hoping that tomorrow would be successful for him so that he could bring home some nice meat for the family and a hide for my mother to tan.[7] I went to bed but could not go to sleep at once, so filled was I with the wonderment and excitement of it all. The next day was to be a test for me. I was to prove to my father whether he was or was not justified in his pride in me. What would be the result of my training? Would I be brave if I faced danger, and would Father be proud of me? Though I did not know it that night, I was to be tried for the strength of my manhood and my honesty in this hunt. Something happened that day which I remember above all things. It was a test of my real character, and I am proud to say that I did not find myself weak but made a decision that has been all these years a **gratification**[8] to me.

The next morning the hunters were catching their horses about daybreak. I arose with my father and went out and caught my pony. I wanted to do whatever he did and show him that he did not have to tell me what to do. We brought our animals to the tepee and got our bows and arrows and mounted. From over the village came the hunters. Most of them were leading their running horses. These running horses were anxious for the hunt and came prancing, their ears straight up and their tails waving in the air. We were joined with perhaps a hundred or more riders, some of whom carried bows and arrows and some armed with guns.

> **WOULD I BE BRAVE IF I FACED DANGER, AND WOULD FATHER BE PROUD OF ME?**

---

[5] **commodity**—something of basic value because of its usefulness.

[6] quirt—small riding whip.

[7] tan—turn an animal hide into leather.

[8] **gratification** (GRAT•uh•fih•KAY•shuhn)—source of pleasure and satisfaction.

THE VERY PRESENCE OF QUIET WAS EVERYWHERE

Evening campfires make the walls of the tepees glow at an encampment of Blackfeet in northwestern Montana around 1900. ▶

The buffalo were reported to be about five or six miles away as we should count distance now. At that time we did not measure distance in miles. One camping distance was about ten miles, and these buffalo were said to be about one half camping distance away.

Some of the horses were to be left at a stopping place just before the herd was reached. These horses were pack animals which were taken along to carry extra blankets or weapons. They were trained to remain there until the hunters came for them. Though they were neither hobbled[9] nor tied, they stood still during the shooting and noise of the chase.

My pony was a black one and a good runner. I felt very important as I rode along with the hunters and my father, the chief. I kept as close to him as I could.

Two men had been chosen to scout or to lead the party. These two men were in a sense policemen whose work it was to keep order. They carried large sticks of ash wood, something like a policeman's billy,[10] though longer. They rode ahead of the party while the rest of us kept in a group close together. The leaders went ahead until they sighted the herd of grazing buffalo. Then they stopped and waited for the rest of us to ride up. We all rode slowly toward the herd, which on sight of us had come together, although they had been scattered here and there over the plain. When they saw us, they all ran close together as if at the command of a leader. We continued riding slowly toward the herd until one of the leaders

---

[9] hobbled (HAHB•uhld)—tied around the legs to limit movement.

[10] billy—short wooden club.

shouted, "Ho-ka-he!" which means, "Ready, go!" At that command every man started for the herd. I had been listening, too, and the minute the hunters started, I started also.

Away I went, my little pony putting all he had into the race. It was not long before I lost sight of Father, but I kept going just the same. I threw my blanket back, and the chill of the autumn morning struck my body, but I did not mind. On I went. It was wonderful to race over the ground with all these horsemen about me. There was no shouting, no noise of any kind except the pounding of the horses' feet. The herd was now running and had raised a cloud of dust. I felt no fear until we had entered this cloud of dust and I could see nothing about me—only hear the sound of feet. Where was Father? Where was I going? On I rode through the cloud, for I knew I must keep going.

Then all at once I realized that I was in the midst of the buffalo, their dark bodies rushing all about me and their great heads moving up and down to the sound of their hoofs beating upon the earth. Then it was that fear overcame me and I leaned close down upon my little pony's body and clutched him tightly. I can never tell you how I felt toward my pony at that moment. All thought of shooting had left my mind. I was seized by blank fear. In a moment or so, however, my senses became clearer, and I could distinguish other sounds beside the clatter of feet. I could hear a shot now and then, and I could see the buffalo beginning to break up into small bunches. I could not see Father nor any of my companions yet, but my fear was vanishing and I was safe. I let my pony run. The buffalo looked too large for me to tackle, anyway, so I just kept going. The buffalo became more and more scattered. Pretty soon I saw a young calf that looked about my size. I remembered now what Father had told me the night before as we sat about the fire. Those instructions were important for me now to follow.

ALL THOUGHT OF SHOOTING HAD LEFT MY MIND. I WAS SEIZED BY BLANK FEAR.

I was still back of the calf, being unable to get alongside of him. I was anxious to get a shot, yet afraid to try, as I was still very nervous. While my pony was making all speed to come alongside, I chanced a shot, and to my surprise my arrow landed. My second arrow glanced[11] along the back of the animal and sped on between the horns, making only a slight wound. My third arrow hit a spot that made the running beast slow up in his gait. I shot a fourth arrow, and though it, too, landed, it was not a fatal wound. It seemed to me that it was taking a lot of shots, and I was not proud of my marksmanship. I was glad, however, to see the animal going slower, and I knew that one more shot would make me a hunter. My horse seemed to know his own importance. His two ears stood straight forward, and it was not necessary for me to urge him to get closer to the buffalo. I was soon by the side of the buffalo, and one more shot brought the chase to a close. I jumped from my pony, and as I stood by my fallen game, I looked all around wishing that the world could

---

[11] glanced—struck at an angle and bounced off; grazed.

▲
A Native American hunter takes aim at a buffalo in this 1830 painting by an unknown artist.

see. But I was alone. In my determination to stay by until I had won my buffalo, I had not noticed that I was far from everyone else. No admiring friends were about, and as far as I could see I was on the plain alone. The herd of buffalo had completely disappeared. And as for Father, much as I wished for him, he was out of sight, and I had no idea where he was.

I stood and looked at the animal on the ground. I was happy. Everyone must know that I, Ota K'te,[12] had killed a buffalo. But it looked as if no one knew where I was, so no one was coming my way. I must then take something from this animal to show that I had killed it. I took all the arrows one by one from the body. As I took them out, it occurred to me that I had used five arrows. If I had been a skillful hunter, one arrow would have been sufficient, but I had used five. Here it was that temptation came to me. Why could I not take out two of the arrows and throw them away? No one would know, and then I should be more greatly admired and praised as a hunter. As it was, I knew that I should be praised by Father and Mother, but I wanted more. And so I was tempted to lie.

I was planning this as I took out my skinning knife that Father had sharpened for me the night before. I skinned one side of the animal, but when it came to turning it over, I was too small. I was wondering what to do when I heard my father's voice calling, "To-ki-i-la-la-hu-wo," "Where are you?" I quickly jumped on my pony and rode to the top of a little hill nearby. Father saw me and came to me at once. He was so pleased to see me and glad to know that I was safe. I knew that I could never lie to my father. He was too fond of me and I too proud of him. He had always told me to tell the truth. He wanted me to be an honest man, so I resolved then to tell the truth even if it took from me a little glory. He rode up to me with a glad expression on his face, expecting me to go back with him to his kill. As he came up, I said as calmly as I could, "Father, I have killed a buffalo." His smile changed to surprise, and he asked me where my buffalo was. I pointed to it, and we rode over to where it lay, partly skinned.

> **I KNEW THAT I COULD NEVER LIE TO MY FATHER.**

[12] Ota K'te (OH•tah kuh•TAY)—Lakota Sioux name for Luther Standing Bear, meaning "Plenty Kill."

Father set to work to skin it for me. I had watched him do this many times and knew perfectly well how to do it myself, but I could not turn the animal over. There was a way to turn the head of the animal so that the body would be balanced on the back while being skinned. Father did this for me, while I helped all I could. When the hide was off, Father put it on the pony's back with the hair side next to the pony. On this he arranged the meat so it would balance. Then he covered the meat carefully with the rest of the hide, so no dust would reach it while we traveled home. I rode home on top of the load.

I showed my father the arrows that I had used and just where the animal had been hit. He was very pleased and praised me over and over again. I felt more glad than ever that I had told the truth, and I have never regretted it. I am more proud now that I told the truth than I am of killing the buffalo.

We then rode to where my father had killed a buffalo. There we stopped and prepared it for taking home. It was late afternoon when we got back to camp. No king ever rode in state[13] who was more proud than I that day as I came into the village sitting high up on my load of buffalo meat. Mother had now two hunters in the family, and I knew how she was going to make over me. It is not customary for Indian men to brag about their **exploits**,[14] and I had been taught that bragging was not nice. So I was very quiet, although I was bursting with pride. Always when arriving home I would run out to play, for I loved to be with the other boys, but this day I lingered about close to the tepee so I could hear the nice things that were said about me. It was soon all over camp that Ota K'te had killed a buffalo.

My father was so proud that he gave away a fine horse. He called an old man to our tepee to cry out the news to the rest of the people in camp. The old man stood at the door of our tepee and sang a song of praise to my father. The horse had been led up, and I stood holding it by a rope. The old man who was doing the singing called the other old man who was to receive the horse as a present. He accepted the horse by coming up to me, holding out his hands to me, and saying, "Ha-ye," which means "Thank you." The old man went away very grateful for the horse.

That ended my first and last buffalo hunt. It lives only in my memory, for the days of the buffalo are over.

---

[13] rode in state—rode as a hero or political leader in a formal parade.

[14] **exploits** (EHK•sployts)—adventurous or brave acts.

Questions to Consider

Responding

1. Have you ever felt tempted to lie to make yourself appear better than you are? What did you do?

Analyzing

2. How does the preparation for the hunt tell you about the **significance of the buffalo** to the narrator and his people?

3. How do you think the story would have been different if the boy had lied about the number of arrows he used to kill the buffalo?

4. Why do you think the narrator is more proud of not lying than of killing a buffalo?

Extending

5. How do decisions made in growing up build or establish a person's character?

Literature Connection

Imagery consists of words and phrases that appeal to any of a reader's five senses. Writers use sensory details to help readers imagine how things look, feel, sound, smell, and taste.

1. How does the writer use imagery to help the reader imagine what the Indian camp was like on the night before the buffalo hunt?

2. What types of imagery are used to describe the buffalo hunt?

The Mandan people of the northern Great Plains perform a Buffalo dance.

▼

Activities

Writing About a Decision

Write a personal essay about a decision you made recently that helped to shape your character. Include imagery to add depth to your essay and bring it to life for your readers.

Researching the Buffalo

Using the Internet and library resources, research further the significance of the buffalo in the history of Native Americans in the United States. Be sure to research not only what happened in times past but also the status of buffalo today. Then prepare a poster that includes facts and images about the buffalo and its importance to Native Americans.

THE JOURNEY

BY DUANE BIGEAGLE

About the Author

Duane BigEagle is the son of a Cherokee mother and an Osage father. He was born in 1946 and raised on a reservation in Oklahoma. BigEagle worked in lumber mills, fisheries, and ranches before he became a published writer. Today, he is active in the California Poets in the Schools program. BigEagle also performs the Southern Straight Dance, the formal, traditional men's dance of most of the Oklahoma tribes, including the Osage. In it, the dancer tells the story of a hunt.

About the Selection

In many cultures, the transition from childhood to adulthood is marked by a **rite of passage**, a ritual act that signifies change in the status of an individual. Many rites of passage are connected with birth, maturity, reproduction, and death. Others celebrate cultural changes, such as initiation into a group or accomplishment of a traditional goal, such as a school graduation. Rites may involve an entire community or an individual alone. Often an individual's rite of passage into adulthood is a task, such as a vision quest—a search for a spiritual sign or message.

I had known the train all my life. Its wailing roar rushed through my dreams as through a tunnel and yet I had never even been on one. Now I was to take one on a two thousand kilometer journey half way into a foreign country!

This particular adventure was my fault, if you can call being sick a fault. Mama says finding fault is only a way of clouding a problem and this problem was clouded enough. It began when I was thirteen and I still have tuberculosis scars on my lungs but this illness was more than tuberculosis. The regular doctors were mystified by the fevers and delirium that accompanied a bad cough and nausea. After six months of treatment without improvement, they gave up.

Papa carried me on his back as we left the doctor's office and began our walk to the Mazatlán barrio[1] that was our home. Mama cried as she walked and Papa seemed weighted by more than the weight of my thinned down frame. About half way home Papa suddenly straightened up. I was having a dizzy spell and almost slipped off his back but he caught me with one hand and shouted, "Aunt Rosalie! What a fool I am! Aunt Rosalie Stands Tall!" Papa started to laugh and to

dance around and around on the dirt path in the middle of a field.

"What do you mean?" cried Mama as she rushed around with her hands out, ready to catch me if I fell. From the look on her face, the real question in her mind was more like: Have you gone mad?

"Listen, woman," said Papa, "there are some people who can cure diseases the medical doctors can't. Aunt Rosalie Stands Tall is a medicine woman of the Yaqui[2] people and one of the best! She'll be able to cure Raoul! The only problem is she's married to an Indian in the United States and lives now in Oklahoma. But that can't be helped, we'll just have to go there. Come on, we have plans to make and work to do!"

The planning began that day. We had very little money, but with what we had and could borrow from Papa's many friends there was just enough for a child's ticket to the little town in Oklahoma where Rosalie lived. I couldn't be left alone so Papa decided simply to walk. "I'll take the main highway north to the old Papago[3] trails that go

---

[1] barrio (BAH•ree•oh)—urban district or quarter in a Spanish-speaking country. Mazatlán is a city on the Pacific coast of Mexico.

[2] Yaqui (YAH•kee)—Native American tribe of northwestern Mexico and southern Arizona.

[3] Papago (PAH•pah•goh)—Native American tribe of northern Mexico and the southwestern United States.

across the desert. They'll also take me across the border undetected. Then I'll head east and north to Oklahoma. It should be easy to catch occasional rides once I get to the U.S. When I arrive, I'll send word for Raoul to start."

Papa left one fine spring morning, taking only a blanket, a few extra pairs of shoes, bow and arrows to catch food, and a flint stone for building fires. Secretly I believe he was happy to be traveling again. Travel had always been in his blood. As a young man, Papa got a job on a sailing ship and traveled all over the world. This must have been how he learned to speak English and how he met Mama in the West Indies. Myself, I was still sixty kilometers from the town I was born in and even to imagine the journey I was about to take was more than my fevered brain could handle. But as Mama said, "You can do anything in the world if you take it little by little and one step at a time." This was the miraculous and trusting philosophy our family lived by, and I must admit it has usually worked.

> YOU CAN DO ANYTHING IN THE WORLD IF YOU TAKE IT LITTLE BY LITTLE AND ONE STEP AT A TIME.

Still, the day of departure found me filled with a dread that settled like lead in my feet. If I hadn't been so light headed from the fevers, I'm sure I would have fallen over at any attempt to walk. Dressed in my best clothes, which looked shabby the minute we got to the train station, Mama led me into the fourth-class carriage and found me a seat on a bench near the windows. Then she disappeared and came back a minute later with a thin young man with sallow[4] skin and a drooping Zapata mustache.[5] "This is your second cousin, Alejandro. He is a conductor on this train and will be with you till you get to Juarez; you must do whatever he says."

At that time, the conductors on trains in Mexico were required to stay with a train the entire length of its journey, which perhaps accounted for Alejandro's appearance. He did little to inspire my confidence in him. In any case, he disappeared a second later and it was time for Mama to go too. Hurriedly, she reminded me that there was money in my coat to buy food from the women who came onto the

---

[4] sallow—having a sickly, yellowish color.

[5] Zapata (zah•PAH•tah) mustache—thick, dark, drooping mustache like that of Emiliano Zapata, a hero of the Mexican Revolution.

I BEGAN MY JOURNEY

UPSIDE DOWN

▲ An imaginary railroad floats above the clouds in Oscar Steven Senn's painting *Made Up*.

train at every stop and that there was a silver bracelet sewn into the cuff of my pants to bribe the guards at the border. With one last tearful kiss and hug, she was gone and I was alone. The train started with a jerk that knocked me off my bench and I began my journey upside down in a heap on top of my crumpled cardboard suitcase. I didn't even get a chance to wave goodbye.

I soon got used to the jerking starts of the train, and unsmiling Alejandro turned out to be a guardian angel which was fortunate because my illness began to get worse as the journey went along. Many times I awoke to find Alejandro shuffling some young thief away from my **meager**[6] possessions or buying me food at the last stop before a long stretch of desert. He would bring me things too, fresh peaches and apples and leftover bread and pastries from the first-class carriages where he worked. Once, in the middle of the desert he brought me a small ice-cold watermelon, the most refreshing thing I'd ever tasted—who knows where he got it?

[6] **meager**—scanty.

To this day, I'm not sure exactly which of the things I saw through the window of the train were real and which were not. Some of them I know were not real. In my **delirium**,[7] a half-day's journey would pass in the blink of an eye. Often I noticed only large changes in the countryside, from plains to mountains to desert. Broad valleys remain clearly in my mind and there were many of these. Small scenes, too, remain—a family sitting down to dinner at a candle-lit table in a hut by a river. And a few more sinister ones—once between two pine trees, I caught a glimpse of one man raising a large club to strike another man whose back was turned. I cried out but there was nothing to be done; the train was moving too fast on a downgrade and probably couldn't have been stopped. But then, did I really see them at all? My doubt was caused by the girl in the dark red dress.

> IN MY DELIRIUM, A HALF-DAY'S JOURNEY WOULD PASS IN THE BLINK OF AN EYE.

I think I began to see her about halfway through the journey to Juarez. She was very beautiful, high cheekbones, long black hair and very dark skin. She was about my height and age or maybe a little older. Her eyes were very large and her mouth seemed to have a ready smile. The first time I saw her, at a small station near a lake, she smiled and waved as the train pulled away. Her sensuality embarrassed me and I didn't wave back. I regretted it immediately. But she was back again the next day at a station in the foothills of the mountains, this time dressed in the white blouse and skirt that the Huichol[8] women wear.

She became almost a regular occurrence. Sometimes she was happy, sometimes serious and most of the time she was wearing the dark red dress. Often I would only see her in passing; she'd be working in a field and raise up to watch the train go by. Gradually, my condition grew worse. My coughing fits grew longer and I slept more so I began not to see the girl so much. Still, the last time I saw her really gave me a shock.

---

[7] **delirium** (dih•LIHR•ee•um)—temporary dreamlike state of mental confusion and clouded consciousness, often characterized by hallucinations.

[8] Huichol (HWEE•chohl)—Native American tribe of Mexico.

The mountains of the Sierra Madre Oriental[9] range are very rugged and are cut in places by deep gorges called barrancas. The train was in one of these gorges on a ledge above the river and was about to go around a bend. For some reason, I looked back the way we had come and there, imbedded in the mountain with her eyes closed, was the face of the girl, thirty feet high! For the first time, I noticed the small crescent-shaped[10] scar in the middle of her lower lip.

The vision, or whatever it was, quickly disappeared as the train rounded the curve. I sank back on to the bench with a pounding heart and closed my eyes. I must have slept, or perhaps I fell into a coma because I remember very little of the last part of the trip. I awoke once while Alejandro was carrying me across the border and delivering me to a friend of his on the train to Dallas. How I got from Dallas to Oklahoma I may never know because I remember nothing. But it happened. And finally, I awoke for a minute in my father's arms as he carried me off the train.

Then, there was a sharp pain in the center of my chest. And a pounding. Rhythmic pounding. A woman's voice began to sing in a very high pitch. My eyes opened of themselves. At first I couldn't make it out, arched crossing lines, flickering shadows. I was in the center of an oval-shaped lodge built of bent willow limbs covered with skins and lit by a small fire. A tall woman came into view; she was singing and dancing back and forth. Somehow I knew this was Rosalie Stands Tall, the medicine woman. The pain hit me again and I wanted to get away, but hands held me still.

THEN, THERE WAS A SHARP PAIN IN THE CENTER OF MY CHEST.

Papa's voice said in my ear, "She is calling her spirit helpers, you must try and sit up." I was sitting up facing the door of the lodge. There was a lizard there and he spoke in an old man's voice, words I couldn't understand. Rosalie sang again and there was a

[9] Sierra Madre Oriental (see•EHR•ah MAH•dray OHR•ee•ehn•tuhl)—eastern part of Mexico's Sierra Madre mountain chain that runs along the Gulf of Mexico.
[10] crescent-shaped—shaped like the quarter moon, in a curved slice.

small hawk there. The pain rose up higher in my chest. There was a coyote in the door and his words were tinged with mocking laughter. The pain rose into my throat. There was a small brown bear in the door, his fur blew back and forth in the wind. The pain rose into the back of my mouth. I felt a need to cough. Rosalie put two porcupine quills together and bound them with a strip of leather to make a pair of tweezers. She held my lips closed with them, painfully tight. A pair of wings beat against the top of the lodge. I needed badly to cough. There was something hot in my mouth, it was sharp, it was hurting my mouth, it needed to come out! IT WAS OUT!

I awoke in bed in a small room lit by a coal-oil lamp. There was a young woman with her back to me preparing food by the side of the bed. She had very long black hair. She put the tray down on the table beside the bed. As she turned to leave the room, I saw a small crescent-shaped scar in the middle of her lower lip. I started to call her back, but there was no need. I knew who she was. An immense peacefulness settled over me. It was warm in the bed. Papa sat on the

▲

Retrato de Mujer ("Portrait of a Woman") was painted by Mexican artist Alfredo Ramos Martinez (1871–1946), whose art focused on the daily lives of his people and their cultural heritage.

other side of the bed. He seemed very happy when I turned and looked at him. He said softly, "Raoul, you have changed completely. You're not anymore the young boy left in Mazatlán." I wanted to tell him everything! There was so much to say! But all I could get out was, "Yes, I know, Papa, I've come on a journey out of childhood." And then I went to sleep again.

Questions to Consider

Responding

1. What is your opinion of the value of Mama's philosophy, "You can do anything in the world if you take it little by little and one step at a time"?

Analyzing

2. How does Raoul's journey serve as a **rite of passage** for him in growing up?

3. What is Alejandro's role in Raoul's rite of passage?

4. Once he has fully recovered, how do you think Raoul might explain the girl in the dark red dress to his father?

Extending

5. How important are formal rites of passage in helping young people through the experience of growing up?

Literature Connection

The mood or atmosphere of a literary work is the feeling that it conveys. A mood is frequently described with words such as dark, light-hearted, dreamlike, and so on.

1. In "The Journey," what words would you use to describe the mood of the story up to the point when the narrator begins his train trip?

2. How does the mood change during the train trip?

Activity

Performing the Story

Experiment with producing the mood of a story through lighting and sound effects. Read several stories and identify their moods. Then plan the lighting and sound effects you would use for an oral reading of each story. In your plans, explain how the effects you have designed will support or enhance the story's mood. Working with a partner, stage an oral reading of one of the stories, using your effects. Get feedback from your audience about your work.

Epiphany: The Third Gift

by Lucha Corpi

About the Author

Lucha Corpi is a Mexican-American poet, novelist, and children's book author. She was born in Veracruz, Mexico, in 1945, and moved to the San Francisco Bay Area when she was nineteen. Among her novels are three mysteries featuring the Chicana private detective Gloria Damasco. Her children's book When Fireflies Dance presents stories about her childhood in Veracruz told in both Spanish and English.

About the Selection

*Traditionally, most cultures provided very different education for boys and girls. **Education for girls** was based on the assumption that their primary roles in life would be those of wives and mothers. As you read "Epiphany: The Third Gift," notice how this assumption operated in the author's upbringing.*

Ever since I was four years old, women insisted on giving me dolls. By age seven I had an assortment of them, made of papier-maché, clay, and cloth. Using my older cousin's torn silky stockings, my grandmother had also made a few of them for me. And one of my mother's friends had brought me a porcelain "little lady" from Mexico City, which was kept in my mother's wardrobe so I wouldn't break or damage it.

As a child I didn't understand why everyone around me insisted on giving me dolls especially since I had made it clear that I really didn't like to play with them.

I much more enjoyed climbing trees and running around with the boys—my older brother, a cousin, and their friends. I loved playing marbles, spinning tops until they hummed. Playing walk-the-high-wire on a narrow brick fence or, in Tarzan-like fashion, swinging on long vines from the rubber tree to the fence thrilled me no end. But most of all I preferred reading.

During recess and after school, I would go into the area in the principal's office that doubled as the school library. There I would look at the illustrations and read over and over the few natural sciences and biology books on the table. At home, after doing my homework, I would **avidly**[1] consume any text lying around.

At the time, my father, who worked for the Mexican National Telegraph Company, had undergone a cornea[2] transplant and had to wear a patch over one of his eyes for a while. Straining his other eye, he slowly read the daily reports coming into his office, but by the time he went home, that eye burned inside its lid.

Since I could read well, he asked me to read selections to him after supper from *La Opinión*, the region's daily newspaper. I was happy

> **I would avidly consume any text lying around.**

to do something for my father, whom I loved very much, but reading to him also gave me an opportunity to learn new words, for my father would patiently explain anything I didn't understand.

Although I didn't fully grasp the issues reported in the news articles, my world nonetheless expanded, for I also began to learn about international, national, and regional politics, geography, and literature.

---

[1] **avidly**—eagerly.

[2] cornea (KAWR•nee•uh)—transparent coating that covers the eyeball.

◀ This girl and her doll were photographed by Charles Hewitt in 1952.

Naturally, reading and looking at my small tropical world from high above the tallest trees became more exciting activities for me than playing with those cute celluloid[3] creatures that could do nothing but stare into empty space. Every so often I'd rub my face against the silky surface of the cloth dolls, feel the warm terseness[4] of the papier-maché under my fingers or the smooth coolness of the porcelain whenever my mother allowed me to hold the doll in her wardrobe. But most of the time, to my mother's **chagrin**,[5] the dolls rested one upon the other like fallen dominoes alongside a wall in my room.

For a few months after my seventh birthday, no one—including my mother—had given me any dolls, and I thought the adults around me had finally gotten over their need to do so. But I was wrong, for the sixth of January neared.

Like millions of children in Mexico, at home we received presents on the Twelfth Night after the birth of

---

[3] celluloid (SEHL•yuh•loid)—early plastic material.
[4] terseness—smoothness (an obsolete sense).
[5] **chagrin** (shuh•GRIHN)—keen disappointment.

Jesus Christ—Epiphany—a time to commemorate the revealing of baby Jesus to the Magi[6] and their offering to him of myrrh, incense, and gold.

On that January 6, 1952, my parents gave me three gifts: a doll (no great surprise!), a doll's house, and a book—a children's version of *The Arabian Nights*, which came wrapped in red tissue paper.

I used the wrapping tissue as a book cover and was just getting ready to read when my mother walked into my room.

"Isn't your doll just beautiful?" my mother asked. I looked at the doll—I'll have to call her "She" because I never gave her a name. *She* was a fair celluloid creature with light brown hair and blue eyes that matched the color of her ruffled dress. Her apron and socks were white.

I puckered my lips and raised my eyebrows, not really knowing how to let my mother down easily.

"But this one is different," my mother explained, trying to talk me into playing with the toy. "Look, " my mother emphasized, "this doll talks; she says, 'Mommy.'"

Then my mother turned the doll over, raised her tiny dress, and pulled on a chain to wind the doll's voice mechanism.

Something must have been wrong with the mechanism, because the noises *She* made sounded more like a cat's cries than a baby's babbles. My grandmother had often told me that our neighbor's cat cried like that because it needed love.

"*Anda buscando amor*—it's looking for love," my grandmother would explain, purposely neglecting to elaborate on the kind of love a cat in heat desires.

Interpreting my grandmother's comment literally, on several occasions I had tried to hug the cat to give it love, but it had scratched me and run away. Sure, nonetheless, that the doll needed love, I hugged her tightly for a long time. Useless, I said to myself finally, for the doll kept making the cat-looking-for-love noises. I decided to play instead with the doll's house, which my father had set down on the front porch, where it was cool in the afternoon. I went out to play with it. But since inspecting and rearranging the tiny furniture seemed to be the only activity possible, I quickly lost interest.

---

[6] Magi (MAY•jy)—in the Bible, three "wise men" from the East who traveled to Bethlehem to pay homage to the infant Jesus.

I could hear my friends in the yard talking and egging each other on to walk the high wire. Bending over or squatting to play with the doll's house had left my body and spirit in need of physical activity. So I went into my room to put on my shoes to join my friends in the yard. I was tying my shoelaces when I saw again the third of my gifts—*The Arabian Nights*—wrapped in the red tissue paper, and I began to read it. From that moment on, the doll and the doll's house began to collect dust, and *Scheherazada*[7] became my constant companion.

Every day, after doing my homework, I climbed the guava tree my father had planted a few years before. Nestled among its branches, during the next three weeks, I read and reread the stories in *The Arabian Nights* to my heart's content. But I was unaware that my mother had become concerned as she noticed that I wasn't playing with either the doll or the little house.

My parents had always encouraged us to read. My mother wouldn't have dreamed of asking me to give up my reading session, but she began to insist that I take the doll up the tree with me.

Trying to read on a branch fifteen feet off the ground while holding on to the silly doll was not an easy feat. Not even for an artist of *the high wire and the flying trapeze*. After nearly falling off the branch twice, I finally had to devise a way to please my mother and keep my neck intact. Cutting two thin vines off a tree, I removed their skin and tied them together into one long rope; then I tied one end around the doll's neck and the opposite one around the branch. This way I could just let the doll hang in midair while I read.

I was always looking out for my mother, though. I sensed that my playing with the doll was of great importance to her. So every time I heard my mother coming, I lifted the doll up and hugged her. The smile in my mother's eyes told me my plan worked. Before suppertime, I entered the house through the kitchen so my mother could see me holding the doll.

During the next few days, my mother, the doll, and I were quite happy. But the **inevitable**[8] happened one afternoon. Totally absorbed in the

---

[7] *Scheherezada* (sheh•hehr•uh•ZAHD•ah)—Spanish form of the name Scheherezade, chief narrator of the stories in the *Arabian Nights*.

[8] **inevitable** (ihn•EHV•ih•tuh•buhl)—unavoidable; certain to happen.

reading, I did not hear my mother calling me until she was right under the tree. When I looked down, I saw my mother, her mouth open in disbelief, staring at the dangling doll. Fearing the worst of scoldings, I climbed down in a flash, reaching the ground just as my mother was untying the doll.

"What is this? " she asked as she smoothed out the doll's dress.

My mother always asked me that or a similar rhetorical question[9] when she wanted me to admit to some wrongdoing. From that point on, we would both follow an unwritten script. After my giving the appropriate answer for the particular situation we faced—"It's a doll, hanging," in this case—my mother would then ask me a second question. In this case, she would have asked, "And why is this doll hanging from the tree? "

To my surprise, on this occasion my mother wasn't following the script. Dumbfounded, she kept on staring at the doll, then she glanced at me. I swallowed hard. At that moment, I realized I had just accomplished the impossible: *I had rendered my mother speechless!*

I also sensed for the first time in my seven years that I had done something *terribly, terribly* wrong— perhaps even unforgivable.

Making me carry the doll in my arms, my mother led me back to the house, still without a **reprimand.**[10] But I was sure that I would be paying for my **transgression**[11] by nightfall when my father came home. By suppertime, I feared the storm would hover right above my head. But my father came home, and supper came and went, and I went to bed at my usual time with my ears, hands, and butt untouched.

The day after the hanging-doll incident, my father came home early and suggested that he and I play with the doll's house. He had stopped by my grandmother's house a block away and had picked up some tiny clay bowls, glasses, and pots she had bought for me. Among the kitchenware there was even a tiny metate,[12] in case we wanted to grind *masa* to make tortillas, he said.

> **I had rendered my mother speechless!**

[9] rhetorical question—question to which no answer is expected.

[10] **reprimand**—severe criticism.

[11] **transgression**—offense.

[12] metate (meh•TAH•teh)—shallow dish to grind masa, or corn meal.

Already dust had collected on the little house's roof and on the tiny furniture, and it took us fifteen minutes to wipe everything clean before we could begin to put the kitchenware and the furniture back in the rooms.

A short while later I realized that playing with the doll's house this second time was just as boring as the first time. But my father seemed to be having so much fun I didn't have the heart to inform him I wasn't in the least interested. So quietly I slipped out of the room and picked up *Scheherazada* on my way to the yard. Absorbed as he was in arranging and rearranging the tiny furniture, he didn't even take notice of my quick exit.

At suppertime, again, I expected a good *jalón de orejas*.[13] Instead, waving a finger but laughing, my father said, "Ah, *mi chaparrita traviesa*[14] (my naughty little woman).

---

[13] *jalón de orejas* (hah•LOHN deh oh•REH•hahs)—Spanish for "tug on the ears."

[14] *mi chaparrita traviesa*—(mee chah•pah•REE•tah trah•vee•EHS•ah).

◀ English illustrator Edmund Dulac (1882–1953) painted this illustration for one of the tales of the *Arabian Nights*.

"Miguel Angel, you're spoiling this child, " my mother mildly objected.

My father's only reply was a chuckle.

Almost twenty years passed before I found out from both my parents why the hanging-doll episode had been so significant for them. By then I had already moved to California, my father had been diagnosed with terminal cancer, and I was a parent myself.

After recounting the episode of the hanging doll amid my father's and my laughter, my mother, teary eyed and sentimental, confessed that all those years she had been afraid I would turn out to be an unnatural mother because, as a child, I had hung the doll from the branch. She was delighted I had turned out to be a most loving and understanding mother to my three-year-old son Arturo.

During my nineteen years at home, neither my father nor my mother ever gave up trying to socialize me— "civilize" me, my mother would often say.

Throughout those years, they **inculcated**[15] in me that intellectually and artistically I was as capable as my brothers. So they provided me with the best education they could afford. They made clear to me, nonetheless, that all this was being done not just to satisfy my own needs as an individual; above all, I was being educated to serve the needs of the family I would one day have.

"When you educate a man," my father would often tell my younger sister and me, "you educate an individual. But when you educate a woman, you educate the whole family." Then he would caress my sister's cheek and mine as he added, "I don't remember who said that a child's education begins twenty years before he's born. But whoever said it was surely right. My grandchildren's education begins with yours, *mis chaparritas*."

It wasn't unusual for Mexican fathers—almost regardless of class— to deny their daughters the advantages of formal schooling on the false **premise**[16] that as women they would always be supported and protected by their husbands. The important thing

> **When you educate a woman, you educate the whole family.**

---

[15] **inculcated** (ihn•KUHL•kayt•ihd)—taught by frequent instruction.
[16] **premise** (PREHM•ihs)—assumption.

was, then, my uncles **perfunctorily**[17] stated, to get as successful a husband as could be found for the girls in the family. Problem solved.

My father was not quite the typical Mexican father in this respect. But even this atypical man, who has been and will continue to be one of the most influential people in my life, was subject to the social norms and pressures that made the education of a woman a separate (if equal) experience.

> **Your children will grow up having a zombie for a mother, and you'll die young**.

Consistently throughout my life I was convinced by both my father and my mother that what I truly wanted—a career as either a medical doctor or an astronomer—was not what was best for me.

"As a medical doctor you will have to care for and examine male patients; you will be subject to men's low designs," my father warned every time I brought up the subject.

"You will suffer," my mother added, waving her finger admonishingly, to emphasize what she really wanted to say: *"Conform."*

With **impeccable**[18] logic my father would state the advantages for a woman of a career in dentistry: independence (not working for a man), flexibility of schedule (time to take care of the children as well), and great financial rewards.

Relentlessly I would plead for a second wish, a career in astronomy. My father would caress my check gently and say, "But, my little woman, an astronomer has to work at night. When would you spend time with your children? And your husband? Surely, he would find someone else to keep him company at night. "

"And you will suffer," my mother would interject in her usual manner. "Your children will grow up having a zombie for a mother, and you'll die young, " she would state to strengthen her argument, with a stern and sad face, as if I were already the victim of an ancient curse.

Because I wanted to pursue a career, I eventually agreed to attend the school of dentistry in San Luis. I was happy the first two years, since my classmates and I carried the same subjects as first-year medical students,

---

[17] **perfunctorily** (puhr•FUNGK•tuh•rih•lee)— routinely; without interest or enthusiasm.
[18] **impeccable**—flawless; perfect.

in addition to dental labs. But when I stared into a real open mouth for the first time, I began to suspect that I was not cut out to be a good dentist. The first time I sweated out the extraction of a molar, my suspicions were confirmed. After the first ten tooth fillings, I knew I would surely go insane one day.

For a couple of years I had been going steady with Guillermo, who was preparing to move to Berkeley, where he hoped to attend the University of California. As painful as it was to leave my family and my country, I had no qualms in quitting dentistry school, marrying him, and moving to California.

Through my relationship with my husband I rediscovered the pleasure of reading for my own enjoyment. Although I would not start writing poetry for another five years after my arrival in Berkeley, I knew I wanted to make the study of literature my life's pursuit.

By the time I began to write poetry, I was already undergoing a painful separation from my husband, feeling cut off from the cultural and emotional support of family and friends, working as a bilingual secretary to support my son and put myself through college at Berkeley, grieving for my late father and expressing my daily thoughts and experiences in a language not yet my own.

For the next few years, in an almost manic manner, I wrote at least one poem a day, possessed by the terrifying notion that if I stopped writing I would stop breathing as well.

Every so often, when I visit my mother in Mexico, she recalls the incident of the hanging doll and thanks God aloud for making me a good parent. Then she sighs as she inventories my **vicissitudes**[19] in life, pointing out that I would be a rich dentist and a happily married woman now, living still in Mexico, instead of being a divorced woman, a poor schoolteacher, and a Chicana poet in California.

I look back at that same childhood incident, recall my third gift, the book I wrapped in red tissue paper, and for a fleeting instant I, too, take inventory of the experiences that have made me who and what I am. I pause to marvel at life's wondrous ironies.

---

[19] **vicissitudes** (vih•SIHS•ih•toods)—changes; ups and downs.

Questions to Consider

Responding

1. Of all the gifts you received growing up, which one has had the most influence on your life up to now?

Analyzing

2. How are assumptions about appropriate roles for women reflected in the gifts the author received as a child?

3. What kind of child does the author seem to have been?

4. How was the author's father untypical in his views about **education for girls**?

5. What lesson does the author seem to have learned by thinking about this childhood experience?

Extending

6. What is your opinion on the question of whether there should be any differences in the way boys and girls are educated?

Literature Connection

A **theme** is a message about life or human nature that is communicated by a literary work. The theme of a literary work is not the same as its subject. The subject is what the work is about, such as the natural world, romantic love, or old age. The theme is a statement of what the author is saying concerning this subject. Sometimes the theme is stated directly. In many cases, however, a reader must infer what the writer's message is.

1. What is the subject of this memoir?

2. How would you state the theme?

Activity

Writing About Gifts

Create a list of the gifts you received as a child that meant the most to you and then select one as the basis of a brief autobiographical essay. Describe the occasion when you received the gift, why it was so important to you, what happened to the gift later, and any other details that will help your reader appreciate why you valued it.

HOLLYWOOD AND THE PITS

by Cherylene Lee

About the Author

Cherylene Lee was born in Los Angeles. She was a child actor in Hollywood and later earned degrees in paleontology and geology. Lee began writing fiction, poetry, and plays in 1983. Her play Arthur and Leila *appeared in* Women Playwrights: The Best Plays of 1993. *Lee is a fourth-generation Chinese American and writes mostly about the Chinese-American perspective. She says she is fascinated by which aspects of Chinese culture are passed on through generations and which are lost in the process of becoming American.*

About the Selection

*Throughout much of the 20th century, images of **Asians in the media** were generally racist or stereotypical, like those of most other American ethnic groups. Asians have been presented more realistically in recent movies, television, advertising, cartoons, and other media. Growing up, Asian Americans look to the media to see reflections of themselves and their experience, just as other Americans do. Note the issues the narrator points out about Asian Americans in the media as you read "Hollywood and the Pits."*

In 1968 when I was fifteen, the pit opened its secret to me. I breathed, ate, slept, dreamed about the La Brea Tar Pits.[1] I spent summer days working the archaeological dig and in dreams saw the bones glistening, the broken pelvises, the skulls, the vertebrae looped like a woman's pearls hanging on an invisible cord. I welcomed those dreams. I wanted to know where the next skeleton was, identify it, record its position, discover whether it was whole or not. I wanted to know where to dig in the coarse, black, gooey sand. I lost myself there and found something else.

> I grew up in Hollywood, a place where dreams and nightmares can often take the same shape.

My mother thought something was wrong with me. Was it good for a teenager to be fascinated by death? Especially animal death in the Pleistocene?[2] Was it normal to be so obsessed by a sticky brown hole in the ground in the center of Los Angeles? I don't know if it was normal or not, but it seemed perfectly logical to me. After all, I grew up in Hollywood, a place where dreams and nightmares can often take the same shape. What else would a child actor do?

"Thank you very much, dear. We'll be letting you know."

I knew what that meant. It meant I would never hear from them again. I didn't get the job. I heard that phrase a lot that year.

I walked out of the plush office, leaving behind the casting director, producer, director, writer, and whoever else came to listen to my reading for a semiregular role on a family sitcom. The carpet made no sound when I opened and shut the door.

I passed the other girls waiting in the reception room, each **poring**[3] over her script. The mothers were waiting in a separate room, chattering about their daughters' latest commercials, interviews, callbacks, jobs. It sounded like every Oriental kid in Hollywood was working except me.

---

[1] La Brea (BRAY•uh) Tar Pits—springs in Los Angeles, California, that ooze crude oil and contain the fossilized remains of many Ice Age animals.

[2] Pleistocene (PLY•stuh•SEEN)—Ice Age, geologic period in Earth's development, marked by the spread of glaciers over large parts of the earth and by the appearance of human beings.

[3] **poring**—reading or studying carefully.

My mother used to have a lot to say in those waiting rooms. Ever since I was three, when I started at the Meglin Kiddie Dance Studio, I was dubbed "The Chinese Shirley Temple"[4]—always the one to be picked at auditions and interviews, always the one to get the speaking lines, always called "the one-shot kid," because I could do my scenes in one take—even tight close-ups. My mother would only talk about me behind my back because she didn't want me to hear her brag, but I knew that she was proud. In a way I was proud too, though I never dared admit it. I didn't want to be called a show-off. But I didn't exactly know what I did to be proud of either. I only knew that at fifteen I was now being passed over at all these interviews when before I would be chosen.

My mother looked at my face hopefully when I came into the room. I gave her a quick shake of the head. She looked bewildered. I felt bad for my mother then. How could I explain it to her? I didn't understand it myself. We left saying polite good-byes to all the other mothers.

We didn't say anything until the studio parking lot, where we had to

▲
Cherylene Lee and her older sister appeared on the television show of entertainer Dinah Shore in 1959.

search for our old blue Chevy among rows and rows of parked cars baking in the Hollywood heat.

"How did it go? Did you read clearly? Did you tell them you're available?"

"I don't think they care if I'm available or not, Ma."

---

[4] Shirley Temple—(c. 1927–) popular American child star in movies of the 1930s.

◄ Lee performs with dancer
Gene Kelly in 1958.

"Didn't you read well? Did you remember to took up so they could see your eyes? Did they ask you if you could play the piano? Did you tell them you could learn?"

The **barrage**[5] of questions stopped when we finally spotted our car. I didn't answer her. My mother asked about the piano because I lost out in an audition once to a Chinese girl who already knew how to play.

My mother took off the towel that shielded the steering wheel from the heat. "You're getting to be such a big girl," she said, starting the car in neutral. "But don't worry, there's always next time. You have what it takes. That's special." She put the car into forward and we drove through a parking lot that had an endless number of identical cars all facing the same direction. We drove back home in silence.

*In the La Brea Tar Pits many of the excavated bones belong to juvenile mammals. Thousands of years ago thirsty young animals in the area were drawn to watering holes, not knowing they were traps. Those inviting pools had false bottoms made of sticky tar, which **immobilized**[6] its victims and preserved their bones when they died. Innocence trapped by ignorance. The tar pits record that well.*

---

[5] **barrage** (buh•RAZH)—rapid series.
[6] **immobilized**—made unable to move.

I suppose a lot of my getting into show business in the first place was a matter of luck—being in the right place at the right time. My sister, seven years older than me, was a member of the Meglin Kiddie Dance Studio long before I started lessons. Once during the annual recital held at the Shrine Auditorium, she was spotted by a Hollywood agent who handled only Oriental performers. The agent sent my sister out for a role in the CBS *Playhouse 90* television show *The Family Nobody Wanted*. The producer said she was too tall for the part. But true to my mother's training of always having a positive reply, my sister said to the producer, "But I have a younger sister . . ." which started my show-biz career at the tender age of three.

My sister and I were lucky. We enjoyed singing and dancing, we were natural hams, and our parents never discouraged us. In fact they were our biggest fans. My mother chauffeured us to all our dance lessons, lessons we begged to take. She drove us to interviews, took us to studios, went on location with us, drilled us on our lines, made sure we kept up our schoolwork and didn't sass back the tutors hired by studios to teach us for three hours a day. She never complained about being a stage mother. She said that we made her proud.

My father must have felt pride too, because he paid for a choreographer to put together our sister act: "The World Famous Lee Sisters," fifteen minutes of song and dance, real vaudeville[7] stuff. We joked about that a lot, "Yeah, the Lee Sisters—Ug-Lee and Home-Lee," but we definitely had a good time. So did our parents. Our father especially liked our getting booked into Las Vegas at the New Frontier Hotel on the Strip. He liked to gamble there, though he said the craps tables in that hotel were "cold," not like the casinos in downtown Las Vegas, where all the "hot" action took place.

In Las Vegas our sister act was part of a show called "Oriental Holiday." The show was about a Hollywood producer going to the Far East, finding undiscovered talent, and bringing it back to the U.S. We did two shows a night in the main showroom, one at eight and one at twelve,

---

[7] vaudeville (VAUD•vihl)—stage entertainment such as song-and-dance routines.

and on weekends a third show at two in the morning. It ran the entire summer often to standing-room-only audiences—a thousand people a show.

Our sister act worked because of the age and height difference. My sister then was fourteen and nearly five foot two; I was seven and very small for my age—people thought we were cute. We had song-and-dance routines to old tunes like "Ma He's Making Eyes at Me," "Together," and "I'm Following You, " and my father hired a writer to adapt the lyrics to "I Enjoy Being a Girl," which came out "We Enjoy Being Chinese." We also told corny jokes, but the Las Vegas audience seemed to enjoy it. Here we were, two kids, staying up late and jumping around, and getting paid besides. To me the applause sometimes sounded like static, sometimes like distant waves. It always amazed me when people applauded. The owner of the hotel liked us so much, he invited us back to perform in shows for three summers in a row. That was before I grew too tall and the sister act didn't seem so cute anymore.

Many of the skeletons in the tar pits are found incomplete—particularly the skeletons of the young, which have only soft cartilage connecting the bones. In life the soft tissue allows for growth, but in death it dissolves quickly. Thus the skeletons of young animals are more apt to be scattered, especially the vertebrae protecting the spinal cord. In the tar pits, the central ends of many vertebrae are found unconnected to any skeleton. Such bone fragments are shaped like valentines, disks that are slightly lobed—heart-shaped shields that have lost their connection to what they were meant to protect.

I never felt my mother pushed me to do something I didn't want to do. But I always knew if something I did pleased her. She was generous with her praise, and I was sensitive when she withheld it. I didn't like to disappoint her.

I took to performing easily, and since I had started out so young, making movies or doing shows didn't feel like anything special. It was a part of my childhood—like going to the dentist one morning or going to school the next. I didn't wonder if I wanted a particular role or wanted to be in a show or how I would feel if I didn't get in. Until I was fifteen, it never occurred to me that one day I wouldn't get parts or that I might not "have what it takes."

When I was younger, I got a lot of roles because I was so small for my age. When I was nine years old, I could pass for five or six. I was really short. I was always teased about it when I was in elementary school, but I didn't mind because my height got me movie jobs. I could read and memorize lines that actual five-year-olds couldn't. My mother told people she made me sleep in a drawer so I wouldn't grow any bigger.

But when I turned fifteen, it was as if my body, which hadn't grown for so many years, suddenly made up for lost time. I grew five inches in seven months. My mother was amazed. Even I couldn't get used to it. I kept knocking into things, my clothes didn't fit right, I felt awkward and clumsy when I moved. Dumb things that I had gotten away with, like paying children's prices at the movies instead of junior admission, I couldn't do anymore. I wasn't a shrimp or a small fry any longer. I was suddenly normal.

Before that summer my mother had always claimed she wanted me to be normal. She didn't want me to become spoiled by the attention I received when I was working at the studios. I still had chores to do at home, went to public school when I wasn't working, was punished severely when I behaved badly. She didn't want me to feel I was different just because I was in the movies. When I was eight, I was interviewed by a reporter who wanted to know if I thought I had a big head.

"Sure," I said.

"No you don't," my mother interrupted, which was really unusual, because she generally never said anything. She wanted me to speak for myself.

I didn't understand the question. My sister had always made fun of my head. She said my body was too tiny for the weight—I looked like a walking Tootsie Pop. I thought the reporter was making the same observation.

I grew five inches in seven months. My mother was amazed.

"She better not get that way," my mother said fiercely. "She's not any different from anyone else. She's just lucky and small for her age."

The reporter turned to my mother, "Some parents push their children to act. The kids feel like they're used."

"I don't do that—I'm not that way," my mother told the reporter.

But when she was sitting silently in all those waiting rooms while I was being turned down for one job after another, I could almost feel her wanting to shout, "Use her. Use her. What is wrong with her? Doesn't she have it anymore?" I didn't know what I had had that I didn't seem to have anymore. My mother had told the reporter that I was like everyone else. But when my life was like everyone else's, why was she disappointed?

What is wrong with her? Doesn't she have it anymore?

The churning action of the La Brea Tar Pits makes interpreting the record of past events extremely difficult. The usual order of deposition—the oldest on the bottom, the youngest on the top—loses all meaning when some of the oldest fossils can be brought to the surface by the movement of natural gas. One must look for an undisturbed spot, a place untouched by the action of underground springs or natural gas or human interference. Complete skeletons become important, because they indicate areas of least disturbance. But such spots of calm are rare. Whole blocks of the tar pit can become displaced, making false sequences of the past, skewing[8] the interpretation for what is the true order of nature.

That year before my sixteenth birthday, my mother seemed to spend a lot of time looking through my old scrapbooks, staring at all the eight-by-ten glossies of the shows that I had done. In the summer we visited with my grandmother often, since I wasn't working and had lots of free time. I would go out to the garden to read or sun-bathe, but I could hear my mother and grandmother talking.

"She was so cute back then. She worked with Gene Kelly[9] when she was five years old. She was so smart for her age. I don't know what's wrong with her."

"She's fifteen."

---

[8] skewing (SKYOO•ing)—distorting.
[9] Gene Kelly—(1912–1996) American dancer and movie star.

"She's too young to be an ingenue[10] and too old to be cute. The studios forget so quickly. By the time she's old enough to play an ingenue, they won't remember her."

"Does she have to work in the movies? Hand me the scissors."

My grandmother was making false eyelashes using the hair from her hairbrush. When she was young she had incredible hair. I saw an old photograph of her when it flowed beyond her waist like a cascading black waterfall. At seventy, her hair was still black as night, which made her few strands of silver look like shooting stars. But her hair had thinned greatly with age. It sometimes fell out in clumps. She wore it brushed back in a bun with a hairpiece for added

---

[10] ingenue (AN•zhuh•noo)—actress who plays roles of innocent young girls.

◀ Many skeletons of Ice Age animals such as this mammoth have been recovered from the La Brea Tar Pits.

COMPLETE SKELETONS BECOME IMPORTANT

fullness. My grandmother had always been proud of her hair, but once she started making false eyelashes from it, she wasn't proud of the way it looked anymore. She said she was proud of it now because it made her useful.

It was painstaking work—tying knots into strands of hair, then tying them together to form feathery little crescents. Her glamorous false eyelashes were much sought after. Theatrical make-up artists waited months for her work. But my grandmother said what she liked was that she was doing something, making a contribution, and besides it didn't cost her anything. No overhead. "Till I go bald," she often joked.

She tried to teach me her art that summer, but for some reason strands of my hair wouldn't stay tied in knots.

"Too springy," my grandmother said. "Your hair is still too young." And because I was frustrated then, frustrated with everything about my life, she added, "You have to wait until your hair falls out, like mine. Something to look forward to, eh?" She had laughed and patted my hand.

My mother was going on and on about my lack of work, what might be wrong, that something she couldn't quite put her finger on. I heard my grandmother reply, but I didn't catch

it all: "Movies are just make-believe, not real life. Like what I make with my hair that falls out—false. False eyelashes. Not meant to last."

The remains in the La Brea Tar Pits are mostly of carnivorous animals. Very few herbivores[11] are found—the ratio is five to one, a perversion[12] of the natural food chain. The ratio is easy to explain. Thousands of years ago a thirsty animal sought a drink from the pools of water only to find itself trapped by the bottom, gooey with subterranean oil. A shriek of agony from the trapped victim drew flesh-eating predators, which were then trapped themselves by the very same ooze which provided the bait. The cycle repeated itself countless times. The number of victims grew, lured by the image of easy food, the deception of an easy kill. The animals piled on top of one another. For over ten thousand years the promise of the place drew animals of all sorts, mostly predators and scavengers—dire wolves, panthers, coyotes, vultures—all hungry for their chance. Most were sucked down against their will in those watering holes destined to be called the La Brea Tar Pits in a place to be named the City of Angels, home of Hollywood movie stars.

---

[11] carnivorous animals. . . herbivores—meat-eating and plant-eating animals.

[12] perversion (puhr•VUR•zhuhn)—unnatural or abnormal change.

I spent a lot of time by myself that summer, wondering what it was that I didn't have anymore. Could I get it back? How could I if I didn't know what it was?

That's when I discovered the La Brea Tar Pits. Hidden behind the County Art Museum on trendy Wilshire Boulevard, I found a job that didn't require me to be small or cute for my age. I didn't have to audition. No one said, "Thank you very much, we'll call you." Or if they did, they meant it. I volunteered my time one afternoon, and my fascination stuck—like tar on the bones of a saber-toothed tiger.

My mother didn't understand what had changed me. I didn't understand it myself. But I liked going to the La Brea Tar Pits. It meant I could get really messy and I was doing it with a purpose. I didn't feel awkward there. I could wear old stained pants. I could wear T-shirts with holes in them. I could wear disgustingly filthy sneakers and it was all perfectly justified. It wasn't a costume for a role in a film or a part in TV sit-com. My mother didn't mind my dressing like that when she knew I was off to the pits. That was okay so long as I didn't track tar back into the house. I started going to the pits every day, and my mother wondered why. She couldn't believe I would rather be **groveling**[13] in tar than going on auditions or interviews.

While my mother wasn't proud of the La Brea Tar Pits (she didn't know or care what a fossil was), she didn't discourage me either. She drove me there, the same way she used to drive me to the studios.

"Wouldn't you rather be doing a show in Las Vegas than scrambling around in a pit?" she asked.

"I'm not in a show in Las Vegas, Ma. The Lee Sisters are retired." My older sister had married and was starting a family of her own.

"But if you could choose between . . ."

"There isn't a choice."

"You really like this tar-pit stuff, or are you just waiting until you can get real work in the movies?"

I didn't answer.

My mother sighed. "You could do it if you wanted, if you really wanted. You still have what it takes."

I found a job that didn't require me to be small or cute for my age.

---

[13] **groveling** (GRAHV•uhl•ihng)—bowing or working low to the ground.

I didn't know about that. But then, I couldn't explain what drew me to the tar pits either. Maybe it was the bones, finding out what they were, which animal they belonged to, imagining how they got there, how they fell into the trap. I wondered about that a lot.

At the La Brea Tar Pits, everything dug out of the pit is saved—including the sticky sand that covered the bones through the ages. Each bucket of sand is washed, sieved,[14] and examined for pollen grains, insect remains, any evidence of past life. Even the grain size is recorded—the percentage of silt to sand to gravel that reveals the history of deposition, erosion, and disturbance. No single fossil, no one observation, is significant enough to tell the entire story. All the evidence must be weighed before a semblance[15] of truth emerges.

The tar pits had its lessons. I was learning I had to work slowly, become observant, to concentrate. I learned about time in a way that I would never experience—not in hours, days, and months, but in thousands and thousands of years. I imagined what the past must have been like, envisioned Los Angeles as a sweeping basin, perhaps slightly colder and more humid, a time before people and studios arrived. The tar pits recorded a warming trend; the kinds of animals found there reflected the changing climate. The ones unadapted disappeared. No trace of their kind was found in the area. The ones adapted to warmer weather left a record of bones in the pit. Amid that collection of ancient skeletons, surrounded by evidence of death, I was finding a secret preserved over thousands and thousands of years. There was something cruel about natural selection and the survival of the fittest. Even those successful individuals that "had what it took" for adaptation still wound up in the pits.

I never found out if I had what it took, not the way my mother meant. But I did adapt to the truth: I wasn't a Chinese Shirley Temple any longer, cute and short for my age. I had grown up. Maybe not on a Hollywood movie set, but in the La Brea Tar Pits.

---

[14] sieved—sifted.

[15] semblance (sehm•bluhns)—outward appearance; likeness.

Responding

1. Have you ever felt the pressure to "have what it takes"? How did you handle it?

Analyzing

2. What does the narrator's account of her career growing up as an actor suggest about the image of **Asians in the media** at that time?

3. How does the last line of each paragraph about the tar pits tie into the next section on Hollywood?

4. How does the narrator's attitude about her future as an actor change as she grows up?

Extending

5. What are you losing or gaining as you grow out of childhood?

Literature Connection

A character's motivation *is the reason he or she acts, feels, or thinks a certain way. Motivation is a driving force in a story's development because it makes characters do something.*

1. What do you think is the mother's motivation for encouraging her daughter to pursue a movie career?

2. Why do you think the narrator seems to be confused about her own motivation to go to the tar pits so often?

▲

Cherylene Lee (right) dances in a scene from the film version of *Flower Drum Song.*

Activity

Commenting on Films

Cherylene Lee appeared in the stage and film versions of The Flower Drum Song, *a musical with a large cast of Asian Americans. Do a survey of past and recent American movies with Asian characters. With help from the Internet and a film book, locate popular American movies with Asian actors (or with white actors portraying Asians). View as many of those movies as possible. After viewing each movie, write a paragraph on a notecard about the impression the movie gives of Asians or Asian Americans. Share your comment cards with your classmates.*

AMIGO BROTHERS

BY PIRI THOMAS

About the Author

Poet, writer, and storyteller Piri Thomas was born in New York City's Spanish Harlem in 1928. He wrote his autobiography, Down These Mean Streets *(1967), while completing a prison sentence. It tells about his hard life as a Puerto Rican and African American boy in the ghetto. Thomas has continued to write and today hosts a web site about his life and work.*

About the Selection

Growing up, most people are affected by sports in one way or another. Youthful members of America's ethnic groups have frequently viewed **success in sports** *as a way to escape poverty or to gain recognition in a society that often denied them other career paths. As you read "Amigo Brothers," examine what seems to drive Antonio and Felix to pursue success in sports.*

Antonio Cruz and Felix Vargas were both seventeen years old. They were so together in friendship that they felt themselves to be brothers. They had known each other since childhood, growing up on the lower east side of Manhattan in the same tenement building on Fifth Street between Avenue A and Avenue B.

Antonio was fair, lean, and lanky, while Felix was dark, short, and husky. Antonio's hair was always falling over his eyes, while Felix wore his black hair in a natural Afro style.

Each youngster had a dream of someday becoming lightweight champion of the world. Every chance they had the boys worked out, sometimes at the Boys Club on 10th Street and Avenue A and sometimes at the pro's gym on 14th Street. Early morning sunrises would find them running along the East River Drive, wrapped in sweatshirts, short towels around their necks, and handkerchiefs Apache style around their foreheads.

While some youngsters were into street negatives, Antonio and Felix slept, ate, rapped, and dreamt positive. Between them, they had a collection of *Fight* magazines second to none, plus a scrapbook filled with torn tickets to every boxing match they had ever attended and some clippings of their own. If asked a question about any given fighter, they would immediately zip out from their memory banks divisions,[1] weights, records of fights, knockouts, technical knockouts, and draws or losses.

Each had fought many bouts representing their community and had won two gold-plated medals plus a silver and bronze medallion. The difference was in their style. Antonio's lean form and long reach made him the better boxer, while Felix's short and muscular frame made him the better slugger. Whenever they had met in the ring for sparring sessions, it had always been hot and heavy.

Now, after a series of elimination bouts,[2] they had been informed that they were to meet each other in the division finals that were scheduled for the seventh of August, two weeks away—the winner to represent the Boys Club in the Golden Gloves Championship Tournament.

The two boys continued to run together along the East River Drive. But even when joking with each other, they both sensed a wall rising between them.

---

title *amigo* (ah•MEE•goh)—Spanish for "friend."

[1] divisions—weight groups into which boxers are placed.

[2] elimination bouts—fights to determine which boxers will move on in competition.

One morning less than a week before their bout, they met as usual for their daily workout. They fooled around with a few jabs at the air, slapped skin, and then took off, running lightly along the dirty East River's edge.

Antonio glanced at Felix, who kept his eyes purposely straight ahead, pausing from time to time to do some fancy leg work while throwing one-twos followed by upper cuts to an imaginary jaw. Antonio then beat the air with a barrage of body blows and short devastating lefts with an overhand, jaw-breaking right. After a mile or so, Felix puffed and said, "Let's stop a while, bro. I think we both got something to say to each other."

WE BOTH KNOW THAT IN THE RING THE BETTER MAN WINS.

Antonio nodded. It was not natural to be acting as though nothing unusual was happening when two ace boon buddies were going to be blasting . . . each other within a few short days.

They rested their elbows on the railing separating them from the river. Antonio wiped his face with his short towel. The sunrise was now creating day.

Felix leaned heavily on the river's railing and stared across to the shores of Brooklyn. Finally, he broke the silence.

". . . , man. I don't know how to come out with it."

Antonio helped. "It's about our fight, right?"

"Yeah, right." Felix's eyes squinted at the rising orange sun.

"I've been thinking about it too, *panin*.[3] In fact, since we found out it was going to be me and you, I've been awake at night, pulling punches[4] on you, trying not to hurt you."

"Same here. It ain't natural not to think about the fight. I mean, we both are *cheverote*[5] fighters, and we both want to win. But only one of us can win. There ain't no draws in the eliminations."

Felix tapped Antonio gently on the shoulder. "I don't mean to sound like I'm bragging, bro. But I wanna win, fair and square."

Antonio nodded quietly. "Yeah. We both know that in the ring the better man wins. Friend or no friend, brother or no . . ."

---

[3] *panin* (pah•NEEN)—American Spanish for "buddy."

[4] pulling punches—holding back while hitting.

[5] *cheverote* (cheh•veh•ROH•teh)—American Spanish for "really cool."

ONLY ONE OF US CAN WIN

David Grossman photographed this young boxer training at Gleason's Gym for the Golden Gloves in the early 1990s. ▶

Felix finished it for him. "Brother. Tony, let's promise something right here. Okay?"

"If it's fair, *hermano*,[6] I'm for it." Antonio admired the courage of a tugboat pulling a barge five times its welterweight[7] size.

"It's fair, Tony. When we get into the ring, it's gotta be like we never met. We gotta be like two heavy strangers that want the same thing, and only one can have it. You understand, don'tcha?"

"*Sí*, I know." Tony smiled. "No pulling punches. We go all the way."

"Yeah, that's right. Listen, Tony. Don't you think it's a good idea if we don't see each other until the day of the fight? I'm going to stay with my Aunt Lucy in the Bronx. I can use Gleason's Gym for working out. My manager says he got some sparring partners with more or less your style."

Tony scratched his nose **pensively**.[8] "Yeah, it would be better for our heads." He held out his hand, palm upward. "Deal?"

"Deal." Felix lightly slapped open skin.

"Ready for some more running?" Tony asked lamely.

---

[6] *hermano* (ehr•MAH•noh)—Spanish for "brother."

[7] welterweight—weight group for boxers with a maximum weight of 147 pounds.

[8] **pensively** (PEHN•sihv•lee)—thoughtfully.

"Naw, bro. Let's cut it here. You go on. I kinda like to get things together in my head."

"You ain't worried, are you?" Tony asked.

"No way, man." Felix laughed out loud. "I got too much smarts for that. I just think it's cooler if we split right here. After the fight, we can get it together again like nothing ever happened."

The *amigo* brothers were not ashamed to hug each other tightly.

BOTH FIGHTERS HAD A LOT OF PSYCHING UP TO DO BEFORE THE BIG FIGHT.

"Guess you're right. Watch yourself, Felix. I hear there's some pretty heavy dudes up in the Bronx. *Suavecito,*[9] okay?"

"Okay. You watch yourself too, *sabe*?"[10]

Tony jogged away. Felix watched his friend disappear from view, throwing rights and lefts. Both fighters had a lot of psyching up to do before the big fight.

The days in training passed much too slowly. Although they kept out of each other's way, they were aware of each other's progress via the ghetto grapevine.

The evening before the big fight, Tony made his way to the roof of his tenement. In the quiet early dark, he peered over the ledge. Six stories below, the lights of the city blinked, and the sounds of cars mingled with the curses and the laughter of children in the street. He tried not to think of Felix, feeling he had succeeded in psyching his mind. But only in the ring would he really know. To spare Felix hurt, he would have to knock him out, early and quick.

Up in the South Bronx, Felix decided to take in a movie in an effort to keep Antonio's face away from his fists. The flick was *The Champion* with Kirk Douglas, the third time Felix was seeing it.

The champion was getting . . . beat . . . , his face being pounded into raw, wet hamburger. His eyes were cut, jagged, bleeding, one eye swollen, the other almost shut. He was saved only by the sound of the bell.

Felix became the champ and Tony the challenger.

The movie audience was going out of its head, roaring in blood lust at the butchery going on. The champ hunched his shoulders, grunting and

---

[9] *Sauvecito* (swah•veh•SEE•toh)—American Spanish for "Take it easy."

[10] *sabe?* (SAH•beh)—Spanish for "You know?"

sniffing red blood back into his broken nose. The challenger, confident that he had the championship in the bag, threw a left. The champ countered with a dynamite right that exploded into the challenger's brains.

Felix's right arm felt the shock. Antonio's face, superimposed on the screen, was shattered and split apart by the awesome force of the killer. Felix saw himself in the ring, blasting Antonio against the ropes. The champ had to be forcibly restrained. The challenger was allowed to crumble slowly to the canvas, a broken, bloody mess.

When Felix finally left the theatre, he had figured out how to psyche himself for tomorrow's fight. It was Felix the Champion vs. Antonio the Challenger.

He walked up some dark streets, deserted except for small pockets of wary-looking kids wearing gang colors. Despite the fact that he was Puerto Rican like them, they eyed him as a stranger to their turf. Felix did a fast shuffle, bobbing and weaving, while letting loose a torrent of blows that would demolish whatever got in its way. It seemed to impress the brothers, who went about their own business.

Finding no takers, Felix decided to split to his aunt's. Walking the streets had not relaxed him, neither had the fight flick. All it had done was to stir him up. He let himself quietly into his Aunt Lucy's apartment and went straight to bed, falling into a fitful sleep with sounds of the gong for Round One.

Antonio was passing some heavy time on his rooftop. How would the fight tomorrow affect his relationship with Felix? After all, fighting was like any other profession. Friendship had nothing to do with it. A gnawing doubt crept in. He cut negative thinking real quick by doing some speedy fancy dance steps, bobbing and weaving like mercury. The night air was blurred with **perpetual**[11] motions of left hooks and right crosses. Felix, his *amigo* brother, was not going to be Felix at all in the ring. Just an opponent with another face. Antonio went to sleep, hearing the opening bell for the first round. Like his friend in the South Bronx, he prayed for victory via a quick, clean knockout in the first round.

> **HOW WOULD THE FIGHT TOMORROW AFFECT HIS RELATIONSHIP WITH FELIX?**

---

[11] **perpetual** (puhr•PEHCH•oo•uhl)—continual.

Large posters plastered all over the walls of local shops announced the fight between Antonio Cruz and Felix Vargas as the main bout.

The fight had created great interest in the neighborhood. Antonio and Felix were well liked and respected. Each had his own loyal following. Betting fever was high and ranged from a bottle of Coke to cold, hard cash on the line.

Antonio's fans bet with unbridled[12] faith in his boxing skills. On the other side, Felix's admirers bet on his dynamite-packed fists.

Felix had returned to his apartment early in the morning of August 7th and stayed there, hoping to avoid seeing Antonio. He turned the radio on to *salsa*[13] music sounds and then tried to read while waiting for word from his manager.

The fight was scheduled to take place in Tompkins Square Park. It had been decided that the gymnasium of the Boys Club was not large enough to hold all the people who were sure to attend. In Tompkins Square Park, everyone who wanted could view the fight, whether from ringside or window fire escapes or tenement rooftops.

The morning of the fight, Tompkins Square was a beehive of activity with numerous workers setting up the ring, the seats, and the guest speakers' stand. The scheduled bouts began shortly after noon, and the park had begun filling up even earlier.

The local junior high school across from Tompkins Square Park served as the dressing room for all the fighters. Each was given a separate classroom, with desktops, covered with mats, serving as resting tables. Antonio thought he caught a glimpse of Felix waving to him from a room at the far end of the corridor. He waved back just in case it had been him.

The fighters changed from their street clothes into fighting gear. Antonio wore white trunks, black socks, and black shoes. Felix wore sky blue trunks, red socks, and white boxing shoes. Each had dressing gowns to match their fighting trunks with their names neatly stitched on the back.

The loudspeakers blared into the open window of the school. There were speeches by dignitaries, community leaders, and great boxers of yesteryear. Some were well prepared, some

---

[12] unbridled—uncontrolled.

[13] *salsa* (SAHL•suh)—popular form of Latin-American dance music.

improvised[14] on the spot. They all carried the same message of great pleasure and honor at being part of such a historic event. This great day was in the tradition of champions emerging from the streets of the lower east side.

Interwoven with the speeches were the sounds of the other boxing events. After the sixth bout, Felix was much relieved when his trainer, Charlie said, "Time change. Quick knockout. This is it. We're on."

Waiting time was over. Felix was escorted from the classroom by a dozen fans in white T-shirts with the word FELIX across their fronts.

Antonio was escorted down a different stairwell and guided through a roped-off path.

As the two climbed into the ring, the crowd exploded with a roar. Antonio and Felix both bowed gracefully and then raised their arms in acknowledgment.

Antonio tried to be cool, but even as the roar was in its first birth, he turned slowly to meet Felix's eyes looking directly into his. Felix nodded his head and Antonio responded. And both as one, just as quickly, turned away to face his own corner.

Bong, bong, bong. The roar turned to stillness.

"Ladies and Gentlemen. Señores y Señoras."

The announcer spoke slowly, pleased at his bilingual efforts.

"Now the moment we have all been waiting for—the main event between two fine young Puerto Rican fighters, products of our lower east side."

"*Loisaida*,"[15] called out a member of the audience."

"In this corner, weighing 131 pounds, Felix Vargas. And in this corner, weighing 133 pounds, Antonio Cruz. The winner will represent the Boys Club in the tournament of champions, the Golden Gloves. There will be no draw. May the best man win."

The cheering of the crowd shook the windowpanes of the old buildings surrounding Tompkins Square Park. At the center of the ring, the referee was giving instructions to the youngsters.

"Keep your punches up. No low blows. No punching on the back of the head. Keep your heads up. Understand. Let's have a clean fight. Now shake hands and come out fighting."

Both youngsters touched gloves and nodded. They turned and danced quickly to their corners. Their head

---

[14] **improvised** (IHM•pruh•veyezd)—performed without preparation.

[15] *Loisaida* (loh•ee•SY•dah)—Hispanic slang pronunciation for Lower East Side.

towels and dressing gowns were lifted neatly from their shoulders by their trainers' nimble fingers. Antonio crossed himself. Felix did the same.

BONG! BONG! ROUND ONE. Felix and Antonio turned and faced each other squarely in a fighting pose. Felix wasted no time. He came in fast, head low, half hunched toward his right shoulder, and lashed out with a straight left. He missed a right cross as Antonio slipped the punch and countered with one-two-three lefts that snapped Felix's head back, sending a mild shock coursing through

him. If Felix had any small doubt about their friendship affecting their fight, it was being neatly **dispelled**.[16]

Antonio danced, a joy to behold. His left hand was like a piston pumping jabs one right after another with seeming ease. Felix bobbed and weaved and never stopped boring in. He knew that at long range he was at a disadvantage. Antonio had too much reach on him. Only by coming in close could Felix hope to achieve the dreamed-of knockout.

---

[16] **dispelled** (dihs•PEHLD)—driven away or scattered.

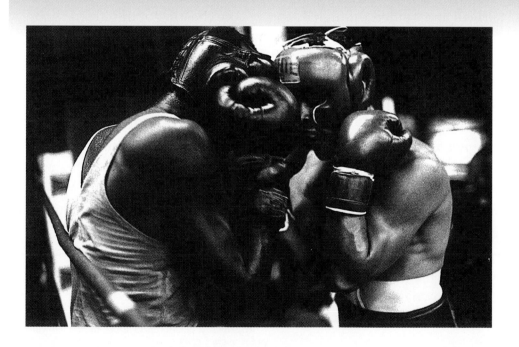

▲
These two young fighters sparring were photographed by David Grossman.

Antonio knew the dynamite that was stored in his *amigo* brother's fist. He ducked a short right and missed a left hook. Felix trapped him against the ropes just long enough to pour some punishing rights and lefts to Antonio's hard midsection. Antonio slipped away from Felix, crashing two lefts to his head, which set Felix's right ear to ringing.

Bong! Both *amigos* froze a punch well on its way, sending up a roar of approval for good sportsmanship.

Felix walked briskly back to his corner. His right ear had not stopped ringing. Antonio gracefully danced his way toward his stool none the worse, except for glowing glove burns, showing angry red against the whiteness of his midribs.

"Watch that right, Tony." His trainer talked into his ear. "Remember Felix always goes to the body. He'll want you to drop your hands for his overhand left or right. Got it?"

Antonio nodded, spraying water out between his teeth. He felt better as his sore midsection was being firmly rubbed.

Felix's corner was also busy.

"You gotta get in there, fella." Felix's trainer poured water over his curly Afro locks. "Get in there or he's gonna chop you up from way back."

Bong! Bong!

Round two. Felix was off his stool and rushed Antonio like a bull, sending a hard right to his head. Beads of water exploded from Antonio's long hair.

> **GET IN THERE OR HE'S GONNA CHOP YOU UP FROM WAY BACK.**

Antonio, hurt, sent back a blurring barrage of lefts and rights that only meant pain to Felix, who returned with a short left to the head followed by a looping right to the body. Antonio countered with his own flurry, forcing Felix to give ground. But not for long.

Felix bobbed and weaved, bobbed and weaved, occasionally punching his two gloves together.

Antonio waited for the rush that was sure to come. Felix closed in and feinted[17] with his left shoulder and threw his right instead. Lights suddenly exploded inside Felix's head as

---

[17] feinted (FAYNT•ehd)—pretended to attack one way to draw attention away from the intended purpose or target.

Antonio slipped the blow and hit him with a pistonlike left catching him flush on the point of his chin.

Bedlam[18] broke loose as Felix's legs momentarily buckled. He fought off a series of rights and lefts and came back with a strong right that taught Antonio respect.

Antonio danced in carefully. He knew Felix had the habit of playing possum when hurt, to sucker an opponent within reach of the powerful bombs he carried in each fist.

A right to the head slowed Antonio's pretty dancing. He answered with his own left at Felix's right eye that began puffing up within three seconds.

Antonio, a bit too eager, moved in too close, and Felix had him entangled into a rip-roaring, punching toe-to-toe slugfest that brought the whole Tompkins Square Park screaming to its feet.

Rights to the body. Lefts to the head. Neither fighter was giving an inch. Suddenly a short right caught Antonio squarely on the chin. His long legs turned to jelly, and his arms flailed[19] out desperately. Felix, grunting like a bull, threw wild punches from every direction. Antonio, groggy, bobbed and weaved, evading[20] most of the blows. Suddenly his head cleared. His left flashed out hard and straight catching Felix on the bridge of his nose.

Felix lashed back with a haymaker, right off the ghetto streets. At the same instant, his eye caught another left hook from Antonio. Felix swung out trying to clear the pain. Only the frenzied screaming of those along ringside let him know that he had dropped Antonio. Fighting off the growing haze, Antonio struggled to his feet, got up, ducked, and threw a smashing right that dropped Felix flat on his back.

Felix got up as fast as he could in his own corner, groggy but still game.[21] He didn't even hear the count. In a fog, he heard the roaring of the crowd, who seemed to have gone insane. His head cleared to hear the bell sound at the end of the round. He was very glad. His trainer sat him down on the stool.

In his corner, Antonio was doing what all fighters do when they are hurt. They sit and smile at everyone.

---

[18] Bedlam (BEHD•luhm)—loud confusion.

[19] flailed—waved or swung vigorously; thrashed.

[20] evading—escaping or avoiding by cleverness.

[21] game—ready to continue.

The referee signaled the ring doctor to check the fighters out. He did so and then gave his okay. The cold water sponges brought clarity to both *amigo* brothers. They were rubbed until their circulation ran free.

Bong! Round three—the final round. Up to now it had been tic-tac-toe, pretty much even. But everyone knew there could be no draw and this round would decide the winner.

This time, to Felix's surprise, it was Antonio who came out fast, charging across the ring. Felix braced himself but couldn't ward off the barrage of punches. Antonio drove Felix hard against the ropes.

The crowd ate it up. Thus far the two had fought with *mucho corazón.*[22] Felix tapped his gloves and commenced his attack anew. Antonio, throwing boxer's caution to the winds, jumped in to meet him.

Both pounded away. Neither gave an inch, and neither fell to the canvas. Felix's left eye was tightly closed. Claret[23] red blood poured from Antonio's nose. They fought toe-to-toe.

The sounds of their blows were loud in contrast to the silence of a crowd gone completely mute. The referee was stunned by their savagery.

Bong! Bong! Bong! The bell sounded over and over again. Felix and Antonio were past hearing. Their blows continued to pound on each other like hailstones.

Finally the referee and the two trainers pried Felix and Antonio apart. Cold water was poured over them to bring them back to their senses.

They looked around and then rushed toward each other. A cry of alarm surged through Tompkins Square Park. Was this a fight to the death instead of a boxing match?

The fear soon gave way to wave upon wave of cheering as the two *amigos* embraced.

No matter what the decision, they knew they would always be champions to each other.

Bong! Bong! Bong! "Ladies and Gentlemen. *Señores* and *Señoras*. The winner and representative to the Golden Gloves Tournament of Champions is. . . "

The announcer turned to point to the winner and found himself alone. Arm in arm, the champions had already left the ring.

---

[22] *mucho corazón* (MOO•choh koh•rah•ZOHN)—Spanish for "a lot of heart" or "courage."

[23] Claret—wine of dark red color.

Questions to Consider

Responding

1. How is the relationship between the *amigo* brothers similar or different from the relationships you have with your friends?

Analyzing

2. What do you think motivates Antonio and Felix to pursue **success in sports** as they are growing up?

3. How does the ending of the story support what happened before?

4. How do you think the outcome of the fight will change the relationship of Antonio and Felix?

Extending

5. If you found yourself competing with a friend, how do you think this situation would affect both your competition and your friendship?

Literature Connection

In literature, conflict is the struggle between opposing forces. It may be external, as in a struggle between two or more characters or between characters and an outside force such as nature. It also may be internal, as in a struggle within a character about an issue or action.

1. What external conflicts do both boys face?

2. What internal conflicts do they face?

Activities

Writing About Conflict

About his childhood in the harsh world of New York's slums, Piri Thomas wrote, "Reading helped me to realize that there was a world out there far vaster than the narrow confines of El Barrio. I learned that there were people who didn't care about color being a measure of superiority or inferiority. What mattered was the dignity of one's heart and the honor of one's word." Write a paragraph that explains how reading helps or might help you to overcome or deal with conflict in your life.

Performing a Skit

With a partner, write an original skit in which you portray teenagers who dream of escaping from the poverty of the ghetto by means of success in sports, music, the arts, or academics. Have the characters clearly express their bond with each other, but show conflict too. Make one character hopeful and the other skeptical. Perform your skit for your class.

The "Black Table" Is Still There

BY LAWRENCE OTIS GRAHAM

About the Author

Lawrence Otis Graham earned degrees from Princeton University and Harvard Law School. In 1997, Graham left his job as an attorney, went undercover as a busboy at an all-white country club, and then wrote an article on the discrimination there. Graham has written a number of books, including Our Kind of People: Inside America's Black Upper Class (1999). He currently works as a commentator and journalist.

About the Selection

*When people voluntarily divide themselves by race, ethnicity, social class, religion, or common interests such as athletics or a particular type of music, **self-segregation** may result. Self-segregation is a term given to situations in which people group themselves in such a way that they give the impression they want to associate only with people from that group. Often the term is applied to situations where people group themselves by race or ethnicity. As you read "The 'Black Table' Is Still There," think about why young people growing up tend to do this and the narrator's view on its effects.*

During a recent visit to my old junior high school in Westchester County, I came upon something that I never expected to see again, something that was a source of fear and dread for three hours each school morning of my early adolescence: the all-black lunch table in the cafeteria of my predominantly white suburban junior high school.

As I look back on 27 years of often being the first and only black person integrating such activities and institutions as the college newspaper, the high school tennis team, summer music camps, our all-white suburban neighborhood, my eating club at Princeton or my private social club at Harvard Law School, the one **scenario**[1] that puzzled me the most then and now is the all-black lunch table.

Why was it there? Why did the black kids separate themselves? What did the table say about the integration that was supposedly going on in home rooms and gym classes? What did it say about the black kids? The white kids? What did it say about me when I refused to sit there, day after day, for three years?

Each afternoon, at 12:03 P.M., after the fourth period ended, I found myself among 600 12-, 13- and 14-year-olds who marched into the brightly-lit cafeteria and dashed for a seat at one of the 27 blue formica lunch tables.

No matter who I walked in with— usually a white friend—no matter what mood I was in, there was one thing that was certain: I would not sit at the black table.

I would never consider sitting at the black table.

What was wrong with me? What was I afraid of?

I would like to think that my decision was a heroic one, made in order to express my **solidarity**[2] with the theories of integration that my community was espousing.[3] But I was just 12 at the time, and there was nothing heroic in my actions.

I was afraid that by sitting at the black table I'd lose all my white friends.

---

[1] **scenario** (sih•NAHR•ee•oh)—outline or model of an expected or supposed sequence of events.

[2] **solidarity**—union of purposes and ideas held by a group.

[3] espousing (ih•SPOWZ•ihng)—giving support to.

I avoided the black table for a very simple reason: I was afraid that by sitting at the black table I'd lose all my white friends. I thought that by sitting there I'd be making a racist, anti-white statement.

Is that what the all-black table means? Is it a rejection of white people? I no longer think so.

At the time, I was angry that there was a black lunch table. I believed that the black kids were the reason why other kids didn't mix

more: I was ready to believe that their self-segregation was the cause of white **bigotry**.[4]

Ironically, I even believed this after my best friend (who was white) told me I probably shouldn't come to his bar mitzvah[5] because I'd be the only black and some people would feel uncomfortable. I even believed this after my Saturday afternoon visit,

[4] **bigotry**—attitude or act of intolerance.
[5] bar mitzvah (bar•MIHTS•vuh)—ceremony celebrating the coming of age of a 13-year-old Jewish boy.

Susie Fitzhugh photographed these African-American students seated at a cafeteria table in a school in Baltimore. ▶

Why do all those black kids *sit together?*

at age 10, to a private country club pool prompted incensed[6] white parents to pull their kids from the pool in terror.

In the face of this blatantly[7] racist (anti-black) behavior, I still somehow managed to blame only the black kids for being the barrier to integration in my school and my little world. What was I thinking?

I realize now how wrong I was. During that same time, there were at least two tables of athletes, an Italian table, a Jewish girls' table, a Jewish boys' table (where I usually sat), a table of kids who were into heavy metal music and smoking pot, a table of middle class Irish kids. Weren't these tables just as segregationist as the black table? At the time, no one thought so. At the time, no one even acknowledged the segregated nature of these other tables.

Maybe it's the color difference that makes all-black tables or all-black groups attract the scrutiny[8] and wrath of so many people. It scares and angers people; it **exasperates**.[9] It did those things to me, and I'm black.

As an integrating black person, I know that my decision not to join the black lunch table attracted its own kind of scrutiny and wrath from my classmates. At the same time that I heard angry words like "Oreo"[10] and "white boy" being hurled at me from the black table, I was also dodging impatient questions from white classmates: "Why do all those black kids sit together?" or "Why don't you ever sit with the other blacks?"

The black lunch table, like those other segregated tables, is a comment on the superficial inroads that integration has made in society. Perhaps I should be happy that even this is a long way from where we started. Yet, I can't get over the fact that the 27th table in my junior high school cafeteria is still known as the "black table"—14 years after my adolescence.

---

[6] incensed—very angry.

[7] blatantly—obviously and offensively.

[8] **scrutiny** (skroot•nee)—careful, close examination or study.

[9] **exasperates** (ihg•ZAHS•puh•rayts)—greatly annoys.

[10] Oreo—derogatory term that suggests a black person is white on the inside—meaning that the black person thinks and acts like a white person.

Questions to Consider

Responding

1. Have you ever discovered that some action of yours you had thought was all right was probably wrong all along? How did you handle your new awareness?

Analyzing

2. Was Graham's stubbornness about sitting at a white table a denial of the reality of racism?

3. How does Graham support his point about the color factor in people's reactions to **self-segregation**?

4. What point does Graham make about the success of integration?

Extending

5. What do you think of segregated tables or areas at your school?

Literature Connection

The tone of a literary work expresses the writer's attitude toward a subject. Words such as angry, sad, *or* humorous *can be used to describe tone.*

1. What is the subject of this essay?

2. How would you describe the writer's tone?

Activities

Writing About Self-segregation

Write a short story told from the perspective of a person in an established situation of self-segregation. Explore the feelings and thoughts of the person regarding the situation. Give background about how the situation came about and why it continues. Include a description of someone (the narrator or another person) who tries to or succeeds in breaking through or breaking away from the situation.

Role Playing

Working with other students in your class, role play a self-segregation situation. It might be at lunch, at a dance, or some other place. Role play what happens when one or more students acts to integrate the segregated groups. Role play how teachers, parents, and other adults might become involved. After your role plays, hold a class discussion of what happened and how it might translate to dealing with similar situations in real life.

Part Four

Families

An ethnic group is, in one sense, a large family. Ethnic identity is based on family life. Our family life, in turn, is often defined by the ethnic group or groups to which we belong.

◀ This large Latino family has gathered for a casual portrait.

Mi Familia

BY CARMEN TAFOLLA

About the Author

Carmen Tafolla (tah•FOY•ah) was one of the most successful Texas poets to emerge in the 1970s. Tafolla was born in 1951 in the westside barrios (or Hispanic neighborhoods) of San Antonio. She grew up discovering and savoring her Mexican-American ancestry. Tafolla was a dedicated student who earned a doctoral degree in bilingual education. She and her husband founded a company to improve education for minority children. In addition to poetry, Tafolla writes short stories, nonfiction, and plays. She is well known for her one-woman theatrical performances in which she portrays characters from various races and walks of life.

About the Selection

The **concept of family** in modern America is a broad one. It encompasses more than a group of people related biologically or legally. In general, a family may be defined as a set of individuals who share deep personal connections and provide support for each other. Families often include members who are adopted or divorced. They may include those who are in foster or kinship care. Many families include individuals from various races and ethnicities and a range of age groups. Single-parent, teen-parent, and two-parent families are all "typical" today. As you read, "Mi Familia," think about who makes up the author's family.

I know when I began—or at least when I was born, on July 29th, 1951, at 8:41 P.M.—but that isn't really the whole story. My beginnings were somehow rooted in memories passed on to me through my grandmother's sayings and my father's songs, and my mother's stories, and in some mountains that I saw once from the highway, and in the thread of a dream below the voice and between the words of someone whose name I don't know but whose voice and dream I still carry.

The way I defined family was much like the old funerals I remember. In the front rows were the next of kin, the most greatly affected by the loss, behind them those close, behind them the friends, then the acquaintances and always, somewhere, the people of whom no one knew the exact relationship to the departed, but that didn't matter—those people knew, and that was enough reason to be there. In fact, one's own internal reasons were the guiding law for anyone's presence, and no one had to make explanations at a time like that. Modern "family sections" later served to cut off, to make people separate off, who was family from who wasn't,

who was "immediate family" from who was "distant." None of this was necessary in the old Mexicano funerals I remembered. The cousin (*prima hermana*,[1] to emphasize how close the relationship really was) who'd spent eighty years of her life with the deceased didn't have to be turned away from the three skimpy rows of "Family Section" just in order to allow room for younger **siblings**[2] and spouse, nieces and nephews, who'd only spent twenty to sixty-some-odd years with the deceased. There was no having to judge "degree" of relationship, in competition with the others present. One merely found one's place according to one's own intuition.

Family was like that. There was the little boy in second grade that I was proud to claim as my "third step cousin-in-law" and there were the friends for whom no blood connection existed, but who counted in every way as cousins, to whom there was a life-long commitment and a life-long connection.

It was a big family. It seemed I had several dozen aunts and uncles, and at least fifty of the immediate cousins.

---

[1] *prima hermana* (PREE•mah ehr•MAH•nah)—Spanish for "first cousin" (female).

[2] **siblings**—brothers or sisters.

It was a context that provided variety and contrast. "Somos como los frijoles pintos," my grandmother would say, "algunos güeros, algunos morenos, y algunos con pecas." (We're like pinto beans in this family—some light, some dark, and some with freckles.) I knew my grandmother so well, through all her sayings, but these had been told to me by my father, years after her death. I knew her through my father, even the details of her death, a death that happened shortly after my first birthday. Still, she guides me through many days, telling me "No hay sábado sin sol ni domingo sin misa." (There's no Saturday that doesn't have some sunshine, no Sunday that doesn't have a Mass.) Still, she warns me "Díme con quien andas y te diré quien eres." (Tell me who you hang around with, and I'll tell you who you are.)

She was from Mexico, a proud, quiet woman, who spoke little and said much, whose skirts always touched the ground, who never raised her voice or lowered her sense of dignity. Her high cheekbones were echoed in my father's face and in my own. I find it hard to imagine her as a noisy child, as a noisy anything.

My grandfather, on the other hand, lived by words. Words were his tools, and he was a man who valued tools. "Cómprate un fierro con cada día de pago" (Buy yourself one tool every payday), he gave my father as *consejo*,[3] and he taught his sons carpentry, plumbing, construction, and a hunger to build things. My father would later teach me, perhaps more randomly than he would have constructed the lessons for a boy, but still I knew how to use a hammer and a drill, how to putty the nail holes and clean a carburetor,[4] and most importantly, how to hunger to build things. Had the training been less random, less riddled with gaps, I would have known *how* to build things. As it is, I sit with pen and paper today, and try to plan and guess how I could put together a table or a house, how to do it right, for it would not do to make one not solid, not "*macizo*."[5]

> **Tell me who you hang around with, and I'll tell you who you are.**

---

[3] *consejo* (kohn•SAY•hoh)—Spanish for "advice."
[4] carburetor (KAHR•buh•RAY•tuhr)—device in an engine that mixes air and fuel.
[5] "*macizo*" (mah•KEE•zoh)—Spanish for "filled in."

▲
Mexican-American artist Martina López used family photographs as the basis for her painting *Heirs Come to Pass* (1991).

Yet my grandfather's main occupation in life was using words as tools. The preacher, teacher, leader, he was the first in the family (possibly in the whole barrio) to own a typewriter. I don't know how old he was when he got it, but it was still his, marked with his work and his determination, used solidly and squarely as any of his tools, the fountain of many letters, that somehow always looked as individual as if he'd marked them by fountain pen and fingerprint.

His name was Mariano Tafolla. It was his grandfather's name, my father's name, and my father's oldest brother's name. Searching through the Santa Fe **archives**[6] a few years ago, I found his grandfather's signature. It was almost a duplicate of my father's. I keep the name Tafolla, although my signature, perhaps even my personality, is far different.

---

[6] **archives** (AHR•KYVZ)—collections of records, documents, or other materials of historical interest.

Perhaps it has something to do with words. With finding your place in the old Mexicano funerals, by internal guide, by intuition. This is who I am.

I have always considered my life one of great fortune, and the barrio was one of these points of fortune. It was a place rich in story and magic, warmth and wisdom. So magic it was that even the police would not come there, despite calls or complaints, unless they came in twos, with their car doors locked. We played baseball in the streets, shot off firecrackers on the Fourth of July, and raised our Easter chicks to fully grown (and temporarily spoiled) chickens.

When I was, years later, to hear about slums and ghettos, cultural deprivation, and poverty-warped childhoods—there was no identification in my mind with these. In our own view, we were wealthy—we had no deprivation of cultural experiences, but rather a double dose of *cultura*. Yes, my cousins from "up north" would come to visit, and they had so many more "facts" at hand, seemed to know so much and do so much in their schools. Our school had no interscholastic activities, no spelling bees or science fairs, no playground equipment, nor even a fence.

The main thing the schools tried to teach us was not to speak Spanish. The main thing we learned was not to speak Spanish in front of the teachers, and not to lose Spanish within ourselves. Perhaps that is why so many good independent and critical minds came out of that time period. Or perhaps that is why so many good independent and critical minds dropped out of school. We learned— oh, did we learn, but it was not what the school district had planned for us to learn. It was much bigger than that.

An Encounter with Life was painted by Martina López in 1996.

▼

We became filled with a hunger— I call it now, sometimes, Latino Hunger. A hunger to see ourselves, our families and friends, our values and lives and realities reflected in something other than our own minds. We wanted proof that we really existed—a proof documented in those many schoolbooks filled with Toms and Susans, and Dicks and Janes, but no Chuys or Guadalupes or Juanas, no Adelitas or Santos or Esperanzas. And we definitely needed Esperanzas,[7] if we were to dream of anything at all beyond the sirens, the friskings, and the punishments for the sin of having spoken Spanish at school. There was a hunger and a place in our lives that needed to be filled with Esperanzas and Milagros.[8]

So what we didn't see, we invented. Even the national anthem became our cultural playground: "Jo—o—sé, can you see—ee?" And we filled TV with our own *raza*,[9] hidden between the lines and in the shadows of people's pasts.

My roots in New Mexico go back for centuries—*españoles*[10] arriving in the 17th century to *indios parientes*[11] already there. The move to Texas happened between 1848 and 1865 (a few wars got in the way, causing strange demographic[12] reshuffles). My great-great-grandmother was already there, and had a seamstress shop in "downtown" San Antonio; my great-grandmother washed clothes in the San Antonio River; her *tío*[13] had brought word in 1836 to Juan Seguín and the *tejanos* at the Alamo that Santa Ana's army was coming in great force.[14] (They didn't listen.) She later married two (one at a time) Confederate veterans. Growing up, I teased that I had relatives on all sides of all wars.

> **We wanted proof that we really existed.**

---

[7] Esperanzas (ehs•pehr•AHN•zahs)—names from *esperanza*, Spanish for "hope."

[8] Milagros (mee•LAH•grohs)—names from *milagro*, Spanish for "miracle."

[9] *raza* (rah•zah)—Spanish for "race."

[10] *españoles* (ehs•pahn•YOH•lehs)—Spanish for "Spaniards."

[11] *indios parientes* (EEN•dee•ohs pah•ree•EHN•tays)— Spanish for "Indian relatives."

[12] demographic (DEHM•uh•GRAF•ihk)—related to the study of human populations.

[13] *tío* (TEE•oh)—Spanish for "uncle."

[14] Juan Seguín . . . force—Juan Seguín (wahn seh•GEEN) led a band of 25 *tejanos* (tay•HAH•nohs), Texans of Mexican descent, in support of the defenders of the Alamo against the Mexican general Santa Ana in 1836.

The Tafollas' roots were in New Mexico, the Salinas' in San Antonio, the Sánchez' in Montemorelos,[15] the Duartes' and Morenos' in Spain, but somehow it was San Antonio that won out. San Antonio is in my blood. Maybe that's because its earth was worn smooth by so many first-step baby feet kissed by mothers before my mother. Maybe because its air was charged by the anger and tension and passion of fights between family members and then warmed by the *abrazos*[16] between them, healing their hearts. Maybe it's that the sunshine captured the laughter, or the river collected the tears from my own eyes and a thousand crying family eyes before me, and then returned the same life-moisture in rain to celebrate, and in honest sweat from good work done. Maybe it's the softness of the grass, the softness of the earth, that holds the softness of all those buried there by blood or heart related: my grandparents, my aunts, my father, my first-born child, and a thousand cousins and cousins of cousins for centuries held together by the warmth of *familia*.

From the *vaqueros*, *rancheros*, *soldados*,[17] preachers, teachers and storytellers on my father's side and the metalworkers, maids, nursemaids, and servant people on my mother's side come the family members that sit by my side as I write today. So do the mesquite trees and *vacas*, coyotes and *ríos* of their lives, and the *molcajetes* and *gatos*, *libros*[18] and computers, friends and strangers, races, telephones and headlines—of mine. They are all a part of my *familia*, that huge network of creatures in coexistence, sharing places and times and feelings, sharing commitment, sharing care about each other . . .

But that only tells part of the story. Because we don't have photographs or even mental images of most of the people that form our *familia*—we don't even know who they were, or who they will be. And everything and everyone I see out there, and the even more numerous ones I don't see, are all the real members of my *familia*. And when we speak of family, who can we really leave out?

---

[15] Montemorelos (MOHN•tay•moh•RAY•lohs)—city in northeastern Mexico.

[16] *abrazos* (ah•BRAH•zohs)—Spanish for "hugs."

[17] *vaqueros* (vah•KEHR•ohs), *rancheros* (rahn•CHEHR•ohs), *soldados* (sohl•DAH•dohs)—Spanish for "cowboys, ranchers, soldiers."

[18] *vacas* (VAH•kahs), *ríos* (REE•ohs), *molcajetes* (mohl•kah•HAY•tays), *gatos* (GAH•tohs), *libros* (LEE•brohs)—Spanish for "cows, rivers, mortars and pestles, cats, books."

Questions to Consider

Responding

1. How would you define your **concept of family**?

Analyzing

2. How do the funerals the narrator remembers help define her concept of family?

3. What does the narrator mean when she says that she and the other children of the barrio learned "not to lose Spanish within ourselves"?

4. How is San Antonio related to the narrator's concept of family?

Extending

5. What does the narrator mean when she says that we don't even know most of the people who form our families? What do you think about this idea?

Literature Connection

A **proverb** is an "old saying," a sentence or phrase that expresses a recognized truth or a perceptive observation about life. For example, "Blood is thicker than water" is a proverb meaning that family ties are more important than other ties. Traditionally, proverbs are passed on orally from generation to generation.

1. How did the grandmother's proverbs help to make the narrator think of her as one who "spoke little and said much"?

2. How was the grandfather's advice about tools different from the grandmother's proverbs?

Activities

Making a Family Record

Create a family record about members of your family. You can limit yourself to basic information, such as dates of births, marriages, and deaths; or you can include other interesting items about individuals, like their nicknames. You can also decide whether you will include people who are not closely related to you—or perhaps not related at all—but who are still considered part of your "family."

▲
After the Civil War, many African Americans used charts like this to keep track of their family histories.

My Mother Pieced Quilts

BY TERESA PALOMO ACOSTA

About the Author

Texan Teresa Palomo Acosta was born in 1949. She earned degrees in ethnic studies at the University of Texas and journalism at Columbia University. She then took up work as a journalist and teacher. During a creative writing class, she wrote her most famous poem, "My Mother Pieced Quilts." She originally had no intention of publishing the poem. Today, Acosta's poems appear in several collections. She attributes her interest in literature to the stories her Mexican-American grandfather told her as a child.

About the Selections

The traditional **role of mother**s focuses on childcare and housekeeping. In the United States today, more women work outside the home than ever before; however, the primary perception of a mother remains a woman who spends most of her time nurturing her children. Certainly, the mother-child bond is strong. It is rooted in biological urges and society's values. As you read the "My Mother Pieced Quilts" and "My Mother Juggling Bean Bags" (page 226), think about what the speakers value about that bond.

they were just meant as covers
in winters
as weapons
against pounding january winds

but it was just that every morning I awoke to these
october ripened canvases
passed my hand across their cloth faces
and began to wonder how you pieced
all these together
these strips of gentle communion[1] cotton and flannel nightgowns
wedding organdies
dime store velvets

how you shaped patterns square and oblong and round
positioned
balanced
then cemented them
with your thread
a steel needle
a thimble

how the thread darted in and out
galloping along the frayed edges, tucking them in
as you did us at night
oh how you stretched and turned and re-arranged
your michigan spring faded curtain pieces
my father's santa fe work shirt[2]
the summer denims, the tweeds of fall

---

[1] communion—one of the sacraments of the Roman Catholic Church. Usually, those receiving Communion for the first time wear white for the ceremony.

[2] sante fe work shirt—work clothes named for the Santa Fe Railroad.

A quilt is being aired on a porch in *Gilley's House*, a lithograph by North Carolina artist Bob Timberlake. ▶

patterns

square and oblong

in the evening you sat at your canvas
—our cracked linoleum floor the drawing board
me lounging on your arm
and you staking out the plan:
whether to put the lilac purple of easter against the red plaid of winter-going-
into-spring

whether to mix a yellow with blue and white and paint the
corpus christi[3] noon when my father held your hand
whether to shape a five point star from the
somber black silk you wore to grandmother's funeral

you were the river current
carrying the roaring notes
forming them into pictures of a little boy reclining
a swallow flying
you were the caravan master at the reins
driving your threaded needle **artillery**[4] across the **mosaic**[5] cloth bridges
delivering yourself in separate **testimonies**[6]

oh mother you plunged me sobbing and laughing
into our past
into the river crossing at five
into the spinach fields
into the plainview[7] cotton rows
into tuberculosis wards
into braids and muslin dresses
sewn hard and taut to withstand the thrashings of twenty-five years.

stretched out they lay
armed/ready/shouting/celebrating

knotted with love
the quilts sing on

---

[3] corpus christi—Corpus Christi is a city in southern Texas.
[4] **artillery**—large guns, such as cannons.
[5] **mosaic**—picture or decorative design made by setting small colored pieces, as of stone, glass, or tile, into a surface.
[6] **testimonies**—declarations or public statements.
[7] plainview—Plainview is a Texas town known for cotton.

My Mother Juggling Bean Bags

BY JAMES MITSUI

About the Author

James Mitsui (mit•SOO•ee) was born in 1940 in Skykomish, Washington. His parents were Japanese immigrants. When he was one year old, his family was forced into a wartime relocation camp. This experience made a lasting impression on Mitsui. His novels, stories, and poems deal with his Japanese heritage and with political issues.

At 71, my mother juggled three,
even four bean bags
while shouting *"yeeaaat"*[8]

and *"yoi-cho"*[9] between her gold
front teeth. My children
stooped to pick up

her mistakes. They watched,
mouths shaped like little *o*'s,
as "Little Grandma"

laughed in a language
anyone could understand.
On visitation weekends

---

[8] *yeeaaat*—Japanese expression used to mean something like "Yes!" or "All right!" when doing something well or right.

[9] *yoi-cho*—Japanese expression used to mean something like "one, two, three" when exerting an effort, especially with a group.

we visited her low-income apartment
and shared 7-UP, too many
British jelly cookies

and potato chips.
Now, over twenty years later,
I value my mother's humor.

As a child I had one-present
Christmases, but there was always
roast turkey on holidays,

 Photographer Joel Gordon took this portrait of a smiling Japanese-American grandmother.

jeans with no holes, and a first-base
glove from Montgomery Ward
that they really couldn't afford.

I remember the night when two girls
from the Class of '59
had driven ten miles from Odessa[10]

just to show my mother how to
short-sheet[11] my bed. I can still hear
her laughter in the dark.

I can also remember my mother
chasing me with a stick of firewood
around the trash burner in the parlor,

using my father's railroad swear
    words.
She always managed not
to catch me. Now I warn my
    children—

when I turn 71, I may turn from
    poetry
to juggling oranges. I owe it to my
    mother;
I owe it to my six grandchildren.

---

[10] Odessa—town in east central Washington.

[11] short-sheet—trick in which a sheet is folded in half on a bed to appear as though it is both the bottom sheet and the top sheet, so that when a person gets into bed it is impossible to straighten out their legs.

Questions to Consider

Responding

1. What three words would you choose to express the most important things mothers contribute to family life?

Analyzing

2. In "My Mother Pieced Quilts," what does the speaker feel her mother provided by means of the quilts?

3. In "My Mother Juggling Bean Bags," why do you think the speaker "owes" it to his mother and grandchildren to juggle oranges at 71?

4. What do each of these poems say about the **role of mothers** in their children's lives?

Extending

5. What do you think are the most important gifts you have received from your mother?

Literature Connection

Imagery consists of words and phrases that appeal to a reader's five senses. Writers use sensory details to help readers imagine how things look, feel, sound, smell, and taste.

1. What role does imagery of color have in "My Mother Pieced Quilts"?

2. In "My Mother Juggling Bean Bags," how does the poet use imagery to picture his mother in action?

Activity

Juggling Bean Bags

Otedama is a traditional Japanese form of juggling using colorful beanbags known as ojami. It was once a popular pastime for young girls, particularly in winter when it was too cold to play outside. The girls played singly or in groups. Learn about otedama and do a demonstration for your class.

Those Winter Sundays

BY ROBERT HAYDEN

About the Author

African-American poet Robert Hayden (1913–1980) grew up in
Detroit. To escape family fights during his childhood, he read constantly.
He attended Detroit City College (now Wayne State University) and
the University of Michigan, where he studied with the poet W. H. Auden.
Hayden's poetry gained international recognition in the 1960s. In 1976, he became the first
African American to be named Poet Laureate of the Library of Congress. He is known for
his technique and dramatic style. His poems explore African-American concerns throughout
American history.

About the Selections

The traditional **role of fathers** emphasizes material support, strength,
and authority. These values are good when they do not exclude warmth
and an ability to nurture. As you read "Those Winter Sundays" (page 230)
and "My Father's Song" (page 231), think about what the poems say
about the role of fathers.

Sundays too my father got up early
and put his clothes on in the blueblack cold,
then with cracked hands that ached
from labor in the weekday weather made
banked fires blaze. No one ever thanked him.

I'd wake and hear the cold splintering, breaking.
When the rooms were warm, he'd call,
and slowly I would rise and dress,
fearing the **chronic**[1] angers of that house,

Speaking **indifferently**[2] to him,
who had driven out the cold
and polished my good shoes as well.
What did I know, what did I know
of love's **austere**[3] and lonely offices?[4]

---

[1] **chronic**—habitual; frequently recurring.
[2] **indifferently**—with no interest.
[3] **austere**—strict, severe.
[4] offices—duties, functions.

My Father's Song

BY SIMON ORTIZ

About the Author

Simon Ortiz is an Acoma Pueblo poet who writes with a storyteller's eyes and ears. He was born in New Mexico in 1941, and grew up with a love for the desert landscape and the Native American oral tradition. After graduating from the University of New Mexico and the Iowa Writers Workshop, Ortiz became a professional writer and teacher. He won the Pushcart Prize for Poetry for his collection of poems From Sand Creek *(1981). Ortiz's poems are simple and direct. Many have a conversational feel.*

Wanting to say things,
I miss my father tonight.
His voice, the slight catch,[5]
the depth from his thin chest,
the tremble of emotion
in something he has just said
to his son, his song:

We planted corn one Spring at Acu[6]—
we planted several times

---

[5] catch—choking or stopping of the breath or voice.
[6] Acu—Acoma Pueblo, Ortiz's childhood home in New Mexico.

but this one particular time
I remember the soft damp sand
in my hand.

My father had stopped at one point
to show me an overturned furrow;[7]
the plowshare[8] had unearthed
the burrow nest of a mouse
in the soft moist sand.

Very gently, he scooped tiny pink animals
into the palm of his hand
and told me to touch them.
We took them to the edge
of the field and put them in the shade
of a sand moist clod.

I remember the very softness
of cool and warm sand and tiny alive mice
and my father saying things.

---

7 furrow—long, narrow, shallow trench made in the ground by a plow.

8 plowshare—cutting blade of a plow.

Daniel DeSiga's painting *Campesino*
(1976) expresses the close relationship
between the farmer and the earth. ▶

Questions to Consider

Responding

1. What three words would you choose to express the most important things fathers contribute to family life?

Analyzing

2. What does each of these poems say about the **role of fathers** in their children's lives?

3. In "Those Winter Sundays," how does the author's use of imagery contribute to the speaker's memories of the father?

4. Why does the speaker talk "indifferently" to the father?

5. What imagery is used to make you feel the tenderness between the father and son in "My Father's Song"?

6. Why do you think the father told his son to touch the mice?

Extending

7. Why do you think it is hard sometimes for people to express their love to parents or other caregivers?

Literature Connection

*The **tone** of a literary work expresses the writer's attitude toward a subject. Words such as angry, sad, or humorous can be used to describe tone. Look at the following lines from "Those Winter Sundays:"*

> What did I know, what did I know
> of love's austere and lonely offices?

1. What do these lines suggest about the speaker's attitude toward his father?

2. What words would you use to describe the tone of this poem?

3. How does the tone of "My Father's Song" differ from that of "Those Winter Sundays"?

Activity

Interviewing Your Father

Interview your father, someone who serves as a father to you, or another father you know concerning the roles of fathers. Ask questions such as the following: What are the roles of the modern father? How do fathers affect their children? Are good fathers born or made? What roles will fathers play in the families of tomorrow? Tape-record the interview. Then, transcribe it (write it out). Edit out phrases such as "uh" and "um." You may then wish to organize it in a question-and-answer format, or summarize what your interview subject said.

BOWLING

TO FIND A LOST

FATHER

BY MEE HER

About the Author

Mee Her is a Hmong who was born in Laos. The Hmong (hmawng) are a people who live in the mountains of southern China and the northern areas of Thailand, Vietnam, and Laos. Mee Her came with her family to the United States as a child in 1976. They were political refugees like the other Hmong immigrants of that time. She attended college, studying psychology, and earned a master's degree. Through her writing, she explores issues related to the experiences of Hmong immigrants, a new group of Asian Americans.

About the Selection

*According to Asian tradition, **duty to parents** is a person's primary responsibility. This ideal requires that children should always be respectful, polite, loyal, helpful, and obedient toward their parents. Those who do not live up to this standard of conduct are viewed as shameful. As you read "Bowling to Find a Lost Father," think about how this ideal affects the author's family life. (The Chinese characters shown here are those for "father" (top) and "mother.")*

We all held our breath as the ball slowly rolled down the alley. Then, just as it was about to hit the pins, it dropped into the gutter. Ahhh. . . . he sighed in disappointment. My father slowly turned toward us. His eyes sparkled like those of a little boy, and a big smile was printed on his face. Then he joyfully chuckled as he walked to his seat. I never thought my father would enjoy playing with us. In fact, I never thought he'd enjoy fun. But on that evening when I taught him how to bowl, I did more than teach him how to hit pins. I had taken the first step toward bridging a gap which had been created between him and his children.

My father had never played with us. I guess that came with his Hmong **orientation**[1] in valuing hard work. He told us that play was a waste of meaningful time which could be better used for productivity.

If we were still living in Laos where children don't have to go to school, and all they do is work in the field with parents, my father's orientation would be the ideal. There, children would work hard on the farms, then, during break times, they would listen to parents tell stories of their own childhood. Parents also either would teach "music" lessons to their children with instruments that they created out of bamboo sticks or they would teach them how to blow and make music out of leaves. This kept the relationship between children and their parents close. But in this country, where everything is so sophisticated, parents don't know how to be close to their children.

I remembered my relationship with my father as a child. We went everywhere together. He took me to the hospital

> SINCE WE CAME TO THIS COUNTRY, MY RELATIONSHIP WITH MY FATHER HAS CHANGED.

where he worked, to the fields, or to feed the stock on the farm. I remember the times my father took me to the hospital with him. My father would teach me how his medical instruments were used, or he would show me to his patients. I felt so close to him. However, since we came to this country, my relationship with my father has changed. He no longer knows

---

[1] **orientation**—inclination; tendency of thought.

how to be the father he used to be for us. He began to build walls around us by becoming so overly protective. He did not let us play outside or go out with our friends, using concepts of hard work to keep us at home like dutiful Hmong children. I felt emotionally distant from him. Somehow the gap seemed so great that neither he nor his children knew how to bridge it. As it turned out, I ignored our relationship altogether.

It wasn't until my third year in college that I decided to make my first move to recreate the relationship between my father and me. I had moved away from home when I started college. The time and distance made me miss the closeness that I used to have with him. I was beginning to see the need for closeness between my parents and the other children too. My father must have tried to keep the gap from getting larger when he became overly protective of us. It must have been frightening to live with children who did not live in the same world that he did. He couldn't play video games

with them and couldn't understand ear-busting rock 'n roll. He didn't even know how to play soccer or volleyball! And those were the things that his children did for enjoyment in this country.

Poor Dad. It was not his fault that he did not know how to be included in our lives. It was just that he didn't know how to get involved with his children. That was why my brothers and sisters and I decided to introduce my father to bowling.

I remember that day well when my brother, sisters, dad, and I went bowling. Dad was a little hesitant to come with us, but we all persuaded him. When we got to the bowling alley, we showed him how to hold the ball. Then we taught him how to throw the ball. It was a little bit foreign for me to be the one teaching my father, and I sensed that Father felt odd, too. But once he got the hang of it, he did well. He even made a couple of strikes!

I think it was much more than bowling that father enjoyed. It was the emotional closeness that he felt with us which made him come back to bowl again. The next time we went bowling, he was teaching the younger children to bowl. As I watched him beam so happily with the kids, it occurred to me that this was the beginning of building a bridge across a long-created gap between Dad and his children. Another thought came to my mind too. I wonder why it had taken me so long to show my father how to bowl. Was I waiting for him to make the first move? Was I waiting for him to teach me instead? But how could he have done that when he didn't know how?

▲
This Hmong family was photographed by Leonard Freed in Wisconsin.

Questions to Consider

Responding

1. Do you sometimes have trouble getting close to your parents? How do you handle it?

Analyzing

2. Why had the writer's father never played with his children?

3. How had he related to them?

4. Why do you think he began to feel overprotective of his children when they moved to the United States?

5. How does the writer learn to bridge the emotional gap between her father and his children?

Extending

6. In what ways are traditional American values of individualism and independence in conflict with the Asian ideal of **duty to parents**?

Literature Connection

A personal essay is a short informal work of nonfiction that presents the writer's ideas on a topic of personal interest. These essays are usually loose in their organization. Some may be organized by categories; that is, by the different subjects discussed. Other personal essays may be in time order.

1. How is this essay organized?

2. What does it say about the roles of parents and children in families of immigrants?

3. What does it say about the roles of work and play in people's lives?

Activities

Researching the Hmong

Many Hmong came to the United States in the mid-1970s as political refugees after the Vietnam War. The Hmong were being persecuted in Laos and Vietnam for helping the United States during the war. Using the Internet and library resources, research the situation for Hmong refugees—then and now. Did refugee programs prepare immigrant families for their new lives? Did the children adapt better than the parents? Did the Hmong concept of hard work help them in the United States? Present your findings in a short speech or report.

◀ Hmong girls wear traditional dress at a festival.

EVA & DANIEL

BY TOMÁS RIVERA

About the Author

Tomás Rivera (1935–1984) is one of the major figures in Chicano literature. Rivera worked in the fields of Texas with his family until he entered junior college. He went on to earn advanced degrees in English, Spanish literature, and educational administration. He then taught in Texas schools and universities in the Southwest. Rivera began writing when he was about twelve. "I was fascinated by the whole world of imagination and wanted to create," he said. His novel about South Texas migrant workers, . . . And the Earth Did Not Devour Him (1971), has become a modern American classic.

About the Selection

Marriage *is the focus of a great deal of attention in all cultures. Until fairly recent times, marrying "for love" was not the norm in many ethnic groups. Marriages were "arranged" for a young couple by family members. As you read "Eva and Daniel," note how their families influence the young couple's relationship.*

People still remember Eva and Daniel. They were both very good looking, and in all honesty it was a pleasure to see them together. But that's not the reason people remember them. They were very young when they got married or, rather, when they **eloped**.[1] Her parents hardly got angry at all, and, if they did, it was for a very short time and that was because everyone who knew Daniel liked him very much and had many good reasons to like him. They eloped up north during the County Fair that was held every year in Bird Island.

Both families lived on the same ranch. They worked together in the same fields, they went to town in the same truck and they just about had their meals together; they were that close. That's why no one was surprised when they started going together. And, even though everyone knew about it, no one let on, and even Eva and Daniel, instead of talking with one another, would write letters to each other once in a while. I remember very clearly that that Saturday when they eloped they were going happily to the fair in the truck. Their hair was all messed up by the wind, but when they got to the fair they didn't even remember to comb it.

They got on every ride, then they separated from the group and no one saw them again until two days later.

"Don't be afraid. We can take a taxi to the ranch. Move over this way, come closer, let me touch you. Don't you love me?"

"Yes, yes."

"Don't be afraid. We'll get married. I don't care about anything else. Just you. If the truck leaves us behind, we'll go back in a taxi."

"But they're going to get after me."

"Don't worry. If they do, I'll protect you myself. Anyway, I want to marry you. I'll ask your father for permission to court you if you want me to. What do you say? Shall we get married?"

At midnight, when all the games were closed and the lights of the fair were turned off and the explosions of the fireworks were no longer heard, Eva and Daniel still hadn't shown up. Their parents started to worry then, but they didn't notify the police. By one-thirty in the morning the other people became impatient. They got on and off the truck every few minutes and, finally, Eva's father told the driver to drive off. Both families were

---

[1] **eloped**—ran away together, usually with the intention of getting married.

worried. They had a feeling that Eva and Daniel had eloped and they were sure they would get married, but they were worried anyway. And they would keep on worrying until they saw them again. What they didn't know was that Eva and Daniel were already at the ranch. They were hiding in the barn, up in the loft where the boss stored hay for the winter. That's why, even though they looked for them in the nearby towns, they didn't find them until two days later when they came down from the loft very hungry.

There were some very heated discussions but, finally, Eva's parents consented to their marriage. The following day they took Eva and Daniel to get their blood test, then a week later they took them before the judge and the parents had to sign because they were too young.

◀ The dreamy lovers in *River Diego* were painted by North Carolina artist Daniel Nevins.

SHALL WE GET MARRIED?

"You see how everything turned out all right."

"Yes, but I was afraid when father got all angry. I even thought he was going to hit you when he saw us for the first time."

"I was afraid too. We're married now. We can have children."

"Yes."

"I hope that they grow real tall and that they look like you and me. I wonder how they will be?"

"Just let them be like you and me."

"If it's a girl I hope she looks like you; if it's a boy I hope he looks like me."

"What if we don't have any?"

"Why not? My family and your family are very large."

"I'll say."

"Well, then?"

"I was just talking."

Things really began to change after they were married. First of all because, by the end of the first month of their marriage, Eva was vomiting often, and then also Daniel received a letter from the government telling him

THINGS REALLY BEGAN TO CHANGE AFTER THEY WERE MARRIED.

to be in such and such town so that he could take his physical for the army.[2] He was afraid when he saw the letter, not so much for himself, but he immediately sensed the separation that would come forever.

"You see, son, if you hadn't gone to school you wouldn't have passed the examination."

"Oh, mama. They don't take you just because you passed the examination. Anyway I'm already married, so they probably won't take me. And another thing, Eva is already expecting."

"I don't know what to do, son, every night I pray that they won't take you. So does Eva. You should have lied to them. You should have played dumb so you wouldn't pass."

"Oh, come on, mama."

By November, instead of returning to Texas with his family, Daniel stayed up north, and in a few days he was in the army. The days didn't seem to have any meaning for him—why should there be night, morning or day. Sometimes he didn't care anything about anything. Many times he

---

[2] physical for the army—medical examination given to military draftees or enlistees. This story takes place during the Korean War (1950–1953), when young men were drafted into the armed services.

thought about escaping and returning to his own town so that he could be with Eva. When he thought at all, that was what he thought about—Eva. I think he even became sick, once or maybe it was several times, thinking so much about her. The first letter from the government had meant their separation, and now the separation became longer and longer.

"I wonder why I can't think of anything else other than Eva? If I hadn't known her, I wonder what I would think about. Probably about myself, but now. . ."

Things being what they were, everything marched on. Daniel's training continued at the same pace as Eva's pregnancy. They transferred Daniel to California, but before going he had the chance to be with Eva in Texas. The first night they went to sleep kissing. They were happy once again for a couple of weeks but then right away they were separated again. Daniel wanted to stay but then he decided to go on to California. He was being trained to go to Korea. Later Eva started getting sick. The baby was bringing complications. The closer she came to the day of delivery, the greater the complications.

"You know, *viejo*,[3] something is wrong with that baby."

"Why do you say that?"

"Something is wrong with her. She gets very high fevers at night. I hope everything turns out all right, but even the doctor looks quite worried. Have you noticed?"

"No."

"Yesterday he told me that we had to be very careful with Eva. He gave us a whole bunch of instructions, but it's difficult when you can't understand him. Can you imagine? How I wish Daniel were here. I'll bet you Eva would even get well. I already wrote to him saying that she is very sick, hoping that he'll come to see her, but maybe his superiors won't believe him and won't let him come."

"Well, write to him again. Maybe he can arrange something, if he speaks out."

"Maybe, but I've already written him a number of letters saying the same thing. You know, I'm not too worried about him anymore. Now I worry about Eva. They're both so young."

"Yes they are, aren't they."

---

[3] *viejo* (bee•AY•hoh)—Spanish for "dear" (used with a parent or spouse).

▲

Label for a package of fireworks.

Eva's condition became worse and, when he received a letter from his mother in which she begged him to come see his wife, either Daniel didn't make himself understood or his superiors didn't believe him. They didn't let him go. He went AWOL[4] just before he was to be sent to Korea. It took him three days to get to Texas on the bus. But he was too late.

I remember very well that he came home in a taxi. When he got down and heard the cries coming from inside the house he rushed in. He went into a rage and threw everyone out of the house and locked himself in for almost the rest of the day. He only went out when he had to go to the toilet, but even in there he could be heard sobbing.

He didn't go back to the army and no one ever bothered to come looking for him. Many times I saw him burst into tears. I think he was remembering. Then he lost all interest in himself. He hardly spoke to anyone.

One time he decided to buy fireworks to sell during Christmas time. The package of fireworks which he sent for through a magazine advertisement cost him plenty. When he got them, instead of selling them, he didn't stop until he had set them all off himself. Since that time that's all he does with what little money he earns to support himself. He sets off fireworks just about every night. I think that's why around this part of the country people still remember Eva and Daniel. Maybe that's it.

---

[4] AWOL—military term standing for "absent without leave."

Responding

1. How much do you think young people should let their families influence their decisions about **marriage**?

Analyzing

2. What do you think Eva and Daniel thought their married life would be like?

3. How might Eva and Daniel be considered typical of many young couples?

4. At what point in the story do you begin to worry about Eva and Daniel and why?

5. Why do you think Daniel sets off firecrackers every night?

Extending

6. What should people consider before they marry?

Literature Connection

*The **point of view** of a story is the perspective from which the story is told. If a story is told from a first-person point of view, the narrator is a character in the story. The author uses first-person pronouns, such as I, me, and we. In a story told from the third-person point of view, the narrator is not a character. The author uses third-person pronouns such as he, she, and it. (Note that as a literary term, point of view does not mean "opinion.")*

1. From what point of view is "Eva and Daniel" told?

2. How does the point of view contribute to the feeling this story creates?

3. How do you think this feeling would change if the story were told by Daniel's mother?

Activities

Writing a Letter

Write a letter from Daniel's mother to either Eva or Daniel warning them or encouraging them about marriage. Make it clear whether the letter is written before they elope or just after they marry.

Illustrating the Story

The story of Eva and Daniel is presented in a few brief episodes. Select the five or six events from the story that you think are the most important and would be the most dramatic visually. Decide on an artistic medium you like and create a series of pictures based on these episodes.

Sweet Potato Pie

BY EUGENIA COLLIER

About the Author

Eugenia Collier says that the source of her creativity is "the richness, the diversity, the beauty of my black heritage." She was born in 1928 in Baltimore, where she still lives. Collier earned degrees from Howard University in Washington, D.C., and Columbia University. She was a social worker and a college professor before turning to writing. Her stories, poems, and critical essays have appeared in many anthologies and magazines.

About the Selection

Sharecroppers were families who rented a plot of land to farm. Landowners provided tools, seed, and housing, in return for a share of the crop. After the Civil War, most African Americans in the South—and many poor whites—became sharecroppers on former plantations that had been split into small farms. The work was hard and brought little reward, for share-croppers were usually in debt to landowners, who often cheated them. The sharecroppers' poverty was made worse by floods, droughts, and an insect pest known as the boll weevil that destroyed cotton plants. Families often had barely enough to survive. As a result, many African Americans moved North to the cities. As you read "Sweet Potato Pie," keep in mind the pressures on a family of sharecroppers.

From up here on the fourteenth floor, my brother Charley looks like an insect scurrying among other insects. A deep feeling of love surges through me. Despite the distance, he seems to feel it, for he turns and scans the upper windows, but failing to find me, continues on his way. I watch him moving quickly—gingerly, it seems to me—down Fifth Avenue and around the corner to his shabby taxi-cab. In a moment he will be heading back uptown.

I turn from the window and flop down on the bed, shoes and all. Perhaps because of what happened this afternoon or maybe just because I see Charley so seldom, my thoughts hover over him like hummingbirds. The cheerful, impersonal tidiness of this room is a world away from Charley's walk-up flat in Harlem and a hundred worlds from the bare, noisy shanty where he and the rest of us spent what there was of childhood. I close my eyes, and side by side I see the Charley of my boyhood and the Charley of this afternoon, as clearly as if I were looking at a split TV screen. Another surge of love, seasoned with gratitude, wells up in me.

As far as I know, Charley never had any childhood at all. The oldest children of sharecroppers never do. Mama and Pa were shadowy figures whose voices I heard vaguely in the morning when sleep was shallow and whom I glimpsed as they left for the field before I was fully awake or as they trudged wearily into the house at night when my lids were irresistibly heavy.

They came into sharp focus only on special occasions. One such occasion was the day when the crops were in and the share-croppers were paid. In our cabin there was so much excitement in the air that even I, the "baby," responded to it. For weeks we had been running out of things that we could neither grow nor get on credit. On the evening of that day we waited anxiously for our parents' return. Then we would cluster around the rough wooden table—I on Lil's lap or clinging to Charley's neck, little Alberta nervously tugging her plait,[1] Jamie crouched at Mama's elbow, like a

> **As far as I know, Charley never had any childhood at all.**

---
[1] plait—braid of hair.

African-American artist William H. Johnson painted a Southern farm family around 1940 in *Going to Church.* ▶

panther about to spring, and all seven of us silent for once, waiting. Pa would place the money on the table—gently, for it was made from the sweat of their bodies and from their children's tears. Mama would count it out in little piles, her dark face stern and, I think now, beautiful. Not with the hollow beauty of well-modeled features but with the strong radiance of one who has suffered and never yielded.

"This for store bill," she would mutter, making a little pile. "This for c'llection. This for piece o' gingham[2]. . ." and so on, stretching the money as tight over our collective needs as Jamie's outgrown pants were stretched over my bottom. "Well, that's the crop." She would look up at Pa at last. "It'll do." Pa's face would relax, and a general grin flitted from child to child. We would survive, at least for the present.

[2] gingham—cotton fabric, often checkered, striped, or plaid.

The other time when my parents were solid entities[3] was at church. On Sundays we would don our thread-bare Sunday-go-to-meeting clothes and tramp, along with neighbors similarly attired, to the Tabernacle Baptist Church, the frail edifice[4] of bare boards held together by God knows what, which was all that my parents ever knew of security and future promise.

Being the youngest and therefore the most likely to err, I was plopped between my father and my mother on the long wooden bench. They sat huge and eternal like twin mountains at my sides. I remember my father's still, black profile silhouetted against the sunny window, looking back into dark recesses of time, into some dim antiquity, like an ancient ceremonial mask. My mother's face, usually sternly set, changed with the varying **nuances**[5] of her emotion, its planes shifting, shaped by the soft highlights of the sanctuary, as she progressed from a subdued "amen" to a loud "Help me, Jesus" wrung from the depths of her **gaunt**[6] frame.

My early memories of my parents are associated with special occasions.

The contours of my everyday were shaped by Lil and Charley, the oldest children, who rode herd on the rest of us while Pa and Mama toiled in fields not their own. Not until years later did I realize that Lil and Charley were little more than children themselves.

Lil had the loudest, screechiest voice in the county. When she yelled, "Boy, you better git yourself in here!" you *got* yourself in there. It was Lil who caught and bathed us, Lil who fed us and sent us to school, Lil who punished us when we needed punishing and comforted us when we needed comforting. If her voice was loud, so was her laughter. When she laughed, everybody laughed. And when Lil sang, everybody listened.

> **Charley was taller than anybody in the world, including, I was certain, God.**

Charley was taller than anybody in the world, including, I was certain, God. From his shoulders, where I spent considerable time in the earliest

---

[3] entities (EHN•tih•tees)—people or things that exist.

[4] edifice (EHD•uf•fuhs)—building.

[5] **nuances** (NOO•ahn•sehs)—slight degrees of difference.

[6] **gaunt**—thin and bony.

years, the world had a different perspective. I looked down at tops of heads rather than at the undersides of chins. As I grew older, Charley became more father than brother. Those days return in fragments of splintered memory: Charley's slender, dark hands whittling a toy from a chunk of wood, his face thin and intense, brown as the loaves Lil baked when there was flour. Charley's quick fingers guiding a stick of charred kindling over a bit of scrap paper, making a wondrous picture take shape—Jamie's face or Alberta's rag doll or the spare figure of our bony brown dog. Charley's voice low and terrible in the dark, telling ghost stories so delightfully dreadful that later in the night the moan of the wind through the chinks in the wall sent us scurrying to the security of Charley's pallet,[7] Charley's sleeping form.

Some memories are more than fragmentary. I can still feel the *whap* of the wet dishrag across my mouth. Somehow I developed a stutter, which Charley was determined to cure. Someone had told him that an effective cure was to slap the stutterer across the mouth with a sopping wet dishrag. Thereafter, whenever I began,

"Let's g-g-g—," *whap!* from nowhere would come the **ubiquitous**[8] rag. Charley would always insist, "I don't want hurt you none, Buddy—" and *whap* again. I don't know when or why I stopped stuttering. But I stopped.

Already laid waste by poverty, we were easy prey for ignorance and superstition, which hunted us like hawks. We sought education feverishly—and, for most of us, **futilely**,[9] for the sum total of our combined energies was required for mere brute survival. Inevitably each child had to leave school and bear his share of the eternal burden.

Eventually the family's hopes for learning fastened on me, the youngest. I remember—I *think* I remember, for I could not have been more than five—one frigid day Pa huddled on a rickety stool before the coal stove, took me on his knee and studied me gravely. I was a skinny little thing, they tell me, with large, solemn eyes.

---

[7] pallet—narrow, hard bed.

[8] **ubiquitous** (yoo•BIHK•wih•tuhs)—present or seeming to be present everywhere at the same time.

[9] **futilely** (FYOO•tih•lee)—without useful results.

"Well, boy," Pa said at last, "if you got to depend on your looks for what you get out'n this world, you just as well lay down right now." His hand was rough from the plow, but gentle as it touched my cheek. "Lucky for you, you got a *mind.* And that's something ain't everybody got. You go to school, boy, get yourself some learning. Make something out'n yourself. Ain't nothing you can't do if you got learning."

Charley was determined that I would break the chain of poverty, that I would "be somebody." As we worked our small vegetable garden in the sun or pulled a bucket of brackish[10] water from the well, Charley would tell me, "You ain gon be no poor farmer, Buddy. You gon be a teacher or maybe a doctor or a lawyer. One thing, bad as you is, you ain gon be no preacher."

I loved school with a desperate passion, which became more intense when I began to realize what a monumental struggle it was for my parents and brothers and sisters to keep me there. The cramped, dingy classroom became a battleground where I was victorious. I stayed on top of my class. With glee I outread, outfigured, and outspelled the country boys who mocked my poverty, calling me "the boy with eyes in back of his head"—the "eyes" being the perpetual holes in my hand-me-down pants.

As the years passed, the economic strain was eased enough to make it possible for me to go on to high school. There were fewer mouths to feed, for one thing. Alberta went North to find work at sixteen; Jamie died at twelve.

I finished high school at the head of my class. For Mama and Pa and each of my brothers and sisters, my success was a personal triumph. One by one they came to me the week before commencement, bringing crumpled dollar bills and coins long hoarded, muttering, "Here, Buddy, put this on your gradiation clothes." My graduation suit was the first suit that was all my own.

On graduation night our cabin (less crowded now) was a frantic collage[11] of frayed nerves. I thought Charley would drive me mad.

"Buddy, you ain pressed out them pants right. . . . Can't you git a better shine on them shoes? . . . Lord, you done messed up that tie!"

---

[10] brackish—somewhat salty.

[11] collage (kuh•LAHZH)—collection of diverse things.

Overwhelmed by the combination of Charley's nerves and my own, I finally exploded. "Man, cut it out!" Abruptly he stopped tugging at my tie, and I was afraid I had hurt his feelings. "It's okay, Charley. Look, you're strangling me. The tie's okay."

> **I wasn't necessarily the smartest—only the youngest.**

Charley relaxed a little and gave a rather sheepish chuckle. "Sure, Buddy." He gave my shoulder a rough joggle. "But you gotta look good. You *somebody*."

My valedictory[12] address was the usual idealistic, sentimental nonsense. I have forgotten what I said that night, but the sight of Mama and Pa and the rest is like a lithograph[13] burned on my memory; Lil, her round face made beautiful by her proud smile; Pa, his head held high, eyes loving and fierce; Mama radiant. Years later when her shriveled hands were finally still, my mind kept coming back to her as she was now. I believe this moment was the **apex**[14] of her entire life. All of them, even Alberta down from Baltimore—different now, but united with them in her pride. And Charley, on the end of the row, still somehow the protector of them all. Charley, looking as if he were in the presence of something sacred.

As I made my way through the carefully rehearsed speech, it was as if part of me were standing outside watching the whole thing—their proud, work-weary faces, myself wearing the suit that was their combined strength and love and hope: Lil with her lovely, low-pitched voice, Charley with the hands of an artist, Pa and Mama with God knows what potential lost with their sweat in the fields. I realized in that moment that I wasn't necessarily the smartest—only the youngest.

And the luckiest. The war came along, and I exchanged three years of my life (including a fair amount of my blood and a great deal of pain) for the GI Bill[15] and a college education. Strange how time can slip by like water flowing through your fingers.

---

[12] valedictory (val•ih•DIHK•tuh•ree) address—closing or farewell statement or speech, usually delivered at graduation ceremonies by the top student in the graduating class.

[13] lithograph—type of print.

[14] **apex** (AY•pehks)—highest point; peak.

[15] GI Bill—U.S. government program to help veterans get higher education, home loans, and so forth, at the government's expense.

One by one the changes came—the old house empty at last, the rest of us scattered; for me, marriage, graduate school, kids, a professorship, and by now a thickening waistline and thinning hair. My mind spins off the years, and I am back to this afternoon and today's Charley—still long and lean, still gentle-eyed, still my greatest fan, and still determined to keep me on the ball.

I didn't tell Charley I would be at a professional meeting in New York and would surely visit; he and Bea would have spent days in fixing up, and I would have had to be company. No, I would drop in on them, take them by surprise before they had a chance to stiffen up. I was eager to see them—it had been so long. Yesterday and this morning were taken up with meetings in the posh

African-American artist Charles Alston's *Farm Boy* is the portrait of a sensitive child growing up in poverty.

**break
the chain of
poverty**

Fifth Avenue hotel—a place we could not have dreamed in our boyhood. Late this afternoon I shook loose and headed for Harlem,[16] hoping that Charley still came home for a few hours before his evening run. Leaving the glare and glitter of downtown, I entered the subway that lurks like the dark, inscrutable *id*[17] beneath the surface of the city. When I emerged, I was in Harlem.

Whenever I come to Harlem I feel somehow as if I were coming home—to some mythic ancestral home. The problems are real, the people are real—yet there is some mysterious epic quality about Harlem, as if all black people began and ended there, as if each had left something of himself. As if in Harlem the very heart of Blackness pulsed its beautiful, tortured rhythms. Joining the throngs of people that **saunter**[18] Lenox Avenue late afternoons, I headed for Charley's apartment. Along the way I savored the panorama of Harlem—women with shopping bags trudging wearily home; little kids flitting saucily through the crowd; groups of adolescent boys striding boldly along—some boisterous, some ominously silent; tables of merchandise spread on the sidewalks with hawkers singing their siren songs of irresistible bargains; a blaring microphone sending forth waves of words to draw passersby into a restless bunch around a slender young man whose eyes have seen Truth; defeated men standing around on street corners or sitting on steps, heads down, hands idle; posters announcing Garvey Day;[19] "Buy Black" stamped on pavements; store windows bright with things African; stores still boarded up, a livid scar from last year's rioting. There was a terrible tension in the air; I thought of how quickly dry timber becomes a roaring fire from a single spark.

I mounted the steps of Charley's building—old and in need of paint, like all the rest—and pushed the button to his apartment. The graffiti on the dirty wall recorded the fantasies of past visitors. Some of it was even a

---

[16] Harlem—New York City's African-American district.

[17] *id*—in psychoanalysis, the part of the mind that is the source of instinctual impulses and primitive urges.

[18] **saunter**—stroll.

[19] Garvey Day—annual celebration of the birthday (August 17) of African-American leader Marcus Garvey (1887–1940).

dialogue of sorts. Someone had scrawled, "Call Lola" and a telephone number, followed by a catalog of Lola's friends. Someone else had written, "I called Lola and she is a Dog." Charley's buzzer rang. I pushed open the door and mounted the urine-scented stairs.

"Well, do Jesus—it's Buddy!" roared Charley as I arrived on the third floor. "Bea! Bea! Come here, girl, it's Buddy!" And somehow I was simultaneously shaking Charley's hand, getting clapped on the back, and being buried in the fervor of Bea's gigantic hug. They swept me from the hall into their dim apartment.

"Lord, Buddy, what you doing here? Whyn't you tell me you was coming to New York?" His face was so lit up with pleasure that in spite of the inroads of time, he still looked like the Charley of years gone by, excited over a new litter of kittens.

"The place look a mess! Whyn't you let us know?" put in Bea, suddenly distressed.

"Looks fine to me, girl. And so do you!"

And she did. Bea is a fine-looking woman, plump and firm still, with rich brown skin and thick black hair.

"Mary, Lucy, look, Uncle Buddy's here!" Two neat little girls came shyly from the TV. Uncle Buddy was something of a celebrity in this house.

I hugged them heartily, much to their discomfort. "Charley, where you getting all these pretty women?"

We all sat in the warm kitchen, where Bea was preparing dinner. It felt good there. Beautiful odors mingled in the air. Charley sprawled in a chair near mine, his long arms and legs akimbo.[20] No longer shy, the tinier girl sat on my lap, while her sister darted here and there like a merry little water bug. Bea bustled about, managing to keep up with both the conversation and the cooking.

It felt good there. Beautiful odors mingled in the air.

I told them about the conference I was attending, and, knowing it would give them pleasure, I mentioned that I had addressed the group that morning. Charley's eyes glistened.

"You hear that, Bea?" he whispered. "Buddy done spoke in front of all them professors!"

---

[20] akimbo (uh•KIM•boh)—bowed outward.

"Sure I hear," Bea answered briskly, stirring something that was making an aromatic steam. "I bet he weren't even scared. I bet them professors learnt something, too."

We all chuckled. "Well anyway," I said, "I hope they did."

We talked about a hundred different things after that—Bea's job in the school cafeteria, my Jess and the kids, our scattered family.

"Seem like we don't git together no more, not since Mama and Pa passed on," said Charley sadly. "I ain't even got a Christmas card from Alberta for three-four year now."

"Well, ain't no two a y'all in the same city. An' everybody scratchin' to make ends meet," Bea replied. "Ain't nobody got time to git together."

"Yeah, that's the way it goes, I guess," I said.

"But it sure is good to see you, Buddy. Say, look, Lil told me bout the cash you sent the children last winter when Jake was out of work all that time. She sure 'preciated it."

"Lord, man, as close as you and Lil stuck to me when I was a kid, I owed her that and more. Say, Bea, did I ever tell you about the time—" and we swung into the usual reminiscences.

They insisted that I stay for dinner. Persuading me was no hard job: fish fried golden, ham hocks and collard greens, corn bread—if I'd *tried* to leave, my feet wouldn't have taken me. It was good to sit there in Charley's kitchen, my coat and tie flung over a chair, surrounded by soul food and love.

"Say, Buddy, a couple months back I picked up a kid from your school."

"No stuff."

"I axed him did he know you. He say he was in your class last year."

"Did you get his name?"

"No, I didn't ax him that. Man he told me you were the best teacher he had. He said you were one smart cat!"

"He told you that cause you're my brother."

"Your *brother*—I didn't tell him I was your brother. I said you was a old friend of mine."

I put my fork down and leaned over. "What you tell him *that* for?"

Charley explained patiently as he had explained things when I was a child and had missed an obvious truth. "I didn't want your students to know your brother wasn't nothing but a cab driver. You *somebody*."

"You're a nut," I said gently. "You should've told that kid the truth." I wanted to say, I'm proud of you, you've got more on the ball than most people I know, I wouldn't have been anything at all except for you. But he would have been embarrassed.

Bea brought in the dessert—home made sweet potato pie! "Buddy, I must of knew you were coming! I just had a mind I wanted to make sweet potato pie."

There's nothing in this world I like better than Bea's sweet potato pie! "Lord, girl, how you expect me to eat all that?"

The slice she put before me was outrageously big—and moist and covered with a light, golden crust—I ate it all.

"Bea, I'm gonna have to eat and run," I said at last.

Charley **guffawed.**[21] "Much as you et, I don't see how you gonna *walk*, let alone *run*." He went out to get his cab from the garage several blocks away.

Bea was washing the tiny girl's face. "Wait a minute, Buddy, I'm gon give you the rest of that pie to take with you."

"Great!" I'd eaten all I could hold, but my *spirit* was still hungry for sweet potato pie.

Bea got out some waxed paper and wrapped up the rest of the pie. "That'll do you for a snack tonight." She slipped it into a brown paper bag.

I gave her a long goodbye hug. "Bea, I love you for a lot of things. Your cooking is one of them!" We had a last comfortable laugh together. I kissed the little girls and went outside to wait for Charley, holding the bag of pie reverently.

In a minute Charley's ancient cab limped to the curb. I plopped into the seat next to him, and we headed downtown. Soon we were **assailed** by the **garish**[22] lights of New York on a sultry spring night. We chatted as Charley skillfully managed the heavy traffic. I looked at his long hands on the wheel and wondered what they could have done with artists' brushes.

We stopped a bit down the street from my hotel. I invited him in, but he said he had to get on with his evening run. But as I opened the door to get out, he commanded in the old familiar voice, "Buddy, you wait!"

> **There's nothing in this world I like better than Bea's sweet potato pie!**

---

[21] **guffawed** (guh•FAWD)—laughed heartily.
[22] **garish**—flashy.

For a moment I thought my coat was torn or something. "What's wrong?"

"What's that you got there?"

I was bewildered. "That? You mean this bag? That's a piece of sweet potato pie Bea fixed for me."

"You ain't going through the lobby of no big hotel carrying no brown paper bag."

"Man, you *crazy*! Of course I'm going—Look, Bea fixed it for me— *That's my pie*—"

Charley's eyes were miserable. "Folks in that hotel don't go through the lobby carrying no brown paper bags. That's *country*. And you can't neither. You *somebody*, Buddy. You got to be *right*. Now gimme that bag."

"I want that pie, Charley. I've got nothing to prove to anybody—"

I couldn't believe it. But there was no point in arguing. Foolish as it seemed to me, it was important to him.

"You got to look *right*, Buddy. Can't nobody look dignified carrying a brown paper bag."

So finally, thinking how tasty it would have been and how seldom I got a chance to eat anything that good, I handed over my bag of sweet potato pie. If it was that important to him—

I tried not to show my irritation. "Okay, man—take care now." I slammed the door harder than I had intended, walked rapidly to the hotel, and entered the brilliant, crowded lobby.

"That Charley!" I thought. Walking slower now, I crossed the carpeted lobby toward the elevator, still thinking of my lost snack. I had to admit that of all the herd of people who jostled each other in the lobby, not one was carrying a brown paper bag. Or anything but expensive attaché cases or slick packages from exclusive shops. I suppose we all operate according to the symbols that are meaningful to us, and to Charley a brown paper bag symbolizes the humble life he thought I had left. I was *somebody*.

I don't know what made me glance back, but I did. And suddenly the tears of laughter, toil, and love of a lifetime burst around me like fireworks in a night sky.

For there, following a few steps behind, came Charley, proudly carrying a brown paper bag full of sweet potato pie.

Responding

1. What types of sacrifices should the members of a family be expected to make for each other?

Analyzing

2. How did being **sharecroppers** shape the lives of the members of Buddy's family?

3. In what ways does Buddy consider himself the "luckiest" in his family?

4. How do Buddy's feelings about his parents compare to his feelings about Lil and Charley?

5. Why do you think Charley brought Buddy the pie?

6. The tone of a literary work expresses the writer's attitude toward a subject. What is the tone of this story?

Extending

7. What do you think should be the role of older children in raising their younger brothers and sisters?

Activities

Writing an Essay

Write an essay on what it means to be "somebody." First discuss the topic with your friends, family, and neighbors. In your essay, discuss the views of others as well as your own. Use examples to make your point clear. Make the tone of your essay consistent.

Literature Connection

Conflict is a struggle between opposing forces. In an external conflict, an individual struggles against another person or some outside force. An internal conflict is a struggle within an individual. Look at the following passage from "Sweet Potato Pie," in which the narrator describes his family listening to him deliver a speech at his graduation:

> their proud, work-weary faces, myself wearing the suit that was their combined strength and love and hope: Lil with her lovely, low-pitched voice, Charley with the hands of an artist, Pa and Mama with God knows what potential lost with their sweat in the fields. I realized in that moment that I wasn't necessarily the smartest—only the youngest.

1. What were the external conflicts faced by the narrator's family?

2. What internal conflicts do you think might have been faced by the narrator's parents? by Charley and Lil?

Last Night

by Fae Myenne Ng

About the Author

Novelist and short story writer Fae Myenne Ng (fay myuhn uhng) is a first-generation Chinese American. She was born in San Francisco's Chinatown in 1957 and spoke Cantonese at home. As a child, she helped her mother, who sewed for a living like Hang Fong Toy in "Last Night." Ng feels that the discipline of learning to sew helped give her the stamina to complete her first novel, Bone (1993), which took her ten years to finish. The novel deals with the struggles of two generations of Chinese Americans in San Francisco.

About the Selection

The term **Chinatown** refers to the neighborhood or section of a city that is inhabited chiefly by Chinese people. The oldest and most famous Chinatown in the United States is located in San Francisco. Chinese immigrants settled here at the time of the California Gold Rush in 1849. From that time on, Chinatown has been the focus of the life of San Francisco's Chinese-American community. As you read "Last Night," note what the author tells you about how families live and work in Chinatown.

When Hang Fong Toy finally awakens, she can't tell if the rhythmic pounding is one of her headaches or just the water pipes banging again. She looks around the room, listening. The street light falls through the Venetian blinds; the slanting lines make the room seem larger.

You Thin Toy sleeps curled toward the wall, a brush stroke on the wide bed. He's a retired merchant marine[1] and has sailed the world. Now he spends afternoons at Portsmouth Square, playing chess and telling stories about himself as a young man. "Like a seagull," he says, "I went everywhere, saw everything."

His old-timer friends like to tease him. "So, why do you sit around the Square now?"

"Curiosity," he says. "I want to see how you fleabags have been living."

You Thin knows all the terms for docking a ship; Hang Fong can name the parts and seams of a dress the way a doctor can name bones.

Hang Fong sews in a garment shop. She's only been outside Chinatown for official business: immigration, unemployment and social security. When the children were young, they took her to Market Street, the Emporium and J. C. Penney's, but now, without translators, she's not an adventuress.

There was a time when her desire to return to China was a sensation in her belly, like hunger. Now she only dreams of it, almost tasting those dishes she loved as a young girl. Sometimes she says to You Thin before falling asleep, maybe a visit, eh?

After raising their children, Chinatown has become their world. They feel lucky to have an apartment on Salmon Alley. Louie's Grocery is around the corner on Taylor, and Hang Fong's sewing shop is just down the block. Their apartment is well situated in the back of the alley, far from the traffic fumes of Pacific Avenue.

After raising their children, Chinatown has become their world.

Hang Fong and You Thin like their landlord, an old Italian lady, and her **mute**[2] son so much that they have given them Chinese names. Fay-Poah, Manager Lady, and Ah-Boy, Mute-Son. Manager Lady wears printed pastel dresses that Hang Fong, a sewing lady, admires very much.

---

[1] merchant marine—sailor on a commercial (rather than a military) ship.

[2] **mute**—unable to speak.

Ah-Boy, a big man with a milky smell, works as a porter at the Oasis Club, but during the day he works around the building. When Hang Fong hears his broom on the stairs or the garbage cans rattling in the airshaft, she feels safe. It's good to have a strong man like Ah-Boy nearby. She tells You Thin, Ah-Boy is a good son, and You Thin nods. He likes to think that the anchor tattoo on Ah-Boy's arm makes them comrades of sorts.

*H*ang Fong thinks maybe Manager Lady left her window open. But then the sound becomes **erratic**[3] and sharp. Hang Fong gets up, leans toward the wall. You Thin lets out a long breath.

Hang Fong presses her ear against the wall, listening. Her eyes are wide open. Suddenly she rushes toward her sleeping husband and shakes him. "Get up! Get up! It's the Manager Lady, she's in trouble!"

You Thin stretches out and props himself up on one elbow. He rubs his eyes, trying to wake up. The banging comes again, and the old couple stare at each other. Outside, a car screeches to an urgent stop. They listen to the faint bubbly hum of the fish tank in the other room, and then hear the rumbling icebox motor shut off with a final click. You Thin and Hang Fong look at each other; the silence feels big.

The pounding comes again. Once. Twice.

---

[3] **erratic**—irregular.

"Something's wrong! Manager Lady is trying to tell us that!" Hang Fong throws off her covers. In one motion, her legs whip out and her slippers make a swishing noise as she moves across the room. The overhead fluorescent light flickers and snaps and then is quiet. The room is bright, glaring.

You Thin squints, reaches over, and raps sharply, one-two-three on the wall.

A sound knocks back in return.

Hang Fong slaps the wall with her open palm; the sound is flat and dull. She presses palm and cheek into the wall, and shouts, "Manager, Manager, are you all right? Nothing's wrong, is there?"

"SSHHH!!!" You Thin yanks her away. "Don't talk loud like that, she don't know what you say, maybe she thinks that you yell at her."

You Thin is out of bed, pacing. Hang Fong sits; she pulls her sweater closer around her neck. The sleeves hang limply at her sides.

"Let's see . . . wait a minute, where's Ah-Boy?"

"It's Tuesday; he's got the night shift."

"Oh. Tuesday. Right."

*L*ast week, when You Thin was at Manager Lady's paying the rent, he looked out her kitchen window while waiting for her to come back with the receipt. He saw a Chinese pot beneath a pile of chipped plates. So the next day he returned with a blue vase, its floral pattern similar to many of Manager Lady's dresses.

"I see?" he asked, pointing out the window.

Manager Lady opened her mouth wide, as her hand fluttered toward the window.

"Oh. Si, si," she said.

You Thin pulled the window open. He moved the cream-colored plates and lifted the pot for Manager Lady to see. She nodded, cradling the blue vase to her bosom.

With both hands, You Thin carried the pot back across the hall. Under the running faucet, Hang Fong scrubbed hard. Red, green and yellow, the palace ladies and plum blossoms came clean. You Thin scraped away the last of the dirt with a toothpick. The characters came clear. Good Luck and Long Life. You Thin and Hang Fong laughed, feeling lucky.

"Worth a lot of money, in time," You Thin said.

"Something to pass on to the children," Hang Fong added.

You Thin told everyone on the Square that the pot belonged to a hard-working old-timer who died alone. Hang Fong said that it was a good omen that they were chosen to house this valuable object. "It's very old," she told her sewing-lady friends.

"So, should we call the Rescue Car?" Hang Fong asks.

You Thin looks out the window, distracted. He shakes his head. "Even if they get here in two minutes, best we could do is stand in front of the door with our mouths open."

Hang Fong knows that he wants to climb the fire escape and get inside Manager Lady's apartment. It's risky, she thinks. You Thin isn't a young man and his step isn't always steady. She won't say anything, because the long years of marriage have taught her one thing: he likes his way.

"Well, what do we do?" Hang Fong asks. On the fire escape, a pigeon sleeps, its beak in its chest feathers. Hang Fong watches it. She hears the big engines of the garbage trucks churning up the hill. Foghorns sound in the distance, like help on the way.

Be careful . . . be safe . . . be careful . . . be safe . . .

You Thin asks, "Well, you think I could make that big step across to their fire escape?"

Hang Fong shrugs her shoulders. "Don't know; how do you feel?"

You Thin raises the window, looks out and snaps back in. Before Hang Fong can speak, he's run to the bathroom and clattered his way out carrying the long wooden board they use as a shelf over the bathtub.

"This is how. . . He slaps the board. "This will reach from our fire escape to theirs. You hold this end, just in case, and the rest I can do."

Hang Fong grips hard, but she keeps a harder eye on him. Inside, she repeats over and over, "Be careful . . . be safe . . . be careful . . . be safe. . . " You Thin is a brave man, she thinks; You Thin is a good man.

One leg, then the other, and he is over there. He peers through the window, knocks, and then tries to lift it open. Shut tight. He has to pull hard, two, three times before it comes open.

You Thin feels along the wall for the light switch. All along the way, he speaks to Manager Lady, softly, in Chinese, "You're all right, nothing's wrong, don't be frightened. . ." You Thin believes in the power of the voice: a well-meaning word spoken in the face of ill fortune can turn luck around.

Manager Lady is a wide figure on the floor. Everything around her speaks of her age: the faded covers, the cluttered nightstand, the bottles of lotions and pills. You Thin takes her hands; he's happy hers are warm.

Hang Fong knocks in quick, urgent raps, and You Thin opens the door for her. She moves quickly through the entryway, kneels and takes Manager Lady's head onto her lap, whispering, "Don't be scared, don't be scared." Manager Lady's eyes open. She says something in Italian; the long vowels reach forth and hang heavy in the air. Hang Fong and You Thin look at each other. They understand.

You Thin says, "I go. Go to get Ah-Boy."

"You know where it is then?"

"Uh. let me think . . . where Lee's Rice Shop used to be?"

"No! Across from Chong's Imports."

"Yes, right, I know, I know."

*T*he air outside is sharp. The street lamps cast an orange glow to the empty alley. You Thin moves quickly through Salmon Alley. But when he turns onto Pacific, he rests a moment. The long road before him is marked with globes of light. He runs his hand along the walls for support. On the steep hill, his legs feel strangely heavy when they land on the pavement and oddly light when they bounce off. He chants to himself, "Hurry. Important. Faster."

When he reaches Powell, he leans against the fire hydrant for a moment, glad that he's halfway there. He can see Broadway; it's still brightly lit. He's breathing hard by the time he gets to The Oasis. This late, it's been long closed. You Thin stands outside, banging on the big wooden doors and rapping on the windows. He cups his hands to the barred window, trying to see in. But with the glare from the street lamps, it's like looking into a mirror.

He takes a deep breath. "Ah-Boy, AAHHH-Boy-AAAIII! . . ."

Silence. Then the sound of flapping slippers, and Ah-Boy opens the door, mop in hand.

You Thin throws his arms about, waving toward Pacific. He slaps the restaurant wall, shouting, "Mah-mah. Be sick. Be sick."

Ah-Boy opens his mouth; his head jerks back and forth, but there is no sound. He lets his broom fall with a clatter. The heavy door slams shut.

Ah-Boy is a big man and You Thin can't keep up for long. At Pacific, You Thin waves him on.

You Thin watches for a moment as Ah-Boy moves up the hill. Yes, he nods. Ah-Boy is a good son.

When You Thin gets to the apartment, Ah-Boy is sitting on the floor with his mother's head on his lap, her gray hair loosened from its bun. She is speaking to Ah-Boy in a low voice.

You Thin and Hang Fong stand under the door frame, watching. "Just like last year," Hang Fong says, "just like Old Jue."

On the phone You Thin speaks loud. He pronounces the syllables as if each sound were a single character. "Numbah Two. Sah-moon Alley. Old Lady. Sick. You be the come. Now, sabei? I stand by downdaire, sabei? Numbah Two, Sah-moon Alley"

Hang Fong stands next to him, listening hard. She whispers something to him.

A group in San Francisco's Chinatown play Xiangqi (shee•ahng chee), or "Elephant Game," a Chinese version of chess. ▶

You Thin raises his head, and speaks even louder. "One minute. You know, Old Lady, she be . . . uh, uh . . . Old Lady she be come from Italy. You sabei? Lady not from China."

At the square the next day, You Thin challenges the Newspaper Man to a chess game. You Thin plays with one leg raised on the cement stool. "My Car over your lousy paper Gun, and you're eaten." The Newspaper Man's children fold *The Chinese Times* on the next table. Lame-Leg Fong tries to tell You Thin which pieces to move. The #15 Kearney bus inches down Clay, its brakes squeaking and hissing. Cars honk.

You Thin tells his story about last night in between chess moves. He describes the distance between Salmon Alley and Broadway. His running motions make his blue sleeves go vlop-vlop in the wind. He repeats all the English words he used, tries to use the ones he'd heard, and makes all the faces Ah-Boy made. He walks the line on the ground to show what he did in midair. Little boys run by on their way to the water fountain.

Hang Fong tells the story without looking up. The ladies listen with rounded backs and moving hands. Sheets of fabric run from the machines to the floor. Clumps of thread knot around the chair legs; spools of color ripple above the ladies' bent heads. The overlock machines click; the steam irons hiss. Some ladies sing along with the drum and gong beat of the Cantonese opera[4] playing on the radio. A voice booms over the intercom system, "LAST CHANCE TO HAND IN THOSE TICKETS, RIGHT NOW!" No one looks up. Some ladies cluck their tongues and roll their eyes. Others shake their heads and curse under their breath.

Many of the sewing ladies want to hear Hang Fong's story, but missing a sentence here or there, they can't follow the drama. Is it a story or is it real? The women become heavy-footed; the needles stamp urgent stitches into the fabric. Trousers fly over the work tables; the colorful mounds of clothing clutter the floor.

Eventually the grumble of the machines drowns out the story. A young girl runs in to ask her mother for money as the fish peddler arrives, singing out her catch in a breath as long as thread.

---

[4] Cantonese opera—work of the traditional Chinese musical theater.

Responding

1. What was the greatest benefit you ever received from a neighbor?

Analyzing

2. What impressions does "Last Night" give of **Chinatown** as a community?

3. What kind of relationship do Hang Fong Toy and her husband have with their landlady and her son?

4. At the end of "Last Night," what is different about the way You Thin Toy and Hang Fong Toy each tells the story of the events? What does it reveal about them?

Extending

5. How is a good neighbor like a member of your own family?

Activities

Writing a Narrative

Create a brief narrative showing your view of how neighbors ought to relate to one another. It can be based on an actual experience or be invented.

Creating a Sketch

"Last Night" concludes with You Thin Toy and Hang Fong Toy each telling the story of their experience. Their styles of storytelling form an interesting contrast. With several classmates, create a sketch based on these final scenes from the story and perform it for your class. Be sure to act out all the physical details.

Literature Connection

*The **setting** of a literary work is the time and place of the action. Sometimes the setting is clear and well-defined; at other times it is left to the reader's imagination. Look at the opening of "Last Night":*

When Hang Fong Toy finally awakens, she can't tell if the rhythmic pounding is one of her headaches or just the water pipes banging again. She looks around the room, listening. The street light falls through the Venetian blinds; the slanting lines make the room seem larger.

1. What details of setting does the writer give?

2. What information do they provide about the time and place of the action?

3. What do these details suggest about Hang Fong Toy's life style?

In a Neighborhood in
Los Angeles

by Francisco X. Alarcón

About the Author

Poet and educator Francisco X. Alarcón was born in 1954 in Wilmington, California. Alarcón grew up in Mexico, returning to California at age 18. He earned his undergraduate and graduate degrees from California universities. Alarcón is the author of many books of poetry as well as books on teaching Spanish. Several of his poetry books are bilingual. He has received numerous awards for his writing. Alarcón currently teaches at the University of California, Davis, where he directs the Spanish for Native Speakers Program.

About the Selections

Family memories *form the core of family bonds. The words "Remember when . . . ." begin many discussions among family members. Some family memories are preserved in photographs, scrapbooks, or on video. Others are imprinted on the heart and in the mind only. Whether painful or joyful, family memories are incorporated into reflections and decisions every day. As you read "In a Neighborhood in Los Angeles" (page 270) and "Nikki-Rosa" (page 271) be mindful of the power of family memories in shaping lives.*

I learned
Spanish
from my grandma

mijito[1]
don't cry
she'd tell me

on the mornings
my parents
would leave

to work
at the fish
canneries

my grandma
would chat
with chairs

sing them
old
songs

dance
waltzes with them
in the kitchen

when she'd say
niño barrigón[2]
she'd laugh

with my grandma
I learned
to count clouds

to point out
in flowerpots
mint leaves

my grandma
wore moons
on her dress

Mexico's mountains
deserts
ocean

in her eyes
I'd see them
in her braids

I'd touch them
in her voice
smell them

one day
I was told:
she went far away

but still
I feel her
with me

whispering
in my ear
mijito

Mexican artist María
Izquierdo (1902–1955)
painted *Portrait of an
Old Woman.* ▶

---

[1] *mijito* (mee•HEE•toh)—Spanish contraction of the words *mi hijito*, meaning "my little boy."
[2] *niño barrigón* (NEE•nyoh bahr•ree•GOHN)—Spanish for "big-bellied baby boy."

NIKKI-ROSA

By Nikki Giovanni

About the Author

Poet, essayist, and lecturer Nikki Giovanni was born Yolande Cornelia Giovanni, Jr., in 1943. She was educated at Fisk University, the University of Pennsylvania, and Columbia University. At age 27, she founded her own publishing company. Giovanni's work changes often, supporting her view that change is necessary for growth. Her early poetry served as a major voice in the civil rights movement of the 1960s. Later poems focused on family and her childhood home, Knoxville, Tennessee. Giovanni's recent work has a global outlook.

childhood remembrances are always a drag
if you're Black
you always remember things like living in Woodlawn[3]
with no inside toilet
and if you become famous or something
they never talk about how happy you were to have
your mother
all to yourself and
how good the water felt when you got your bath
from one of those
big tubs that folk in chicago barbecue in

---

[3] Woodlawn—poor African-American neighborhood on Chicago's South Side.

▲

Edwin Rosskam photographed these African-American children enjoying a game on a sidewalk in Chicago in 1941.

and somehow when you talk about home
it never gets across how much you
understood their feelings
as the whole family attended meetings about Hollydale
and even though you remember
your biographers never understand
your father's pain as he sells his stock
and another dream goes
and though you're poor it isn't poverty that
concerns you
and though they fought a lot
it isn't your father's drinking that makes any difference
but only that everybody is together and you
and your sister have happy birthdays and very good christmasses
and I really hope no white person ever has cause
to write about me
because they never understand
Black love is Black wealth and they'll
probably talk about my hard childhood
and never understand that
all the while I was quite happy

Questions to Consider

Responding

1. Why do you think people always assume growing up poor is miserable?

Analyzing

2. How have **family memories** functioned in the speaker's lives in both "In a Neighborhood in Los Angeles" and "Nikki-Rosa"?

3. In "Nikki-Rosa," how does the speaker's statement that "Black love is Black wealth" sum up her poem?

Extending

4. What can you do to avoid judging people based on their economic status or background?

Literature Connection

An author's or narrator's voice *is his or her distinctive style or manner of expression. It is an individual and original presentation of form, attitude, and ideas.*

1. How would you describe the speaker of "In a Neighborhood of Los Angeles," based on his voice in this poem?

2. How would you describe the author of "Nikki-Rosa," based on her voice in this poem?

Activities

Writing a Poem

Write a poem that expresses a truth about your childhood that others might not understand clearly. Incorporate family memories into your poem. Let your voice come through: write in your own way, with your own unique style.

Recording Family Memories

Create a video scrapbook of your family memories. Videotape your family members recalling funny and tender family incidents. Capture images from your photo albums on tape. Videotape objects and places in your home and neighborhood that have significance to your family, commenting while you film. Present your videotape to your family and get their reactions.

Linking Cultures

Family Album

Families are both very different and very much the same. They differ in size, ethnic background, wealth, education, religion, and many other characteristics. They are also similar in many things, such as their affection for each other and the pleasure they take in shared activities. The following images of families display both these differences and similarities.

▲
This family belongs to the Inupiat people of Alaska.

◀ A White Mountain Apache family poses in front of their home in Arizona.

◀ A Puerto Rican family from New York gathers after church.

 Joel Gordon photographed this Zuñi grandmother and her granddaughter.

An African-American girl poses with her great-grandmother after a game of basketball.
▼

A Chinese-American boy points out features on a dragon to his father.

A Latino mother and daughter enjoy a new baby. ▶

◀ An African-American
mother plays a video
game while her two
young sons look on.

This mixed race family reflects one of the fastest growing ethnic groups in the United States today.

An Asian-American family enjoys a picnic.
▼

Joseph Rodríguez took *Mothers on the Stoop* in 1988. ▶

A Samoan family poses on the porch of their home in Seattle.
▼

◀ Several generations of an African-American family pose for photographer Susie Fitzhugh.

Some of the children of this Mexican-American family hang up beach towels to dry while others play with their dog.

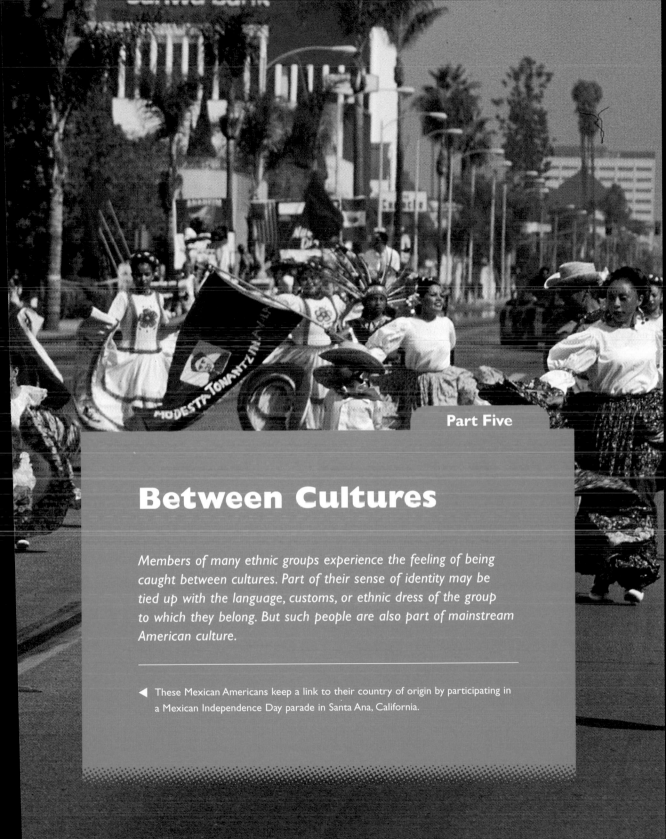

Part Five

Between Cultures

Members of many ethnic groups experience the feeling of being caught between cultures. Part of their sense of identity may be tied up with the language, customs, or ethnic dress of the group to which they belong. But such people are also part of mainstream American culture.

◀ These Mexican Americans keep a link to their country of origin by participating in a Mexican Independence Day parade in Santa Ana, California.

On Being Asian American

BY LAWSON FUSAO INADA

About the Author

Lawson Fusao Inada (1938–   ) is a Sansei (SAHN•say), or third-generation Japanese American. During World War II, he and his family were interned in camps in Arkansas and Colorado. Out of that experience came Before the War: Poems as They Happened *(1971), the first book of poetry by a Japanese American brought out by a major American publisher.*

About the Selections

*Since the late 1800s, when record numbers of immigrants came to the United States, ethnic groups such as Asian Americans have often been referred to as **"hyphenated Americans"** (whether or not the label contains a hyphen.) Both inside and outside these groups, feelings are very mixed about this kind of labeling. As you read "On Being Asian American" and "Saying Yes" (on page 287), think about what attitudes the two writers express toward their dual heritage.*

for Our Children

Of course, not everyone
can be an Asian American.
Distinctions are earned,
and deserve dedication.

Thus, from time of birth,
the journey awaits you—
ventures[1] through time,
the turns of the earth.

When you seem to arrive,
the journey continues;
when you seem to arrive,
the journey continues.

Take me as I am, you cry,
I, I, am an individual.
Which certainly is true.
Which generates an echo.

---

[1] **ventures**—dangerous tasks or assignments.

Who are all your people
assembled in celebration,
with wisdom and strength,
to which you are entitled.

For you are at the head
of succeeding generations[2]
as the rest of the world
comes forward to greet you.

---

[2] succeeding generations—generations to come.

Joel Gordon photographed this young
Japanese-American family. ▶

the
journey
awaits you

Saying Yes

BY DIANA CHANG

About the Author

Diana Chang (1934–   ) is a Chinese-American poet and novelist. Her first novel, Frontiers of Love (1956), dealt with the experiences of Eurasians (people of mixed European and Asian descent). Chang herself is the daughter of a Chinese father and a Eurasian mother. Her novel is considered a forerunner of literature about mixed-race people.

"Are you Chinese?"
"Yes."

"American?"
"Yes."

"*Really* Chinese?"
"No . . . not quite."

"*Really* American?"
"Well, actually, you see . . ."

But I would rather say
yes

Not neither-nor,
not maybe,
but both, and not only

The homes I've had,
the ways I am

I'd rather say it
twice,
yes

Questions to Consider

Responding

1. What do you think is the best thing about a "dual heritage"? What is the worst thing?

Analyzing

2. In "On Being Asian American," what attitude do you think the speaker wants Asian-American children to have toward their dual heritage?

3. In "Saying Yes," what do you think those who are questioning the speaker mean by the categories "*Really* Chinese" and "*Really* American"?

Extending

4. In "Saying Yes," the speaker is made uncomfortable by the need to define herself in simple categories. What experience have you had that was like this? How did you react?

Literature Connection

A **theme** *is a message about life or human nature that is communicated by a literary work. The theme of a literary work is not the same as its subject. The subject is what the work is about, such as the natural world, romantic love, or old age. The theme is a statement of what the author is saying concerning this subject. Sometimes the theme is stated directly. In many cases, however, a reader must infer what the writer's message is.*

1. What is the subject of both of these poems?

2. How would you express the theme of "On Being Asian American"?

3. How would you express the theme of "Saying Yes"?

4. How do the themes of these poems differ?

Activities

Writing About Ethnic Heritage

Write a brief poem or essay, "On Being _____," in which you present your feelings about your own ethnic heritage.

Researching Census Issues

For the first time, the 2000 census allowed Americans to identity themselves as being of more than one race. However, people were still not permitted to simply list themselves as "mixed race." The issues created by the desire of many people to define

themselves as multiracial run all the way from the political to the personal. With another classmate, research some of these issues and do a presentation for your class.

THE STRUGGLE TO BE AN

All-American Girl

BY ELIZABETH WONG

About the Author

Elizabeth Wong is a Chinese-American playwright and journalist. She grew up in San Francisco's Chinatown. Wanting to escape what she saw as the limitations of this environment, she chose as a role model Anna May Wong, Hollywood's first Chinese-American actress. She later wrote a play, China Doll (1995), about the actress. She also wrote some episodes of All-American Girl, which in 1994 became the first television sitcom to feature an Asian-American family.

About the Selections

*One of the most important parts of anyone's identity is the language— or languages—he or she speaks. Some immigrants to the United States embrace English and abandon their native language as the quickest way to become Americanized. Others hold on to their native language as a link to their ethnic heritage. Many Americans are **bilingual**—using both English and the language of the ethnic group to which they belong. They may have very different feelings about the two languages they use. As you read "The Struggle to Be an All-American Girl" and "Grandma's Primo" (on page 293), identify the feelings the speakers express about the different languages in their lives.*

It's still there, the Chinese school on Yale Street where my brother and I used to go. Despite the new coat of paint and the high wire fence, the school I knew 10 years ago remains remarkably, **stoically**[1] the same.

Every day at 5 P.M., instead of playing with our fourth- and fifth-grade friends or sneaking out to the empty lot to hunt ghosts and animal bones, my brother and I had to go to Chinese school. No amount of kicking, screaming, or pleading could **dissuade**[2] my mother, who was solidly determined to have us learn the language of our heritage.

Forcibly, she walked us the seven long, hilly blocks from our home to school, depositing our defiant tearful faces before the stern principal. My only memory of him is that he swayed on his heels like a palm tree, and he always clasped his impatient twitching hands behind his back. I recognized him as a repressed maniacal child killer, and knew that if we ever saw his hands we'd be in big trouble.

We all sat in little chairs in an empty auditorium. The room smelled like Chinese medicine,[3] an imported faraway mustiness. Like ancient moth-balls or dirty closets. I hated that smell.

I favored crisp new scents. Like the soft French perfume that my American teacher wore in public school.

There was a stage far to the right, flanked by an American flag and the flag of the Nationalist Republic of China,[4] which was also red, white and blue but not as pretty.

Although the emphasis at the school was mainly language—speaking, reading, writing—the lessons always began with an exercise in politeness. With the entrance of the teacher, the best student would tap a bell and everyone would get up, kowtow,[5] and chant, "Sing san ho," the phonetic[6] for "How are you, teacher?"

Being ten years old, I had better things to learn than ideographs[7] copied painstakingly in lines that ran right to left from the tip of a *moc but*, a real ink pen that had to be held in an awkward way if blotches were to be avoided. After all, I could do the

---

[1] **stoically** (STOH•ih•kuhl•lee)—showing no emotion. Wong applies a human quality to the building.

[2] **dissuade** (dih•SWAYD)—stop a person from a course of action by persuasion.

[3] Chinese medicine—various substances used in traditional Chinese medical practice.

[4] Nationalist Republic of China—official name for the country consisting of Taiwan and adjacent islands.

[5] kowtow—kneel and touch the forehead to the ground as an expression of deep respect.

[6] phonetic—spoken form of a language.

[7] ideographs (IHD•ee•uh•grafs)—written characters of a language.

multiplication tables, name the satellites of Mars, and write reports on *Little Women* and *Black Beauty*. Nancy Drew,[8] my favorite book heroine, never spoke Chinese.

The language was a source of embarrassment. More times than not, I had tried to **disassociate**[9] myself from the nagging loud voice that followed me wherever I wandered in the nearby American supermarket outside Chinatown. The voice belonged to my grandmother, a fragile woman in her seventies who could outshout the best of the street vendors. Her humor was raunchy, her Chinese rhythmless, patternless. It was quick, it was loud, it was unbeautiful. It was not like the quiet, lilting romance of French or the gentle refinement of the American South. Chinese sounded **pedestrian**.[10] Public.

In Chinatown, the comings and goings of hundreds of Chinese on their daily tasks sounded chaotic and frenzied. I did not want to be thought of as mad, as talking gibberish. When I spoke English, people nodded at me, smiled sweetly, said encouraging words. Even the people in my culture would cluck and say that I'd do well

in life. "My, doesn't she move her lips fast," they would say, meaning that I'd be able to keep up with the world outside Chinatown.

My brother was even more fanatical than I about speaking English. He was especially hard on my mother, criticizing her, often cruelly, for her pidgin[11] speech—smatterings of Chinese scattered like chop suey in her conversation. "It's not 'What it is,' Mom," he'd say in exasperation. "It's 'What *is* it, what *is* it, what *is* it!'" Sometimes Mom might leave out an occasional "the" or "a," or perhaps a verb of being.[12] He would stop her in mid-sentence: "Say it again, Mom. Say it right." When he tripped over his own tongue, he'd blame it on her: "See, Mom, it's all your fault. You set a bad example."

> *Nancy Drew, my favorite book heroine, never spoke Chinese.*

---

[8] Nancy Drew—girl detective in a highly popular series of mystery stories for young people that began appearing in 1930.

[9] **disassociate** (dis•uh•SOH•shee•ayt)—separate.

[10] **pedestrian**—ordinary.

[11] pidgin (PIHJ•uhn)—referring to a simplified form of speech that is usually a mixture of two or more languages.

[12] verb of being—form of the verb *to be* (such as *I am, you are, he is,* and so on.).

▲
These children are studying calligraphy in a Chinese-American school.

What infuriated my mother most was when my brother cornered her on her consonants, especially "r." My father had played a cruel joke on Mom by assigning her an American name that her tongue wouldn't allow her to say. No matter how hard she tried, "Ruth" always ended up "Luth" or "Roof."

After two years of writing with a *moc but* and reciting words with multiples of meanings, I finally was granted a cultural divorce. I was permitted to stop Chinese school.

I thought of myself as multicultural. I preferred tacos to egg rolls; I enjoyed Cinco de Mayo more than Chinese New Year.[13]

At last, I was one of you; I wasn't one of them.

Sadly, I still am.

---

[13] Cinco de Mayo . . . Chinese New Year—Cinco de Mayo ("Fifth of May") is a patriotic Mexican holiday. Chinese New Year is the annual 15-day celebration of the beginning of the new Chinese calendar year.

Grandma's Primo

BY LEROY V. QUINTANA

About the Author

Mexican-American poet Leroy V. Quintana was born in Albuquerque, New Mexico, in 1944, and was raised by his grandparents. They told him many folk tales, which encouraged the love of storytelling that is a basic part of his poetry. He has written six books of poetry and twice won an American Book Award from the Before Columbus Foundation.

Grandma had a cousin
who lived in the big city
and looked like a gringo[14]

He smoked a big cigar
and spoke English as well
as he spoke Spanish

He loved to tell jokes
would always tell them twice—
the first time in Spanish
and the second time in English
to impress us

---

title Primo (PREE•moh)—Spanish for "first (male) cousin."

[14] gringo (GRING•goh)—insulting Spanish slang term for a foreigner in Latin America, especially an American or English person.

Responding

1. If someone was described to you as "all-American," what qualities would you expect him or her to have?

Analyzing

2. How does Elizabeth Wong use exaggeration and comic description to convey humor in "The Struggle to Be an All-American Girl"?

3. What feelings does she express about the Chinese language?

4. What different feelings about English are conveyed in "Grandma's Primo"?

Extending

5. What would be the advantages and disadvantages of being **bilingual**?

Irony can be a contrast between what is expected and what actually happens. Or it can be a contrast between what is said and what is meant. Look at the close of "My Struggle to Be an All-American Girl":

> I thought of myself as multi-cultural. I preferred tacos to egg rolls; I enjoyed Cinco de Mayo more than Chinese New Year.
>
> At last, I was one of you; I wasn't one of them.
>
> Sadly, I still am.

1. How do you think the author expected to feel about being "multicultural"?

2. How does she actually feel about it?

Activities

Translating a Joke

Find a joke in a language that you are familiar with other than English. (If you're not sufficiently familiar with any other language to do this, work with a classmate who is.) Translate the joke into English. As you do so, notice how you have to change language idioms and cultural background. Is the joke still funny? Working with a group of students, translate jokes from several languages and then have a discussion about how humor depends on language and culture.

Researching Language Policy

There have been a number of proposals recently to designate English as the official language of the United States. Supporters say it would help unite the country culturally and would save money currently spent by government on a variety of services to non-English speakers. Opponents say these proposals would lead to "English only" laws unfair to non-English speakers. Research this issue and write an editorial expressing your opinion as to whether English should be designated as the official language of the United States.

A DAUGHTER OF THE
SAMURAI

By Etsu Sugimoto

About the Author

Etsu Sugimoto (1874–1950) was born in Japan at a time when the country's old social order was becoming modernized. Sugimoto was a member of an ancient samurai (SAM•uh•ry) family. The samurai were Japan's traditional military rulers. Sugimoto was raised as a Buddhist and brought up to follow a code of self-discipline, duty, and honor. In 1901, she married a Japanese businessman and emigrated to the United States. Although her family disapproved, Sugimoto eventually adopted western dress, converted to Christianity, and stayed in America until her death. Her memoir, A Daughter of the Samurai (1926), was the first book by a Japanese woman to be popular in the United States.

About the Selection

Cultural symbolism refers to the specific meaning or meanings that physical qualities, objects, and actions have for the members of a culture. Such symbolism often varies significantly from culture to culture. Consider the symbolism of the color white. In the United States, white generally symbolizes purity, and is frequently the color of brides' wedding dresses. In Japan, however, white symbolizes death, and brides often wear red. As you read the following memoir, note the difference between the cultural symbolism of flowers for Americans and Japanese.

When I came to America I expected to learn many things, but I had no thought that I was going to learn anything about Japan. Yet our neighbors, by their questions and remarks, were teaching me every day new ways of looking at my own country.

My closest friend was the daughter of a retired statesman, the General, we called him, who lived just across the steep little **ravine**[1] which divided our grounds from his. Our side was bordered by a hedge of purple lilacs, broken, opposite the path to the well, by a **rustic**[2] drawbridge. One autumn afternoon I was sitting on the shady step of the bridge with a many-stamped package in my lap, watching for the postman. Just about that hour his funny little wagon, looking, with its open side-doors, like a high, stiff *kago*,[3] would be passing on its return trip down the hill, and I was anxious to hurry off my package of white cotton brocade[4] and ribbons of various patterns and colors—the most prized gifts I could send to Japan.

Suddenly I heard a gay voice behind me reciting in a high sing-song:

> Open your mouth and shut your eyes
> And I'll give you something to make you wise.

I looked up at a charming picture. My bright-eyed friend, in a white dress and big lacy hat, was standing on the bridge, holding in her cupped hands three or four grape leaves pinned together with thorns. On this rustic plate were piled some bunches of **luscious**[5] purple grapes.

"Oh, how pretty!" I exclaimed. "That is just the way Japanese serve fruit."

"And this is the way they carry flowers," she said, putting down the grapes on the step and releasing a big bunch of long-stemmed tiger lilies from under her arm. "Why do Japanese always carry flowers upside-down?"

> ***Why do Japanese always carry flowers upside-down?***

[1] **ravine** (ruh•VEEN)—deep, narrow valley.

[2] **rustic**—typical of country life.

[3] *kago* (KAH•goh)—Japanese chair carried on poles by bearers.

[4] brocade (broh•KAYD)—rich, heavy fabric.

[5] **luscious** (LUSH•uhs)—sweet or pleasant to taste or smell.

new ways
of looking at my own country

A Japanese woman wearing a traditional kimono stands in a garden. ▶

I laughed and said, "It looked very odd to me, when I first came, to see everybody carrying flowers with the tops up. Why do you?"

"Why—why—they look prettier so; and that's the way they grow."

That was true, and yet I had never before thought of any one's caring for the appearance of flowers that were being carried. We Japanese have a way of considering a thing invisible until it is settled in its proper place.

"Japanese seldom carry flowers," I said, "except to the temple or to graves. We get flowers for the house from flower-venders who go from door to door with baskets swung from shoulder poles, but we do not send flowers as gifts; and we never wear them."

"Why?" asked Miss Helen.

"Because they wither and fade. And so, to send flowers to a sick friend would be the worst **omen**[6] in the world."

---

[6] **omen**—sign indicating future good or evil.

"Oh, what a lot of pleasure your poor **invalids**[7] in hospitals are losing!" said Miss Helen. "And Japan is the land of flowers!"

Surprised and thoughtful, I sat silent; but in a moment was aroused by a question. "What were you thinking of when I came—sitting here so quietly with that big bundle on your lap? You looked like a lovely, dainty, picturesque little peddler."

"My thoughts were very unlike those of a peddler," I replied. "As I sat here watching the dangling end of the bridge chain I was thinking of a Japanese lover of long ago who crossed a drawbridge ninety-nine times to win his ladylove, and the one hundredth time, in a blinding snowstorm, he failed to see that it was lifted, and so fell to his death in the moat below."

"How tragic!" exclaimed Miss Helen. "What did the poor lady do?"

"It was her fault," I said. "She was vain and ambitious, and when she saw a chance to win the love of a high official at court, she changed her mind about her lover and commanded her attendants not to lower the bridge the day he expected to come triumphant."

"You don't mean that the cold-blooded creature actually planned his death?"

"It was the storm that caused his death," I said. "She was fickle, but not wicked. She thought that when he found the bridge lifted he would know her answer and go away."

"Well, sometimes our girls over here are fickle enough, dear knows," said Miss Helen, "but no American woman would ever do a thing like that. She was actually a murderess."

I was shocked at such a practical way of looking at my romantic tale, and hastened to add that remorseful Lady Komachi[8] became a nun and spent her life in making pilgrimages to various temples to pray for the dead. At last she partially lost her mind, and, as a wandering beggar, lived and died among the humble villagers on the slopes of Mount Fuji.[9] "Her fate is held up by priests," I concluded, "as a warning to all fickle-minded maidens."

"Well," said Miss Helen, drawing a deep breath, "I think she paid pretty dearly for her foolishness, don't you?"

"Why—well, perhaps," I replied, rather surprised at the question, "but

---

[7] **invalids** (IHN•vuh•lihds)—people suffering from illness or injury.

[8] Lady Komachi—(koh•MAH•chee).

[9] Mount Fuji (FOO•jee)—Fujiyama, volcano in central Japan.

we are taught that if a woman so loses her gentle modesty that she can treat with scorn and disrespect the plea of a loyal lover, she is no longer a worthy woman."

"Suppose a man jilts a maid, what then?" quickly asked Miss Helen. "Is he no longer considered a worthy man?"

I did not know how to reply. Instinctively I upheld to myself the teachings of my childhood that man is the protector and guide and woman the helper—the self-respecting, but nevertheless, uncritical, dutiful helper.

Often afterward Miss Helen and I had heart-to-heart talks in which her questions and remarks surprised and sometimes disturbed me. Many of our customs I had taken for granted, accepting the ways of our ancestors without any thought except that thus they had been and still were. When I began to question myself about things which had always seemed simple and right because they were in accordance with laws made by our wise rulers, sometimes I was puzzled and sometimes I was frightened.

◄ *View of Mount Haruna Under Snow* was painted by the Japanese artist Hiroshige (1797–1858).

"I am afraid that I am growing very bold and man-like," I would think to myself, "but God gave me a brain to use, else why do I have it?" All my childhood I had hidden my deepest feelings. Now again it was the same. My American mother would have understood, but I did not know; and so, repressing all outward signs, I puzzled my way alone, in search of higher ideals—not for myself, but for Japan.

> All my childhood I had hidden my deepest feelings. Now again it was the same.

Miss Helen's father was ninety years old when I knew him. He was a wonderful man, tall, with broad shoulders just a trifle stooped and with thick iron-gray hair and bushy eyebrows. A strong face he had, but gentle and humorous when he talked. I looked upon him as an encyclopedia of American history. I had always loved the study of history, in childhood and at school, but I had learned little of the details of America's part in the world; and would sit with the General and his invalid wife listening by the hour while he told stories of early American life. Knowing that incidents of personal history especially appealed to me, he once told me that his own large estate was bought by his father from an Indian chief in exchange for one chair, a gun, and a pouch of tobacco; and that Mother's large home was once an Indian village of bark tents and was purchased for half-a-dozen split-seated kitchen chairs. These incidents seemed to me almost pre-historic; for I had never known any one whose home did not date back into a far past.

When America was a still youthful nation the General had represented his country as a diplomat in Europe, and, with his beautiful young wife, had taken part in the foreign social life in Paris and later in Washington. My first glimpse of American life abroad, I received through the word pictures of this gracious lady, and through her experiences I began to understand, with sympathy, something of the problem in Japan of Americans trying to understand the Japanese, which heretofore I had looked upon only as the problem of Japanese trying to understand Americans.

Responding

1. Why are issues of **cultural symbolism** so important in the world today?

Analyzing

2. Why would the Japanese not wear flowers or send them as a gift for someone who is ill?

3. What is the narrator's view of the role of women?

4. Why does the narrator become troubled by her talks with Miss Helen?

5. Why does the General's story about how his father obtained his estate from the Indians startle the narrator?

Extending

6. What do you think would be the best way to make people sensitive to issues of cultural symbolism?

*An *allusion* is a reference to a famous person, place, event, or work of literature. In A Daughter of the Samurai, the narrator makes an allusion to Lady Komachi, a historical figure who became a famous character in Japanese literature.*

1. How does the narrator view the story of Lady Komachi?

2. How does her American friend Miss Helen view it?

3. What purpose does this allusion serve?

Creating a Cultural Color Chart

Use library or Internet resources to research the cultural symbolism of various colors. Use your research as the basis for a chart in which you indicate what the basic colors mean in different cultures around the world. Share your chart with your classmates and discuss the cultural symbolism of colors.

LIKE MEXICANS

BY GARY SOTO

About the Author

Mexican-American writer Gary Soto was born in Fresno, California, in 1952. Many of his poems and stories are based on what he experienced growing up in Fresno's Mexican-American barrio, or neighborhood. While he was in graduate school, Soto married Carolyn Oda, the daughter of Japanese-American farmers. He describes an event from their courtship in "Like Mexicans." Soto has published nine poetry collections as well as books for young people, memoirs, and film scripts. His 1995 volume, New and Selected Poems, *was nominated for a National Book Award. He lives in Berkeley, California, with his wife and their daughter, Mariko.*

About the Selection

*People sometimes attempt to simplify life by dividing their worlds into **"us" and "them."** At different times, "us" might might be "our ethnic group," or "our religion," or "our nation." "Them" is everybody else. One point when differences between "us" and "them" may become particularly important is when people are deciding who to marry. As you read "Like Mexicans," note how Gary Soto's reactions to the girls he meets reflect divisions into "us" and "them."*

My grandmother gave me bad advice and good advice when I was in my early teens. For the bad advice, she said that I should become a barber because they made good money and listened to the radio all day. "Honey, they don't work como burros,"[1] she would say every time I visited her. She made the sound of donkeys braying. "Like that, honey!" For the good advice, she said that I should marry a Mexican girl. "No Okies, hijo"[2]—she would say— "Look my son. He marry one and they fight every day about I don't know what and I don't know what." For her, everyone who wasn't Mexican, black, or Asian were Okies. The French were Okies, the Italians in suits were Okies. When I asked about Jews, whom I had read about, she asked for a picture. I rode home on my bicycle and returned with a calendar depicting the important races of the world. "Pues sí, son Okies también!"[3] she said, nodding her head. She waved the calendar away and we went to the living room where she lectured me on the virtues of the Mexican girl: first, she could cook and, second, she acted like a woman, not a man, in her husband's home. She said she would tell me about a third when I got a little older.

I asked my mother about it— becoming a barber and marrying Mexican. She was in the kitchen. Steam curled from a pot of boiling beans, the radio was on, looking as squat as a loaf of bread. "Well, if you want to be a barber—they say they make good money." She slapped a round steak with a knife, her glasses slipping down with each strike. She stopped and looked up. "If you find a good Mexican girl, marry her of course." She returned to slapping the meat and I went to the backyard where my brother and David King were sitting on the lawn.

> If you find a good Mexican girl, marry her of course.

I ignored them and climbed the back fence to see my best friend, Scott, a second generation Okie. I called him, and his mother pointed to the side of the house where his bedroom was a small aluminum trailer, the kind you gawk at when they're flipped over on the freeway, wheels spinning in the air. I went around to find Scott pitching horseshoes.

---

[1] como burros—Spanish for "like donkeys."

[2] "No Okies, hijo"—Spanish for "No Okies, son." *Okies* is an insulting term given to migrant workers (many of whom came from Oklahoma) during the Dust Bowl of the 1930s.

[3] "Pues sí . . . también!"—Spanish for "Well yes, they're Okies too!"

we couldn't wait
to become men

◀ Susie Fitzhugh photographed this Latino boy.

I picked up a set of rusty ones and joined him. While we played, we talked about school and friends and record albums. The horseshoes scuffed up dirt, sometimes ringing the iron that threw out a **meager**[4] shadow like a sundial. After three argued-over games, we pulled two oranges apiece from his tree and started down the alley still talking school and friends and record albums. We pulled more oranges from the alley and talked about who we would marry. "No offense, Scott," I said with an orange slice in my mouth," but I would never marry an Okie." We walked in step,

almost touching. "No offense, Gary," Scott said, "but I would *never* marry a Mexican." I looked at him: a fang of orange slice showed from his munching mouth. I didn't think anything of it. He had his girl and I had mine. But our seventh-grade vision was the same: to marry, get jobs, buy cars and maybe a house if we had money left over.

We talked about our future lives until, to our surprise, we were on the downtown mall, two miles from home. We bought a bag of popcorn at Penney's and sat on a bench near the

---

[4] **meager**—thin.

fountain watching Mexican and Okie girls pass. "That one's mine," I pointed with my chin when a girl with eyebrows arched into black rainbows ambled by. "She's cute," Scott said about a girl with yellow hair and a mouthful of gum. We dreamed aloud, our chins busy pointing out girls. We agreed that we couldn't wait to become men and lift them onto our laps.

But the woman I married was not Mexican but Japanese. It was a surprise to me. For years, I went about wide-eyed in my search for the brown girl in a white dress at a dance. I searched the playground at the baseball diamond. When the girls raced for grounders, their hair bounced like something that couldn't be caught. When they sat together in the lunchroom, heads pressed together, I knew they were talking about us Mexican guys. I saw them and dreamed them. I threw my face into my pillow, making up sentences that were good as in the movies.

But when I was twenty, I fell in love with this other girl who worried my mother, who had my grandmother asking once again to see the calendar of the Important Races of the World.

I told her I had thrown it away years before. I took a much-glanced-at snapshot from my wallet. We looked at it together, in silence. Then grandma reclined in her chair, lit a cigarette, and said, "Es pretty."[5] blew and asked with all her worry pushed up to her forehead: "Chinese?"

I was in love and there was no looking back. She was the one. I told my mother who was slapping hamburger into patties. "Well, sure if you want to marry her," she said. But the more I talked, the more concerned she became. Later I began to worry. Was it all a mistake? "Marry a Mexican girl," I heard my mother say in my mind. I heard it at breakfast. I heard it over math problems, between Western Civilization and cultural geography. But then one afternoon while I was hitchhiking home from school, it struck me like a baseball in the back: my mother wanted me to marry someone of my own social class—a poor girl. I considered my fiancée, Carolyn, and she didn't look poor, though I knew she came from a family of farm workers and pull-yourself-up-by-the-bootstraps ranchers. I asked

---

[5] "Es pretty"—"She's pretty."

my brother, who was marrying Mexican poor that fall, if I should marry a poor girl. He screamed "Yeah" above his terrible guitar playing in his bedroom. I considered my sister who had married Mexican. Cousins were dating Mexican. Uncles were remarrying poor women. I asked Scott, who was still my best friend, and he said, "She's too good for you, so you better not."

> **These people are just like Mexicans, I thought. Poor people.**

I worried about it until Carolyn took me home to meet her parents. We drove in her Plymouth until the houses gave way to farms and ranches and finally her house fifty feet from the highway. When we pulled into the drive, I panicked and begged Carolyn to make a U-turn and go back so we could talk about it over a soda. She pinched my cheek, calling me a "silly boy." I felt better, though, when I got out of the car and saw the house: the chipped paint, a cracked window, boards for a walk to the back door. There were rusting cars near the barn. A tractor with a net of spiderwebs under a mulberry. A field. A bale of barbed wire like children's scribbling

leaning against an empty chicken coop. Carolyn took my hand and pulled me to my future mother-in-law who was coming out to greet us.

We had lunch: sandwiches, potato chips, and iced tea. Carolyn and her mother talked mostly about neighbors and the congregation at the Japanese Methodist Church in West Fresno. Her father, who was in khaki work clothes, excused himself with a wave that was almost a salute and went outside. I heard a truck start, a dog bark, and then the truck rattle away.

Carolyn's mother offered another sandwich, but I declined with a shake of my head and a smile. I looked around when I could, when I was not saying over and over that I was a college student, hinting that I could take care of her daughter. I shifted my chair. I saw newspapers piled in corners, dusty cereal boxes and vinegar bottles in corners. The wallpaper was bubbled from rain that had come in from a bad roof. Dust. Dust lay on lamp shades and window sills. These people are just like Mexicans, I thought. Poor people.

Carolyn's mother asked me through Carolyn if I would like a

▲

Japanese *sushi* and other dishes.

sushi.[6] A plate of black and white things were held in front of me. I took one, wide-eyed, and turned it over like a foreign coin. I was biting into one when I saw a kitten crawl up the window screen over the sink. I chewed and the kitten opened its mouth in terror as she crawled higher, wanting in to paw the leftovers from our plates. I looked at Carolyn, who said that the cat was just showing off. I looked up in time to see it fall. It crawled up, then fell again.

We talked for an hour and had apple pie and coffee, slowly. Finally, we got up with Carolyn taking my hand. Slightly embarrassed, I tried to pull away but her grip held me. I let her have her way as she led me down the hallway with her mother right behind me. When I opened the door, I was startled by a kitten clinging to the screen door, its mouth screaming "cat food, dog biscuits, *sushi*. . . ." I opened the door and the kitten, still holding on, whined in the language of hungry animals. When I got into Carolyn's car, I looked back: the cat was still clinging. I asked Carolyn if it was possibly hungry, but she said the cat was being silly. She started the car, waved to her mother, and bounced us over the rain-pocked drive, patting my thigh for being her lover baby. Carolyn waved again. I looked back, waving, then gawking at a window screen where there were now three kittens clawing and screaming to get in. Like Mexicans, I thought. I remembered the Molinas and how the cats clung to their screens—cats they shot down with squirt guns. On the highway, I felt happy, pleased by it all. I patted Carolyn's thigh. Her people were like Mexicans, only different.

[6] *sushi*—Japanese dish of raw fish and rice.

Responding

1. At what points in your life have you found yourself dividing the world into **"us" and "them"**? What caused you to do this?

Analyzing

2. Both Gary Soto's mother and grandmother advise him to marry a Mexican girl. How do the two women's reasons for this advice differ?

4. What does his description of the home of his fiancée's family convey about them?

5. What understanding does he reach after visiting his fiancée's family?

Extending

6. What are some ways of avoiding—or at least controlling—the common human habit of dividing the world into "us" and "them"?

Literature Connection

*A **description** is a picture, in words, of a scene, a character, or an object. Descriptions can be used to appeal to readers' senses or to provide detailed information about characters and events. Look at the narrator's description of his first sight of his fiancée's home in "Like Mexicans":*

> . . . the chipped paint, a cracked window, boards for a walk to the back door. There were rusting cars near the barn. A tractor with a net of spiderwebs under a mulberry. A field. A bale of barbed wire like children's scribbling leaning against an empty chicken coop.

1. What does the description suggest about the fiancée's family?

2. How does the narrator react to what he sees?

Activities

Writing a Description

Gary Soto provides vivid descriptions of various settings in this memoir. Select some familiar place from your own life and recreate it through description. Be sure to include imagery that precisely captures the sights, sounds, smells, and other sensory impressions that are part of your experience of this setting.

Creating an Illustration

Choose one of the scenes in "Like Mexicans," such as Soto's family's kitchen or the outside or inside of the house of his fiancée's family. Create an illustration based on the scene you choose, using pencil, ink, water color, or whatever artistic medium you prefer. Try to give your illustration the same emotional qualities you feel in Soto's description.

Geraldine Moore the Poet

BY TONI CADE BAMBARA

About the Author

Toni Cade Bambara (1939–1996) was born in New York City. Her education included study of mime, theater, dance, and film. Bambara was one of several African-American writers in the 1960s and 1970s who combined writing and political activism. She worked in welfare, for community projects, for literacy programs, and as a director of films and plays about social issues. She produced several collections of short stories and two novels. Her novel The Salt Eaters won the American Book Award in 1981.

About the Selections

Who can be an **artist**? Is art only done by people who make their living as painters, writers, musicians, actors, and so on? Or can anyone who has something significant to say about life be an artist? As you read "Geraldine Moore the Poet" and "Theme for English B" (page 315), think about what are the most important influences of culture on an artist.

*G*eraldine paused at the corner to pull up her knee socks. The rubber bands she was using to hold them up made her legs itch. She dropped her books on the sidewalk while she gave a good scratch. But when she pulled the socks up again, two fingers poked right through the top of her left one.

"That stupid dog," she muttered to herself, grabbing at her books and crossing against traffic. "First he chews up my gym suit and gets me into trouble, and now my socks."

Geraldine shifted her books to the other hand and kept muttering angrily to herself about Mrs. Watson's dog, which she minded two days a week for a dollar. She passed the hot-dog man on the corner and waved. He shrugged as if to say business was very bad.

Must be, she thought to herself. *Three guys before you had to pack up and forget it. Nobody's got hot-dog money around here.*

Geraldine turned down her street, wondering what her sister Anita would have for her lunch. She was glad she didn't have to eat the free lunches in high school any more. She was sick of the funny-looking tomato soup and the dried-out cheese sandwiches and those oranges that were more green than orange.

When Geraldine's mother first took sick and went away, Geraldine had been on her own except when Miss Gladys next door came in on Thursdays and cleaned the apartment and made a meat loaf so Geraldine could have dinner. But in those days Geraldine never quite managed to get breakfast for herself. So she'd sit through social studies class, scraping her feet to cover up the noise of her stomach growling.

Now Anita, Geraldine's older sister, was living at home waiting for her husband to get out of the Army. She usually had something good for lunch—chicken and dumplings if she managed to get up in time, or baked ham from the night before and sweet-potato bread. But even if there was only a hot dog and some baked beans—sometimes just a TV dinner if those soap operas kept Anita glued to the TV set—anything was better than the noisy school lunchroom where monitors kept pushing you into a straight line or rushing you to the tables. Anything was better than that.

Geraldine was almost home when she stopped dead. Right outside her building was a pile of furniture and some boxes. That wasn't anything new. She had seen people get put out in the street before, but this time the ironing board looked familiar. And she recognized the big, ugly sofa standing on its arm, its underbelly showing the hole where Mrs. Watson's dog had gotten to it.

Miss Gladys was sitting on the stoop, and she looked up and took off her glasses. "Well, Gerry," she said slowly, wiping her glasses on the hem of her dress, "looks like you'll be staying with me for a while." She looked at the men carrying out a big box with an old doll sticking up over the edge. "Anita's upstairs. Go on up and get your lunch."

Geraldine stepped past the old woman and almost bumped into the superintendent. He took off his cap to wipe away the sweat.

"Darn shame," he said to no one in particular. "Poor people sure got a hard row to hoe."

"That's the truth," said Miss Gladys, standing up with her hands on her hips to watch the men set things on the sidewalk.

Upstairs, Geraldine went into the apartment and found Anita in the kitchen.

"I dunno, Gerry," Anita said. "I just don't know what we're going to do. But everything's going to be all right soon as Ma gets well." Anita's voice cracked as she set a bowl of soup before Geraldine.

"What's this?" Geraldine said.

"It's tomato soup, Gerry."

Geraldine was about to say something. But when she looked up at her big sister, she saw how Anita's face was getting all twisted as she began to cry.

That afternoon, Mr. Stern, the geometry teacher, started drawing cubes and cylinders on the board. Geraldine sat at her desk adding up a column of figures in her notebook— the rent, the light and gas bills, a new gym suit, some socks. Maybe they would move somewhere else, and she could have her own room. Geraldine turned the squares and triangles into little houses in the country.

"For your homework," Mr. Stern was saying with his back to the class, "set up your problems this way." He wrote GIVEN: in large letters, and then gave the formula for the first problem. Then he wrote TO FIND: and listed three items they were to include in their answers.

Geraldine started to raise her hand to ask what all these squares and angles had to do with solving real problems, like the ones she had. *Better not*, she warned herself, and sat on her hands. *Your big mouth got you in trouble last term.*

In hygiene class, Mrs. Potter kept saying that the body was a wonderful machine. Every time Geraldine looked up from her notebook, she would hear the same thing. "Right now your body is manufacturing all the proteins and tissues and energy you will need to get through tomorrow."

And Geraldine kept wondering, *How? How does my body know what it will need, when I don't even know what I'll need to get through tomorrow?*

▲
The portrait of this African-American high school girl suggests some of Geraldine Moore's outlook.

As she headed down the hall to her next class, Geraldine remembered that she hadn't done the homework for English. Mrs. Scott had said to write a poem, and Geraldine had meant to do it at lunchtime. After all, there was nothing to it—a flower here, a raindrop there, moon, June, rose, nose. But the men carrying off the furniture had made her forget.

"And now put away your books," Mrs. Scott was saying as Geraldine tried to scribble a poem quickly. "Today we can give King Arthur's knights a rest. Let's talk about poetry."

Mrs. Scott moved up and down the aisles, talking about her favorite poems and reciting a line now and then. She got very excited whenever she passed a desk and could pick up the homework from a student who had remembered to do the assignment.

"A poem is your own special way of saying what you feel and what you see," Mrs. Scott went on, her lips moist. It was her favorite subject.

"Some poets write about the light that . . .that . . . makes the world sunny," she said, passing Geraldine's desk. "Sometimes an idea takes the form of a picture—an image."

For almost half an hour, Mrs. Scott stood at the front of the room, reading poems and talking about the lives of the great poets. Geraldine drew more houses, and designs for curtains.

"So for those who haven't done their homework, try it now," Mrs. Scott said. "Try expressing what it is like to be . . . to be alive in this . . . this glorious world."

"Oh, brother," Geraldine muttered to herself as Mrs. Scott moved up and down the aisles again, waving her hands and leaning over the students' shoulders and saying, "That's nice," or "Keep trying." Finally she came to Geraldine's desk and stopped, looking down at her.

"I can't write a poem," Geraldine said flatly, before she even realized she was going to speak at all. She said it very loudly, and the whole class looked up.

"And why not?" Mrs. Scott asked, looking hurt.

"I can't write a poem, Mrs. Scott, because nothing lovely's been happening in my life. I haven't seen a flower since Mother's Day, and the sun don't even shine on my side of the street. No robins come sing on my window sill."

Geraldine swallowed hard. She thought about saying that her father doesn't even come to visit any more, but changed her mind. "Just the rain comes," she went on, "and the bills come, and the men to move out our furniture. I'm sorry but I can't write no pretty poem."

Teddy Johnson leaned over and was about to giggle and crack the whole class up, but Mrs. Scott looked so serious that he changed his mind.

> *I'm sorry, but I can't write no pretty poem.*

"You have just said the most . . . the most poetic thing, Geraldine Moore," said Mrs. Scott. Her hands flew up to touch the silk scarf around her neck. "'Nothing lovely's been happening in my life.'" She repeated it so quietly that everyone had to lean forward to hear.

"Class," Mrs. Scott said very sadly, clearing her throat, "you have just heard the best poem you will ever hear." She went to the board and stood there for a long time staring at the chalk in her hand.

"I'd like you to copy it down," she said. She wrote it just as Geraldine had said it, bad grammar and all.

Nothing lovely's been happening
    in my life.
I haven't seen a flower since
    Mother's Day,
And the sun don't even shine on
    my side of the street.
No robins come sing on my
    window sill.
Just the rain comes, and the bills come,
And the men to move out our
    furniture.
I'm sorry, but I can't write no pretty
    poem.

Mrs. Scott stopped writing, but she kept her back to the class for a long time—long after Geraldine had closed her notebook. And even when the bell rang, and everyone came over to smile at Geraldine or to tap her on the shoulder or to kid her about being the school poet, Geraldine waited for Mrs. Scott to put the chalk down and turn around. Finally Geraldine stacked up her books and started to leave. Then she thought she heard a whimper—the way Mrs. Watson's dog whimpered sometimes—and she saw Mrs. Scott's shoulders shake a little.

Theme for English B

BY LANGSTON HUGHES

About the Author

Langston Hughes (1902–1967) was born in Joplin, Missouri. He traveled widely as a young man, and finally made his home in Harlem. He attended Columbia University and received his degree from Lincoln University in Pennsylvania. Hughes was the first African American to support himself entirely from his writing. He wrote novels, short stories, plays, song lyrics, essays, and radio scripts, but is best known for his poetry. Wherever Hughes went, he wrote poetry in jazz clubs, letting the rhythm of the music emerge in his writing.

◀ The African-American artist Aaron Douglas (1898–1979) painted *Song of the Towers* in 1934. Like Langston Hughes, Douglas was part of the African-American cultural movement known as the Harlem Renaissance.

The instructor said,

Go home and write
a page tonight.
And let that page come out of you—
Then, it will be true.

I wonder if it's that simple?
I am twenty-two, colored, born in Winston-Salem.
I went to school there, then Durham, then here
to this college on the hill above Harlem.
I am the only colored student in my class.
The steps from the hill lead down into Harlem,
through a park, then I cross St. Nicholas,

Eighth Avenue, Seventh, and I come to the Y,
the Harlem Branch Y, where I take the elevator
up to my room, sit down, and write this page:

It's not easy to know what is true for you or me
at twenty-two, my age. But I guess I'm what
I feel and see and hear, Harlem, I hear you:
hear you, hear me—we two—you, me, talk on this page.
(I hear New York, too.) Me—who?
Well, I like to eat, sleep, drink, and be in love.
I like to work, read, learn, and understand life.
I like a pipe for a Christmas present,
or records—Bessie, bop, or Bach.[1]
I guess being colored doesn't make me not like
the same things other folks like who are other races.
So will my page be colored that I write?
Being me, it will not be white.
But it will be
a part of you, instructor.
You are white—
yet a part of me, as I am a part of you.

That's American.
Sometimes perhaps you don't want to be a part of me.
Nor do I often want to be a part of you.
But we are, that's true!
As I learn from you,
I guess you learn from me—
although you're older—and white—
and somewhat more free.

This is my page for English B.

---

[1] Bessie, bop, or Bach—Bessie Smith (1894–1937) was an African-American blues singer. Bop is a style of jazz. Johann Sebastian Bach (1685–1750) was a German composer and organist.

Questions to Consider

Responding

1. What are the most important characteristics for an **artist** to have?

Analyzing

2. In "Geraldine Moore the Poet," what problems does Geraldine face?

3. Why does she feel she can't write a poem?

4. Mrs. Scott says, "A poem is your own special way of saying what you feel and what you see." How does Geraldine's poem fit this definition?

5. In "Theme for English B," what problem does the speaker have with the assignment given him by his instructor?

6. What solution does the speaker arrive at?

Extending

7. What do you think are the most valuable things an artist can do for the society in which he or she lives?

Literature Connection

In literature, conflict is the struggle between opposing forces. It may be external, as in a struggle between two or more characters, or between characters and an outside force, such as nature. It also may be internal, as in a struggle within a character about an issue or action.

1. What external conflicts does Geraldine Moore face?

2. What are her internal conflicts?

3. What conflicts are experienced by the speaker in "Theme for English B"?

Activities

Writing about a Bad Day

There are lots of different approaches to writing about a bad day. You can recreate the experience as a moral lesson. You can exaggerate for humorous effect. You can take an objective, journalistic approach. You can turn it into a heroic saga of obstacles overcome. Write a narrative based on some bad day of your own, using one of these approaches or a different one if you prefer.

IMMIGRANTS

BY PAT MORA

About the Author

Pat Mora has spent most of her life in El Paso, Texas, where she was born in 1942. (Her four grandparents had migrated from Mexico to El Paso to escape a revolution early in this century.) She has said that when she was young, she spoke Spanish at home with her grandmother and aunt but didn't always want her school friends to know that she spoke Spanish. In 1986, Mora received a Kellogg National Fellowship to study ways of preserving cultures. She explains, "I am interested in how we save languages and traditions. What we have inside of our homes and our families is a treasure chest that we don't pay attention to."

About the Selections

Assimilation refers to the process by which a minority group adopts the customs and attitudes of the majority. In the United States, attitudes about the value of assimilation vary a great deal. Some people see it as a highly desirable process that is necessary if minorities are to be success-ful members of American society. Other people feel that it is vital for members of minority groups to preserve their cultural heritage. As you read "Immigrants" and "Refugee Ship" (on page 321) decide what attitude each poem expresses towards the process of assimilation.

wrap their babies in the American flag,
feed them mashed hot dogs and apple pie,
name them Bill and Daisy,
buy them blonde dolls that blink blue
eyes or a football and tiny cleats
before the baby can even walk,
speak to them in thick English,
       hallo, babee, hallo,
whisper in Spanish or Polish
when the babies sleep, whisper
in a dark parent bed, that dark
parent fear, "Will they like
our boy, our girl, our fine american
boy, our fine american girl?"

These children photographed by
Susie Fitzhugh reflect a broad range
of ethnic backgrounds. ▶

REFUGEE SHIP
BY LORNA DEE CERVANTES

About the Author

Lorna Dee Cervantes was born in San Francisco in 1954. She grew up speaking only English, because this was the only language her parents allowed her and her brother to use at home. Of both Native American and Mexican ancestry, she became active as a teenager in both the American Indian Movement (a civil rights group founded in 1968) and in Chicano political movements. Her first book of poetry, Emplumada (1981), won the American Book Award.

Like wet cornstarch, I slide
past my grandmother's eyes. Bible
at her side, she removes her glasses.
The pudding thickens.
Mama raised me without language,

I'm orphaned from my Spanish name.
The words are foreign, stumbling

on my tongue. I see in the mirror
my reflection: bronzed skin, black hair.

I feel I am a captive
aboard the refugee ship.
The ship that will never dock.
El barco que nunca atraca.[1]

---

[1] *"El barco . . . atraca"*—"The ship that never docks."

Responding

1. What do you think it means to "Americanize" someone?

Analyzing

2. In "Immigrants," why do you think newcomers to America do the things the speaker mentions?

3. What attitude toward **assimilation** is expressed in the "dark parent fear"?

4. How closely do you think the speaker in the poem shares this attitude?

5. In "Refugee Ship," what attitude does the speaker seem to have toward Hispanic culture?

6. What is the meaning of the last four lines?

Extending

7. What positive values do you see in the assimilation of minorities into mainstream American culture? What problems might result?

Imagery consists of words and phrases that appeal to the five senses. Writers use sensory details to help readers imagine how things look, feel, smell, sound, and taste. Examine these two poems.

1. What images describe how things look?

2. What images describe how things sound?

3. What other kind of sensory images do you find?

Comparing a Relationship

The speaker in "Refugee Ship" compares her situation between two cultures to that of a passenger aboard a "ship that will never dock." What comparison would you use to express your relationship to both your ethnic background and mainstream American culture? A guest arriving late at a party? A worker on a construction team building a large bridge? Use that comparison as the basis for a short poem.

Expressing Americanization

Create a collage that expresses your views of Americanization. Be sure to present both what you see as the positive and the negative sides.

◀ New American citizens swear allegiance to the United States.

Men on the Moon

by Simon Ortiz

About the Author

Simon Ortiz is a member of the Acoma Pueblo people. He writes with a storyteller's eyes and ears. Ortiz was born in New Mexico in 1941, and grew up with a love for the desert landscape and the Native American oral tradition. After graduating from the University of New Mexico and the Iowa Writers Workshop, Ortiz became a professional writer and teacher. He won the Pushcart Prize for Poetry for his collection of poems From Sand Creek (1981). "Men on the Moon" is the title story of a volume of Ortiz's collected short stories that was published in 1999. Like his poetry, his stories have a conversational feel and often deal with everyday events. "For me," Ortiz has observed, "there's never been a conscious moment without story."

About the Selection

Cultural conflict between ethnic groups can be as important as physical conflict. Native American peoples have frequently seen their cultural values under attack by Western religion, science, and technology. Sometimes it was Christian missionaries who wanted to convert them. Sometimes it was those who wanted to take mineral wealth from their sacred lands. Sometimes it was scientists who wanted to put the bones of their ancestors in museums. As you read "Men on the Moon," think about how an old Acoma Indian reacts to one of America's proudest achievements, the moon landings. (The illustration shows uniformed Native American children at an Indian school in Oklahoma.)

I

Joselita brought her father, Faustin, the TV on Father's Day. She brought it over after Sunday mass[1] and she had her son hook up the antenna. She plugged the TV into the wall socket.

Faustin sat on a worn couch. He was covered with an old coat. He had worn that coat for twenty years.

It's ready. Turn it on and I'll adjust the antenna, Amarosho told his mother. The TV warmed up and then it flickered into dull light. It was snowing.[2] Amarosho tuned it a bit. It snowed less and then a picture formed.

Look, Naishtiya,[3] Joselita said. She touched her father's hand and pointed at the TV.

I'll turn the antenna a bit and you tell me when the picture is clear, Amarosho said. He climbed on the roof again.

After a while the picture turned clearer. It's better, his mother shouted. There was only the tiniest bit of snow falling.

That's about the best it can get I guess, Amarosho said. Maybe it'll clear up on the other channels. He turned the selector. It was clearer on another.

There were two men struggling with each other. Wrestling, Amarosho said. Do you want to watch wrestling? Two men are fighting, Nana. One of them is Apache Red. Chiseh tsah,[4] he told his grandfather.

The old man stirred. He had been staring intently into the TV. He wondered why there was so much snow at first. Now there were two men fighting. One of them was Chiseh, an Apache, and the other was a Mericano.[5] There were people shouting excitedly and clapping hands within the TV.

The two men backed away from each other once in a while and then they clenched. They wheeled mightily and suddenly one threw the other. The old man smiled. He wondered why they were fighting.

Something else showed on the TV screen. A bottle of wine was being poured. The old man liked the pouring sound and he moved his mouth. Someone was selling wine.

The two fighting men came back on the TV. They struggled with each other and after a while one of them didn't get up and then another person

---

[1] Sunday mass—Roman Catholic religious service.

[2] snowing—white specks that appear on a television screen as a result of weak reception.

[3] Naishtiya (nysh•TIH•yah)—Father. The Native American words in this story are from Keres, the language of the Acoma Pueblo people of which the author is a member.

[4] Chiseh tsah (chih•SEH•tsah)—He is Apache.

[5] Mericano—(white) American.

came and held up the hand of the Apache who was dancing around in a feathered headdress.

It's over, Amarosho announced. Apache Red won the fight, Nana.

The Chiseh won. Faustin watched the other one, a light-haired man who looked totally exhausted and angry with himself. He didn't like the Apache too much. He wanted them to fight again.

After a few moments something else appeared on the TV.

What is that? Faustin asked. There was an object with smoke coming from it. It was standing upright.

Men are going to the moon, Nana, his grandson said. It's Apollo.[6] It's going to fly three men to the moon.

That thing is going to fly to the moon?

Yes, Nana.

What is it called again?

Apollo, a spaceship rocket, Joselita told her father.

The Apollo spaceship stood on the ground emitting clouds of something that looked like smoke.

A man was talking, telling about the plans for the flight, what would happen, that it was almost time. Faustin could not understand the man very well because he didn't know many words in Mericano.

He must be talking about that thing flying in the air? he said.

Yes. It's about ready to fly away to the moon.

Faustin remembered that the evening before he had looked at the sky and seen that the moon was almost in the middle phase. He wondered if it was important that the men get to the moon.

Are those men looking for something on the moon? he asked his grandson.

They're trying to find out what's on the moon, Nana, what kind of dirt and rocks there are, to see if there's any life on the moon. The men are looking for knowledge, Amarosho told him.

Faustin wondered if the men had run out of places to look for knowledge on the earth. Do they know if they'll find knowledge? he asked.

They have some information already. They've gone before and come back. They're going again.

Did they bring any back?

They brought back some rocks.

Faustin wondered if the men had run out of places to look for knowledge on the earth.

---

[6] Apollo—Apollo 12, the second manned landing on the moon, which occurred on November 19, 1969.

Rocks. Faustin laughed quietly. The scientist men went to search for knowledge on the moon and they brought back rocks. He thought that perhaps Amarosho was joking with him. The grandson had gone to Indian School for a number of years and sometimes he would tell his grandfather some strange and funny things.

Fire. Faustin had wondered what made it fly.

The old man was suspicious. They joked around a lot. Rocks—you sure that's all they brought back?

That's right, Nana, only rocks and some dirt and pictures they made of what it looks like on the moon.

The TV picture was filled with the rocket, close up now. Men were sitting and moving around by some machinery and the voice had become more urgent. The old man watched the activity in the picture intently but with a slight smile on his face.

Suddenly it became very quiet, and the voice was firm and commanding and curiously pleading. Ten, nine, eight, seven, six, five, four, three, two, liftoff. The white smoke became furious and a muted rumble shook through the TV. The rocket was trembling and the voice was trembling.

It was really happening, the old man marvelled. Somewhere inside of that cylinder with a point at its top and long slender wings were three men who were flying to the moon.

The rocket rose from the ground. There were enormous clouds of smoke and the picture shook. Even the old man became tense and he grasped the edge of the couch. The rocket spaceship rose and rose.

There's fire coming out of the rocket, Amarosho explained. That's what makes it go.

Fire. Faustin had wondered what made it fly. He'd seen pictures of other flying machines. They had long wings and someone had explained to him that there was machinery inside which spun metal blades which made them fly. He had wondered what made this thing fly. He hoped his grandson wasn't joking him.

After a while there was nothing but the sky. The rocket Apollo had disappeared. It hadn't taken very long and the voice from the TV wasn't excited anymore. In fact the voice was very calm and almost bored.

I have to go now, Naishtiya, Joselita told her father. I have things to do.

Me, too, Amarosho said.

Wait, the old man said, wait. What shall I do with this thing. What is it you call it?

TV, his daughter said. You watch it. You turn it on and you watch it.

I mean how do you stop it. Does it stop like the radio, like the mahkina?[7] It stops?

This way, Nana, Amarosho said and showed his grandfather. He turned the dial and the picture went away. He turned the dial again and the picture flickered on again. Were you afraid this one-eye would be looking at you all the time? Amarosho laughed and gently patted the old man's shoulder.

Faustin was relieved. Joselita and her son left. He watched the TV for a while. A lot of activity was going on, a lot of men were moving among machinery, and a couple of men were talking. And then it showed the rocket again.

He watched it rise and fly away again. It disappeared again. There was nothing but the sky. He turned the dial and the picture died away. He turned it on and the picture came on again. He turned it off. He went outside and to a fence a distance from his home. When he finished he studied the sky for a while.

II

That night, he dreamed.

Flintwing Boy[8] was watching a Skquuyuh[9] mahkina come down a hill. The mahkina made a humming noise. It was walking. It shone in the sunlight. Flintwing Boy moved to a better position to see. The mahkina kept on moving. It was moving towards him.

The Skquuyuh mahkina drew closer. Its metal legs stepped upon trees and crushed growing flowers and grass. A deer bounded away frightened. Tshushki[10] came running to Flintwing Boy.

Anaweh,[11] he cried, trying to catch his breath.

The coyote was staring at the thing which was coming towards them. There was wild fear in his eyes.

What is that, Anaweh? What is that thing? he gasped.

It looks like a mahkina, but I've never seen one like it before. It must be some kind of Skquuyuh mahkina.

Where did it come from?

---

[7] makhina (MAH•kih•nah)—machine (with the added sense of something large).

[8] Flintwing Boy—hero from Pueblo oral tradition.

[9] Skquuyuh (SKOO•yuh)—giant, powerful (with the added sense of monstrous, evil).

[10] Tshushki (TSUSH•kih)—Coyote, hero from Pueblo oral tradition.

[11] Anaweh (AH•nah•weh)—Nephew.

Men on the Moon   327

◀ *Osage with Vincent Van Gogh* is by Native American artist T. C. Cannon (1946–1978).

I'm not sure yet, Anaweh, Flintwing Boy said. When he saw that Tshushki was trembling with fear, he said gently, Sit down, Anaweh. Rest yourself. We'll find out soon enough.

The Skquuyuh mahkina was undeterred.[12] It walked over and through everything. It splashed through a stream of clear water. The water boiled and streaks of oil flowed downstream. It split a juniper tree in half with a terrible crash. It crushed a boulder into dust with a sound of heavy metal. Nothing stopped the Skquuyuh mahkina. It hummed.

Anaweh, Tshushki cried, what shall we do? What can we do?

Flintwing Boy reached into the bag at his side. He took out an object. It was a flint arrowhead. He took out some cornfood.

---

[12] undeterred—not slowed or stopped.

Come over here, Anaweh. Come over here. Be calm, he motioned to the frightened coyote. He touched the coyote in several places of his body with the arrowhead and put cornfood in the palm of his hand.

This way, Flintwing Boy said and closed Tshushki's fingers over the cornfood gently. And they faced east. Flintwing Boy said, We humble ourselves again. We look in your direction for guidance. We ask for your protection. We humble our poor bodies and spirits because only you are the power and the source and the knowledge. Help us then—that is all we ask.

They breathed on the cornfood and took in the breath of all directions and gave the cornfood unto the ground.

Now the ground trembled with the awesome power of the Skquuyuh mahkina. Its humming vibrated against everything. Flintwing Boy reached behind him and took several arrows from his quiver.[13] He inspected them carefully and without any rush he fit one to his bowstring.

And now, Anaweh, you must go and tell everyone. Describe what you have seen. The people must talk among themselves and decide what it is about and what they will do. You must hurry but you must not alarm the people. Tell them I am here to meet it. I will give them my report when I find out.

Coyote turned and began to run. He stopped several yards away. Hahtrudzaimeh,[14] he called. Like a man of courage, Anaweh, like a man.

The old man stirred in his sleep. A dog was barking. He awoke and got out of his bed and went outside. The moon was past the midpoint and it would be morning light in a few hours.

III

Later, the spaceship reached the moon.

Amarosho was with his grandfather. They watched a replay of two men walking on the moon.

So that's the men on the moon, Faustin said.

Yes, Nana, that's it.

There were two men inside of heavy clothing and equipment. The

---

[13] quiver—portable case for holding arrows.
[14] Hahtrudzaimeh (HAH•tru•DZY•meh)—(act) with courage.

TV picture showed a closeup of one of them and indeed there was a man's face inside of glass. The face moved its mouth and smiled and spoke but the voice seemed to be separate from the face.

It must be cold. They have heavy clothing on, Faustin said.

It's supposed to be very cold and very hot. They wear the clothes and other things for protection from the cold and heat, Amarosho said.

The men on the moon were moving slowly. One of them skipped and he floated alongside the other.

The old man wondered if they were underwater. They seem to be able to float, he said.

> The old man wondered if they were underwater.

The information I have heard is that a man weighs less than he does on earth, Amarosho said to his grandfather. Much less, and he floats.

And there is no air on the moon for them to breathe, so those boxes on their backs contain air for them to breathe.

He weighs less, the old man wondered, and there is no air except for the boxes on their backs. He looked at Amarosho but his grandson didn't seem to be joking with him.

The land on the moon looked very dry. It looked like it had not rained for a long, long time. There were no trees, no plants, no grass. Nothing but dirt and rocks, a desert.

Amarosho had told him that men on earth—the scientists—believed there was no life on the moon. Yet those men were trying to find knowledge on the moon. He wondered perhaps they had special tools with which they could find knowledge even if they believed there was no life on the moon desert.

The mahkina sat on the desert. It didn't make a sound. Its metal feet were planted flat on the ground. It looked somewhat awkward. Faustin searched vainly around the mahkina but there didn't seem to be anything except the dry land on the TV. He couldn't figure out the mahkina. He wasn't sure whether it could move and could cause fear. He didn't want to ask his grandson that question.

After a while, one of the bulky men was digging in the ground. He carried a long thin hoe with which he scooped dirt and put it into a container. He did this for a while.

Is he going to bring the dirt back to earth too? Faustin asked.

I think he is, Nana, Amarosho said. Maybe he'll get some rocks too. Watch.

Indeed several minutes later the man lumbered over to a pile of rocks and gathered several handsize ones. He held them out proudly. They looked just like rocks from around anyplace. The voice from the TV seemed to be excited about the rocks.

They will study the rocks too for knowledge?

Yes, Nana.

What will they use the knowledge for, Nana?

They say they will use it to better mankind, Nana. I've heard that. And to learn more about the universe we live in. Also some of them say that the knowledge will be useful in finding out where everything began and how everything was made.

The Mimbres people of the American Southwest produced this bowl around 1000 A.D. Such bowls were often placed in graves after they were ritually "killed" by being pierced. ▶

Faustin smiled at his grandson. He said, You are telling me the true facts aren't you?

Why yes, Nana. That's what they say. I'm not just making it up, Amarosho said.

Well then—do they say why they need to know where everything began? Hasn't anyone ever told them?

I think other people have tried to tell them but they want to find out for themselves and also I think they claim they don't know enough and need to know more and for certain, Amarosho said.

> You are telling me the true facts aren't you?

The man in the bulky suit had a small pickaxe in his hand. He was striking at a boulder. The breathing of the man could clearly be heard. He seemed to be working very hard and was very tired.

Faustin had once watched a crew of Mericano drilling for water. They had brought a tall mahkina with a loud motor. The mahkina would raise a limb at its center to its very top and then drop it with a heavy and loud metal clang. The mahkina and its men sat at one spot for several days and finally they found water.

The water had bubbled out weakly, gray-looking and didn't look drinkable at all. And then they lowered the mahkina, put their equipment away and drove away. The water stopped flowing.

After a couple of days he went and checked out the place. There was nothing there except a pile of gray dirt and an indentation in the ground. The ground was already dry and there were dark spots of oil-soaked dirt.

He decided to tell Amarosho about the dream he had.

After the old man finished, Amarosho said, Old man, you're telling me the truth now? You know that you have become somewhat of a liar. He was teasing his grandfather.

Yes, Nana. I have told you the truth as it occurred to me that night. Everything happened like that except that I might not have recalled everything about it.

That's some story, Nana, but it's a dream.

It's a dream but it's the truth, Faustin said.

I believe you, Nana, his grandson said.

Questions to Consider

Responding

1. Has any member of your family ever been puzzled or confused by his or her first experience of new technology? What did you do to help them?

Analyzing

2. Why do you think Faustin suspects his grandson might be teasing him when he tells him the astronauts brought back rocks from the moon?

3. What do you think is the meaning of Faustin's dream?

4. Faustin's grandson tells him that the purpose of the moon landing was to find out "where everything began and how everything was made." The old man asks him, "Hasn't anyone ever told them?" What do you think he means?

Extending

5. Where in today's society do you see **cultural conflict** between traditional values and modern technology?

Literature Connection

Characterization consists of all the techniques writers use to create and develop characters. There are four basic methods of developing a character: (1) physical description of the character; (2) presenting the character's thoughts, speech, and actions; (3) presenting the ways in which other characters think about, speak to, and interact with the character; (4) direct comments about the character's nature.

1. What are the principal ways in which the writer develops the character of Faustin?

2. What words would you use to sum up the character of the old man?

Activities

Writing a Letter

Imagine you are Faustin's grandson Amarosho and you are writing to someone your own age. Describe the episode with your grandfather and the television set.

Drawing What a Character Sees

Draw a picture of the moon landing as you think it might appear to Faustin on the television screen. Keep the old man's comments and cultural background in mind as you depict his view of the moon's surface, the lunar landing vehicle, the astronauts, and so on.

Part Six

Struggles

From the time that Native Americans and Europeans encountered one another, the history of the Americas has been marked by struggles between different ethnic groups. As new groups of immigrants arrived, they also were forced to struggle to establish themselves.

◀ Elliott Pinckney's mural *Visions and Motion* includes portraits of two heroes of ethnic struggle in the United States, Malcolm X and Cesar Chavez.

I WILL FIGHT NO MORE
FOREVER

*by Chief Joseph
of the Nez Perce*

About the Author

Chief Joseph (1840-1904) of the Nez Perce (nez purs) was known by his people as Hin-mah-too-yah-lat-kekt, or "Thunder Rolling Down the Mountain." The Nez Perce were a Native American people of the Northwest. They had years of peaceful relations with the U.S. government. Then gold was discovered on Nez Perce land. In 1877, the government broke its treaty with the tribe and ordered them to move onto a reservation. Chief Joseph tried to lead a peaceful march to the reservation, but war broke out. What followed was a brilliant military retreat by the Nez Perce. Chief Joseph's surrender speech immortalized him in American popular culture. The Nez Perce were split up and placed on reservations in Idaho and Washington.

About the Selections

*From the time of the European arrival in the Western Hemisphere, Native Americans have been forced to struggle to preserve their way of life. The history of many other ethnic groups, such as African Americans, has also been marked by a fierce struggle to survive. This **resistance to oppression** has been through organized group actions and through individual acts. Some resistance has been violent, some nonviolent. As you read "I Will Fight No More Forever" and "If We Must Die" (on page 338), think about the strength required for such struggles.*

I am tired of fighting. Our chiefs are killed. Looking Glass is dead. Toohulhulsote is dead. The old men are all dead. It is the young men who say yes or no. He who led the young men is dead.

It is cold and we have no blankets. The little children are freezing to death. My people, some of them, have run away to the hills and have no blankets, no food. No one knows where they are—perhaps freezing to death. I want to have time to look for my children and see how many I can find. Maybe I shall find them among the dead.

Hear me, my chiefs. I am tired. My heart is sick and sad. From where the sun now stands, I will fight no more forever.

▲
Chief Joseph Rides to Surrender was painted by American artist Howard Terpning (1927–   ).

IF WE MUST DIE

by Claude McKay

About the Author

African-American writer Claude McKay (1890–1948) was born in Jamaica. He moved to the United States at age 23. The racism McKay faced as a black immigrant led him to write about that problem and about black identity. Many of his poems, essays, and novels focused on life in New York's African-American community, Harlem, where he lived for many years. McKay became one of major figures of the Harlem Renaissance of the 1920s. He influenced many younger poets, including Langston Hughes. His autobiography, A Long Way from Home (1937), and a study of Harlem were his last works.

If we must die, let it not be like hogs
Hunted and penned in an inglorious[1]
   spot,
While round us bark the mad and
   hungry dogs,
Making their mock at our accursed
   lot.
If we must die, O let us nobly die,
So that our precious blood may not be
   shed
In vain; then even the monsters we
   defy
Shall be constrained to honor us
   though dead!

O kinsmen! we must meet the
   common foe!
Though far outnumbered let us show
   us brave,
And for their thousand blows deal
   one deathblow!
What though before us lies the open
   grave?
Like men we'll face the murderous,
   cowardly pack,
Pressed to the wall, dying, but
   fighting back!

---

[1] inglorious—disgraceful.

Responding

1. What would be the hardest part of fighting back against injustice? Would it be finding courage to resist or keeping up the fight? Would it be knowing when to quit or fighting on when you couldn't win?

Analyzing

2. What is the main feeling inspired by "I Will Fight No More Forever"?

3. What does Chief Joseph's speech tell you about the sacrifices involved in resistance to oppression?

4. What do you think is the main feeling inspired by "If We Must Die"?

5. How does the message of "If We Must Die" differ from that of "I Will Fight No More Forever"?

Extending

6. Why does resistance to oppression often reveal the strength of the oppressed and the weakness of the oppressors?

A writer may make use of any of various sound devices, techniques used to emphasize important ideas and feelings and to create memorable sound effects. Repetition and rhythm are two of the most common and effective sound devices, especially in poetry. Repetition is the use of any element of language—a word, a phrase, a sound, a grammatical structure—more than once. Rhythm is a pattern of stressed (emphasized) and unstressed syllables in poetry. A consistent pattern of stressed syllables creates a beat.

1. What sound device is used in the opening words of Chief Joseph's speech?

2. What effect does the use of this sound device have on the feeling created by the speech?

3. How does the marching rhythm created in "If We Must Die" contribute to the poem's meaning?

Activities

Writing Historical Fiction

Research the history of Chief's Joseph's war of resistance. Then create a brief fictional narrative of the Nez Perce struggle. Tell your story from the point of view of an imaginary first-person narrator, either one of the Nez Perce or one of the American soldiers who were pursuing them. Illustrate your story with a map showing the route of the Nez Perce retreat.

Performing a Speech

Using the Internet and library resources, locate a speech by someone that addresses resistance to oppression. Read the speech, listening for sound devices that make it effective. Then practice reading the speech aloud. Perform the speech for your class.

Harriet Tubman:

Conductor on the Underground Railroad

BY ANN PETRY

About the Author

Ann Petry (1908–1997) was born in Old Saybrook, Connecticut. She began her career as a pharmacist who wrote for newspapers and magazines. Petry became a noted novelist with The Street *(1946), which was about life in Harlem. Her short story "Like a Winding Sheet" was named Best American Story in 1946. Petry went on to write many more novels, short stories, and children's books. All were about African-American life. Several were about famous African Americans in history, such as Harriet Tubman.*

About the Selection

The **Underground Railroad** *was a secret network of houses and other places used to help slaves escape from the oppression of slavery in the South before the Civil War. The routes ran through various northern states and into Canada. At night, the slaves traveled from one "station" to the next. "Conductors" guided them—providing food, shelter, and hope. Approximately 100,000 African Americans escaped on the Underground Railroad. Harriet Tubman, the most famous conductor, guided more than 300 former slaves on 19 trips to freedom. As you read "Harriet Tubman: Conductor on the Underground Railroad," reflect on what might motivate one person to risk her life for others.*

Along the eastern shore of Maryland, in Dorchester County, in Caroline County, the masters kept hearing whispers about the man named Moses, who was running off slaves. At first they did not believe in his existence. The stories about him were fantastic, unbelievable. Yet they watched for him. They offered rewards for his capture.

They never saw him. Now and then they heard whispered rumors to the effect that he was in the neighborhood. The woods were searched. The roads were watched. There was never anything to indicate his whereabouts. But a few days afterward, a goodly number of slaves would be gone from the plantation. Neither the master nor the overseer had heard or seen anything unusual in the quarter.[1] Sometimes one or the other would vaguely remember having heard a whippoorwill call somewhere in the woods, close by, late at night. Though it was the wrong season for whippoorwills.

Sometimes the masters thought they had heard the cry of a hoot owl, repeated, and would remember having thought that the intervals between the low, moaning cry were wrong, that it had been repeated four times in succession instead of three. There was never anything more than that to suggest that all was not well in the quarter. Yet when morning came, they invariably discovered that a group of the finest slaves had taken to their heels.

Unfortunately, the discovery was almost always made on a Sunday. Thus a whole day was lost before the machinery of pursuit could be set in motion. The posters offering rewards for the fugitives could not be printed until Monday. The men who made a living hunting for runaway slaves were out of reach, off in the woods with their dogs and their guns, in pursuit of four-footed game, or they were in camp meetings saying their prayers with their wives and families beside them.

Harriet Tubman could have told them that there was far more involved in this matter of running off slaves than signaling the would-be runaways by imitating the call of a whippoorwill or a hoot owl, far more involved than a matter of waiting for a clear night when the North Star was visible.

In December 1851, when she started out with the band of fugitives that she planned to take to Canada, she had been in the vicinity of the plantation for days, planning the trip, carefully selecting the slaves that she would take with her.

---

[1] quarter—area on a plantation where the slaves lived.

She had announced her arrival in the quarter by singing the forbidden spiritual—"Go down, Moses, 'way down to Egypt Land"[2]—singing it softly outside the door of a slave cabin late at night. The husky voice was beautiful even when it was barely more than a murmur borne on the wind.

Once she had made her presence known, word of her coming spread from cabin to cabin. The slaves whispered to each other, ear to mouth, mouth to ear, "Moses is here." "Moses has come." "Get ready. Moses is back again." The ones who had agreed to go north with her put ashcake and salt herring in an old bandanna, hastily tied it into a bundle, and then waited patiently for the signal that meant it was time to start.

> The slaves whispered to each other, ear to mouth, mouth to ear, "Moses is here."

There were eleven in this party, including one of her brothers and his wife. It was the largest group that she had ever conducted, but she was determined that more and more slaves should know what freedom was like.

She had to take them all the way to Canada. The Fugitive Slave Law[3] was no longer a great many incomprehensible[4] words down on the country's law books. The new law had become a reality. It was Thomas Sims, a boy, picked up on the streets of Boston at night and shipped back to Georgia. It was Jerry and Shadrach, arrested and jailed with no warning.

She had never been in Canada. The route beyond Philadelphia was strange to her. But she could not let the runaways who accompanied her know this. As they walked along, she told them stories of her own first flight; she kept painting vivid[5] word pictures of what it would be like to be free.

But there were so many of them this time. She knew moments of doubt when she was half-afraid and kept looking back over her shoulder, imagining that she heard the sound of pursuit. They would certainly be pursued. Eleven of them. Eleven thousand dollars' worth of flesh and bone and muscle that belonged to Maryland planters. If they were caught, the eleven runaways would be whipped and sold south, but she—she would probably be hanged.

---

[2] "Go Down . . . Land"—a traditional slave song about Moses leading the Israelites out of Egypt.

[3] Fugitive Slave Law—law passed in 1850 that allowed slave owners to recover escaped slaves even if they had reached free states.

[4] incomprehensible—difficult or impossible to understand.

[5] vivid—evoking lifelike images in the mind.

▲

This portrait of Harriet Tubman shows both the hardships of her life and the strength that helped her endure them.

They tried to sleep during the day, but they never could wholly relax into sleep. She could tell by the positions they assumed, by their restless movements. And they walked at night. Their progress was slow. It took them three nights of walking to reach the first stop. She had told them about the place where they would stay, promising warmth and good food, holding these things out to them as an incentive to keep going.

When she knocked on the door of a farmhouse, a place where she and her parties of runaways had always been welcome, always been given shelter and plenty to eat, there was no answer. She knocked again, softly. A voice from within said, "Who is it?" There was fear in the voice.

She knew instantly from the sound of the voice that there was something wrong. She said, "A friend with friends," the password on the Underground Railroad.

The door opened, slowly. The man who stood in the doorway looked at her coldly, looked with unconcealed astonishment and fear at the eleven **disheveled**[6] runaways who were standing near her. Then he shouted, "Too many, too many. It's not safe. My place was searched last week. It's not safe!" and slammed the door in her face.

She turned away from the house, frowning. She had promised her passengers food and rest and warmth, and instead of that there would be hunger and cold and more walking over the frozen ground. Somehow she would have to **instill**[7] courage into these eleven people, most of them strangers,

---

[6] **disheveled** (dih•SHEHV•uhld)—untidy.
[7] **instill**—implant; gradually introduce.

would have to feed them on hope and bright dreams of freedom instead of the fried pork and corn bread and milk she had promised them.

They stumbled along behind her, half-dead for sleep, and she urged them on, though she was as tired and as discouraged as they were. She had never been in Canada, but she kept painting wondrous word pictures of what it would be like. She managed to **dispel**[8] their fear of pursuit so that they would not become hysterical, panic-stricken. Then she had to bring some of the fear back so that they would stay awake and keep walking though they drooped with sleep.

> She had never been in Canada, but she kept painting wondrous word pictures of what it would be like.

Yet during the day, when they lay down deep in a thicket, they never really slept, because if a twig snapped or the wind sighed in the branches of a pine tree, they jumped to their feet, afraid of their own shadows, shivering and shaking. It was very cold, but they dared not make fires because someone would see the smoke and wonder about it.

She kept thinking, Eleven of them. Eleven thousand dollars' worth of slaves. And she had to take them all the way to Canada. Sometimes she told them about Thomas Garrett, in Wilmington. She said he was their friend even though he did not know them. He was the friend of all fugitives. He called them God's poor. He was a Quaker[9] and his speech was a little different from that of other people. His clothing was different, too. He wore the wide-brimmed hat that the Quakers wear.

She said that he had thick white hair, soft, almost like a baby's, and the kindest eyes she had ever seen. He was a big man and strong, but he had never used his strength to harm anyone, always to help people. He would give all of them a new pair of shoes. Everybody. He always did. Once they reached his house in Wilmington, they would be safe. He would see to it that they were.

She described the house where he lived, told them about the store where he sold shoes. She said he kept a pail of milk and a loaf of bread in the drawer of his desk so that he would have food

---

[8] **dispel**—rid one's mind of; drive away.

[9] Quaker—member of a religious group known as the Society of Friends, whose guiding principle since the 1600s had been that each person, regardless of race or gender, is equal before God.

ready at hand for any of God's poor who should suddenly appear before him, fainting with hunger. There was a hidden room in the store. A whole wall swung open, and behind it was a room where he could hide fugitives. On the wall there were shelves filled with small boxes—boxes of shoes—so that you would never guess that the wall actually opened.

While she talked, she kept watching them. They did not believe her. She could tell by their expressions. They were thinking, New shoes, Thomas Garrett, Quaker, Wilmington—what foolishness was this? Who knew if she told the truth? Where was she taking them anyway?

That night they reached the next stop—a farm that belonged to a German. She made the runaways take shelter behind trees at the edge of the fields before she knocked at the door. She hesitated before she approached the door, thinking, suppose that he, too, should refuse shelter, suppose— Then she thought, Lord, I'm going to steady on to You, and You've got to see me through—and knocked softly.

She heard the familiar **guttural**[10] voice say, "Who's there?"

She answered quickly, "A friend with friends."

He opened the door and greeted her warmly. "How many this time?" he asked.

"Eleven," she said and waited, doubting, wondering.

He said, "Good. Bring them in."

He and his wife fed them in the lamp-lit kitchen, their faces glowing as they offered food and more food, urging them to eat, saying there was plenty for everybody, have more milk, have more bread, have more meat.

They spent the night in the warm kitchen. They really slept, all that night and until dusk the next day. When they left, it was with reluctance. They had all been warm and safe and well-fed. It was hard to exchange the security offered by that clean, warm kitchen for the darkness and the cold of a December night.

Harriet had found it hard to leave the warmth and friendliness, too. But she urged them on. For a while, as they walked, they seemed to carry in them a measure of contentment; some of the serenity and the cleanliness of that big, warm kitchen lingered on inside them. But as they walked farther and farther away from

---

[10] **guttural**—having a harsh, grating quality like certain sounds produced in the back of the throat.

the warmth and the light, the cold and the darkness entered into them. They fell silent, **sullen**,[11] suspicious. She waited for the moment when some one of them would turn **mutinous**.[12] It did not happen that night.

Two nights later she was aware that the feet behind her were moving slower and slower. She heard the irritability in their voices, knew that soon someone would refuse to go on.

She started talking about William Still and the Philadelphia Vigilance Committee.[13] No one commented. No one asked any questions. She told them the story of William and Ellen Craft and how they escaped from Georgia. Ellen was so fair that she looked as though she were white, and so she dressed up in a man's clothing, and she looked like a wealthy young planter. Her husband, William, who was dark, played the role of her slave.

[11] **sullen**—sulky; silently resentful.

[12] **mutinous** (MYOOT•n-uhs)—prepared to rebel against a leader.

[13] Philadelphia Vigilance Committee—organization set up before the Civil War to raise money to help escaping slaves.

the cold and the darkness

entered into them

◀ The tracks of a fugitive slave lead toward the North Star in this square from the Underground Railroad Quilt, which was made by women in Ohio.

Thus they traveled from Macon, Georgia, to Philadelphia, riding on the trains, staying at the finest hotels. Ellen pretended to be very ill—her right arm was in a sling, and her right hand was bandaged, because she was supposed to have rheumatism. Thus she avoided having to sign the register at the hotels, for she could not read or write. They finally arrived safely in Philadelphia and then went on to Boston.

No one said anything. Not one of them seemed to have heard her.

She told them about Frederick Douglass,[14] the most famous of the escaped slaves, of his **eloquence**,[15] of his magnificent appearance. Then she told them of her own first, **vain**[16] effort at running away, evoking the memory of that miserable life she had led as a child, reliving it for a moment in the telling.

But they had been tired too long, hungry too long, afraid too long, foot-sore too long. One of them suddenly cried out in despair, "Let me go back. It is better to be a slave than to suffer like this in order to be free."

She carried a gun with her on these trips. She had never used it—except as a threat. Now as she aimed it, she experienced a feeling of guilt, remembering that time, years ago, when she had prayed for the death of Edward Brodas, the Master, and then not too

long afterward had heard that great wailing cry that came from the throats of the field hands, and knew from the sound that the Master was dead.

One of the runaways said, again, "Let me go back. Let me go back," and stood still and then turned around and said, over his shoulder, "I am going back."

> She carried a gun with her on these trips. She had never used it—except as a threat.

She lifted the gun, aimed it at the despairing slave. She said, "Go on with us or die." The husky, low-pitched voice was grim.

He hesitated for a moment, and then he joined the others. They started walking again. She tried to explain to them why none of them could go back to the plantation. If a runaway returned, he would turn traitor; the master and the overseer would force him to turn traitor. The returned slave would disclose the stopping places, the hiding places, the corn stacks they had used with the full knowledge of the owner of the farm, the name of the

---

[14] Frederick Douglass—(1817–1895) African-American leader, a former slave, who worked to end slavery.

[15] **eloquence** (EHL•uh•kwehns)—skill and power in speaking.

[16] **vain**—failed; fruitless.

German farmer who had fed them and sheltered them. These people who had risked their own security to help runaways would be ruined, fined, imprisoned.

She said, "We got to go free or die. And freedom's not bought with dust."

This time she told them about the long agony of the Middle Passage[17] on the old slave ships, about the black horror of the holds, about the chains and the whips. They too knew these stories. But she wanted to remind them of the long, hard way they had come, about the long, hard way they had yet to go. She told them about Thomas Sims, the boy picked up on the streets of Boston and sent back to Georgia. She said when they got him back to Savannah, got him in prison there, they whipped him until a doctor who was standing by watching said, "You will kill him if you strike him again!" His master said, "Let him die!"

Thus she forced them to go on. Sometimes she thought she had become nothing but a voice in the darkness, **cajoling**,[18] urging, threatening. Sometimes she told them things to make them laugh; sometimes she sang to them and heard the eleven voices behind her blending softly with hers, and then she knew that for the moment all was well with them.

She gave the impression of being a short, muscular, **indomitable**[19] woman who could never be defeated. Yet at any moment she was liable to be seized by one of those curious fits of sleep,[20] which might last for a few minutes or for hours.

Even on this trip, she suddenly fell asleep in the woods. The runaways, ragged, dirty, hungry, cold, did not steal the gun, as they might have, and set off by themselves or turn back. They sat on the ground near her and waited patiently until she awakened. They come to trust her implicitly, totally. They, too, had come to believe her repeated statement, "We got to go free or die." She was leading them into freedom, and so they waited until she was ready to go on.

Finally, they reached Thomas Garrett's house in Wilmington, Delaware. Just as Harriet had promised, Garrett gave them all new shoes and provided carriages to take them on to the next stop.

---

[17] Middle Passage—Atlantic sea route along which Africans were brought to North and South America to become slaves.

[18] **cajoling** (kuh•JOHL•ihng)—urging gently; coaxing.

[19] **indomitable** (ihn•DAHM•ih•tuh•buhl)—unstoppable; unable to be conquered.

[20] curious fits of sleep—spells of dizziness or unconsciousness experienced by Harriet Tubman since being hit on the head as a young woman.

▲

In the 1850s, this African-American family fled slavery in the South for freedom in the Canadian province of Ontario.

By slow stages they reached Philadelphia, where William Still hastily recorded their names and the plantations whence they had come and something of the life they had led in slavery. Then he carefully hid what he had written, for fear it might be discovered. In 1872 he published this record in book form and called it *The Underground Railroad*. In the foreword to his book he said: "While I knew the danger of keeping strict records, and while I did not then dream that in my day slavery would be blotted out,

or that the time would come when I could publish these records, it used to afford me great satisfaction to take them down, fresh from the lips of fugitives on the way to freedom, and to preserve them as they had given them."

William Still, who was familiar with all the station stops on the Underground Railroad, supplied Harriet with money and sent her and her eleven fugitives on to Burlington, New Jersey.

Harriet felt safer now, though there were danger spots ahead. But the biggest part of her job was over. As they went farther and farther north, it grew colder; she was aware of the wind on the Jersey ferry and aware of the cold damp in New York. From New York they went on to Syracuse, where the temperature was even lower.

In Syracuse she met the Reverend J. W. Loguen, known as "Jarm" Loguen. This was the beginning, of a lifelong friendship. Both Harriet and Jarm Loguen were to become friends and supporters of Old John Brown.[21]

From Syracuse they went north again, into a colder, snowier city—

---

[21] John Brown—(1800–1859) antislavery leader executed for leading a raid in 1859 on the arsenal at Harpers Ferry, Virginia (now West Virginia), in the hopes of arming a slave revolt.

Rochester. Here they almost certainly stayed with Frederick Douglass, for he wrote in his autobiography:

"On one occasion I had eleven fugitives at the same time under my roof, and it was necessary for them to remain with me until I could collect sufficient money to get them to Canada. It was the largest number I ever had at any one time, and I had some difficulty in providing so many with food and shelter, but, as may well be imagined, they were not very **fastidious**[22] in either direction, and were well content with very plain food, and a strip of carpet on the floor for a bed, or a place on the straw in the barn loft."

Late in December 1851, Harriet arrived in St. Catharines, Canada West (now Ontario), with the eleven fugitives. It had taken almost a month to complete this journey; most of the time had been spent getting out of Maryland.

That first winter in St. Catharines was a terrible one. Canada was a strange, frozen land, snow everywhere, ice everywhere, and a bone-biting cold the like of which none of them had ever experienced before. Harriet rented a small frame house in the town and set to work to make a home. The fugitives boarded with her. They worked in the forests, felling trees, and so did she. Sometimes she took other jobs, cooking or cleaning house for people in the town. She cheered on these newly arrived fugitives, working herself, finding work for them, praying for them, sometimes begging for them.

Often she found herself thinking of the beauty of Maryland, the mellowness of the soil, the richness of the plant life there. The climate itself made for an ease of living that could never be duplicated in this bleak, barren countryside.

In spite of the severe cold, the hard work, she came to love St. Catharines and the other towns and cities in Canada where black men lived. She discovered that freedom meant more than the right to change jobs at will, more than the right to keep the money that one earned. It was the right to vote and to sit on juries. It was the right to be elected to office. In Canada there were black men who were county officials and members of school boards. St. Catharines had a large colony of ex-slaves, and they owned their own homes, kept them neat and clean and

---

[22] **fastidious** (fa•STIHD•ee•uhs)—difficult to please.

in good repair. They lived in whatever part of town they chose and sent their children to the schools.

When spring came, she decided that she would make this small Canadian city her home—as much as any place could be said to be home to a woman who traveled from Canada to the Eastern Shore of Maryland as often as she did.

In the spring of 1852, she went back to Cape May, New Jersey. She spent the summer there, cooking in a hotel. That fall she returned, as usual, to Dorchester County and brought out nine more slaves, conducting them all the way to St. Catharines, in Canada West, to the bone-biting cold, the snow-covered forests—and freedom.

She continued to live in this fashion, spending the winter in Canada and the spring and summer working in Cape May, New Jersey, or in Philadelphia. She made two trips a year into slave territory, one in the fall and another in the spring. She now had a definite, crystallized purpose, and in carrying it out, her life fell into a pattern which remained unchanged for the next six years.

Harriet Tubman, a mural painted in 1931 by African-American artist Aaron Douglas, shows her as a heroic figure breaking the chains of slavery.

▼

Responding

1. Have you ever been led by a strong person through difficult personal struggles? How did you feel about that person along the way?

Analyzing

2. What do you think was Harriet Tubman's primary motivation in risking her life by serving as a conductor on the **Underground Railroad**?

3. Why was Harriet Tubman's constant "cajoling, urging, and threatening" of the escaping slaves necessary?

4. How was Harriet Tubman like Moses?

5. What different types of people seem to have been associated with the Underground Railroad? What do you think motivated them?

6. What challenges and rewards did the escaped slaves find in their new life in Canada?

Extending

7. Where do you see opportunities today for a heroic leader such as Harriet Tubman?

The point of view of a story is the perspective from which the story is told. If a story is told from a first-person point of view, the narrator is a character in the story. The author uses first-person pronouns, such as I, me, and we. In a story told from the third-person point of view, the narrator is not a character. The author uses third-person pronouns such as he, she, and it.

1. What is the basic point of view used in "Harriet Tubman"?

2. How does the narrator present Harriet Tubman's thoughts and feelings?

3. How would the feeling of the story be different if it were told from the point of view of one of the escaping slaves?

Writing About "Tough Love"

Harriet Tubman helped the escaping slaves she led by "cajoling, urging, threatening,"—in other words, by exercising what is sometimes called "tough love." Write about someone in your life who has helped you through a difficult experience with this combination of encouragement and discipline.

Researching the Antislavery Movement

With two other students, research the role of several notable Quakers in the antislavery cause. Using the Internet and library resources, find out about Quakers such as Lucretia Mott, John Woolman, and Anthony Benezet. Then present your information to the class.

THE BALLAD OF
Gregorio Cortez
ANONYMOUS

About the Author

"The Ballad of Gregorio Cortez" is a famous Mexican corrido, or Border ballad. The ballad exists in at least a dozen versions. The author of the original is unknown.

About the Selection

The Border Country is the region on either side of the Lower Rio Grande River, including parts of both Texas and Mexico. A folk song typical of this region is the corrido (koh•REE•doh), or Border ballad. In 1901, Gregorio Cortez (1875–1916), a Mexican-American cowhand, was convicted of murdering a sheriff in Texas. Cortez became one of the most famous of the **Border ballad heroes.** *Américo Paredes studied both the history and the legend of Gregorio Cortez. Paredes observes that the outlaw heroes of the Border ballads lived by a code summed up in the phrase,"I will break before I bend." As you read "The Ballad of Gregorio Cortez," observe how this code is reflected in the hero's behavior.*

In the country of El Carmen[1]
Look what has occurred,
The Major Sheriff is dead,
And Román[2] lies gravely hurt.

The very next morning
When the people had arrived
They said to one another:
"No one knows who committed the
    crime."

They went about asking questions,
And after a three-hour quest,
They discovered that the wrongdoer
Had been Gregorio Cortez.

Now Cortez is outlawed,
In the whole state he is banned,
Let him be taken dead or alive,
Several have died at his hands.

Then said Gregorio Cortez,
With his pistol in his hand:
"I'm not sorry that I killed him,
My brother's death I would not stand."

Then said Gregorio Cortez,
With his soul all aflame:
"I'm not sorry that I killed him,
Self-defense is my rightful claim."

The Americans started coming,
Their horses seemed to soar,
Because they were all after
The three-thousand-dollar reward.

He set out for Gonzáles,[3]
Several sheriffs saw him go,
They decided not to follow
As they all feared him so.

The bloodhounds began coming,
His trail took him afar,
But tracking down Cortez
Was like following a star.

Then said Gregorio Cortez:
"Why bother scheming around,
When you can't even catch me
With all of your bloodhounds?"

Then said the Americans:
"If we catch him, what should we do?
If we fight him man to man,
The survivors will be few."

He left Brownsville[4] for the ranch,
Some three hundred in that locale
Succeeded in surrounding him,
But he bolted their corral.

---

[1] El Carmen—These events actually took place in
Karnes County, which is southeast of San Antonio.

[2] Román (roh•MAHN)—refers to Romaldo, the brother
of Gregorio Cortez, shot by Sheriff T. T. Morris.

[3] Gonzáles (gohn•ZAH•lehs)—town and county in
southern Texas.

[4] Brownsville—city in southern Texas on the border
between Texas and Mexico.

Gregorio Cortez (played by Edward James Olmos) and his brother Romaldo (played by Pep Serna) face the local sheriff in this scene from the 1983 film based on the life of the Chicano outlaw. ▶

He SHot another SHeriff Dead

Over by El Encinal,[5]
According to what is said,
They got into a gunfight,
And he shot another sheriff dead.

Then said Gregorio Cortez,
With his pistol in his hand:
"Don't run off, cowardly rangers,
From one sole Mexican man."

He struck out for Laredo,[6]
With no fear in his breast:
"Follow me, spineless rangers,
For I am Gregorio Cortez."

---

[5] El Encinal (ehl ehn•SIH•nahl)—Encinal, small town in southern Texas.
[6] Laredo (luh•RAY•doh)—city in southern Texas on the border between Texas and Mexico.

◀ Another scene from the film shows Cortez on the run from Texas Rangers.

Gregorio says to Juan
At the ranch they call Cypress:
"Tell me all the news,
For I am Gregorio Cortez."

Gregorio says to Juan:
"Now you just wait and see,
Go and call the sheriffs,
Tell them to arrest me."

When the sheriffs got there
Gregorio gave himself up to go:
"You can take me because I'm willing.
If you force me, the answer's no."

They've finally caught Cortez,
It's over now, they claim,
And his poor sad family
In their hearts must bear the pain.

With this I bid farewell
In the shade of a cypress,
And thus are sung the final notes
Of the ballad of Gregorio Cortez.

Responding

1. What do you find most admirable about Gregorio Cortez?

Analyzing

2. Why does Gregorio Cortez kill the Major Sheriff?

3. What motivates the Americans who pursue him?

4. What is the meaning of the code of the **Border ballad hero**: "I will break before I bend"?

5. How does Cortez reflect this code?

6. What do you think Gregorio Cortez represented to the Mexican Americans who first listened to this ballad?

Extending

7. Who are today's versions of outlaw heroes such as Gregorio Cortez? How are their deeds celebrated?

A *ballad* is a simple story poem that is intended to be sung or recited. Ballads are often about larger-than-life legendary heroes and extraordinary events. Ballads usually employ simple language and sound devices (page 339) such as repetition, rhythm, and rhyme. These techniques make them easy to memorize.

1. What details in the ballad make Cortez seem larger than life?

Look at the following lines:

> The bloodhounds began coming,
> His trail took them afar,
> But tracking down Cortez
> Was like following a star.

2. What sound devices are used here?

Activities

Writing a Ballad

Write a ballad about an outlaw who was rightfully or wrongfully pursued by the law. The outlaw may be a real person or someone fictional. Use the simple rhyme scheme of the ballad you just read: the second and fourth lines rhyme. You may wish to use the music of another ballad to help you establish the feeling for your ballad. If you like, write music for your ballad too.

Performing a Ballad

Find out the true story behind "The Ballad of Gregorio Cortez," which is also told in a book and a movie. Then locate the music to which it is sung. With accompaniment, perform the ballad for your classmates. Before your performance, tell them the facts about Gregorio Cortez.

I Learned to Sew

xxxxxxxx xxxxxxxx

by Mitsuye Yamada

About the Author

Mitsuye Yamada was born in Japan in 1923 while her parents were there for a visit. She grew up in Seattle, Washington. During World War II, more than 110,000 people of Japanese ancestry—two-thirds of them American citizens—were sent to internment camps in the western United States. Yamada and her family were sent to a camp in Idaho. Her first book of poems, Camp Notes (1976), dealt with her experiences there. One of the issues in her poetry has been the Japanese tradition that demands silence from women. In the following poem, a woman violates this tradition by telling her grandchild about the struggles she has endured in her life.

About the Selection

*One of the most familiar American stories is that of the **struggle of the immigrant** to succeed—or simply survive—in the United States. Many things contribute to this struggle. There is poverty, and the ill-health and ignorance that often result from it. There is the immigrant's homesickness for the world left behind. There is the discrimination immigrants often encounter in their new homes here. As you read "I Learned to Sew," note what contributes to the speaker's struggles in her adopted country and how she deals with her problems.*

How can I say this?
My child
My life is nothing
There is nothing to tell

My family in Japan was too poor
to send me to school
I learned to sew
always I worked to help my family
when I was seventeen years old
and no one made marriage offer
a friend in our village who was going
to Hawaii a picture bride[1]
said to me
Come with me.

I did not want to
my parents did not want me to
My picture was sent to a stranger
    anyway
a young man's photograph and letter
    came
I was already seventeen years old
I went to the island of Hawaii to marry
this photograph.

This man came to the boat
he was too shy to talk to me
the Immigration man said to him
Here
sign here for her

He walked away
The Immigration man came to me
Don't you have relatives in Hawaii?

I said
Yes I have that man who will marry me
He said
Go back to Japan on the next boat
I said
I will wait here for my man
The immigration man said
No
your man is not coming back
he told me he does not want you
he said you are too ugly for him
why don't you go back to Japan
on the next boat?
I said
No
I am not going back
I am staying here

Just
A minute
My child
Put that pen down
Do not write this
I never told this to anybody
Not even to my oldest son, your father
I now tell this story
To you first time in sixty years

---

[1] picture bride—woman who accepted an arranged
marriage with a Japanese or Korean immigrant. Couples
exchanged letters and photographs to get to know each
other. (See page 19.)

I sat at Immigration for a long time
people came and people went
I stayed
I could not see the sky
I could not see the sun
outside the window
I saw a seaweed forest
the crickets made scraping sounds
the geckos[2] went tuk tuk tuk
sometimes a gecko would come into
my room
but I was not afraid to talk to it
it came and it went as it pleased.

I was thinking about Urashima Taro[3]
you know the story?
Urashima disappeared into the sea
lived in the undersea world
married a beautiful princess
returned to his village
a very old man
I was thinking
I will leave this place
only when I am an old lady.

Pretty soon the Immigration man
came to me
We found your cousin
In two weeks a cousin I met once
in Japan came for me
I stayed with him and his wife until
my cousin found a job for me
I worked doing housework
I did this for one year.

My cousin found a husband for me
he was a merchant
we had a small store
and sold dry goods
my husband died after three sons
your father, my oldest son, was six
years old
I could not keep the store
I could not read
I could not write
the only thing I knew how to do was
sew.

I took the cloth from our store
sewed pants and undergarments
put the garments on a wooden cart
ombu[4] the baby on my back
we went from plantation to plantation
sold garments to the workers
I was their only store
sewed more garments at night
I did this for five years.

Your father grew up to love study and
books
my friends called him the professor
he was then eleven years old
I said to him you need a father
He said I want to go to college

---

[2] geckos—lizards.

[3] Urashima Taro (oo•rah•SHEE•mah TAH•roh)—hero of a famous Japanese folk tale. He lives in an undersea fairyland for what seems a brief time. But when he returns home, he finds hundreds of years have passed. He is suddenly transformed into an old man and dies.

[4] *ombu*—carry a child strapped to the back.

Sewing was one of the few jobs available to immigrant Japanese women. ▶

I said to him I will marry any man
    you say
I will marry any man
who will send you to college.

One day he came home and said
I went to a matchmaker[5] and
found a husband for you
he will marry a widow with three
    sons
will send them to college
he is a plantation foreman.

I married this man.

By and by my oldest son went away
to college in Honolulu
but my husband's boss told him
I need workers
your three sons must work
on my plantation like the others.
My husband said
No

He kept his word to my oldest son
and lost his job.

After that we had many hard times
I am nothing
know nothing
I only know how to sew
I now sew for my children and grand-
    children
I turn to the sun every day of my life
pray to Amaterasu Omikami[6]
for the health and
education of my children
for me that is enough

My child
Write this
There   take your pen
There   write it
Say that I am not going back
I am staying here

---

[5] matchmaker—person who arranges marriages.

[6] Amaterasu Omikami (ah•mah•tehr•AH•soo oh•mee•KAH•mee)—sun goddess and ruler of the universe in Japanese mythology.

Responding

1. Why is the speaker telling the story of her life to her grandchild?

Analyzing

2. The speaker says neither she nor her parents wanted her to go to Hawaii. Why do you think she went?

3. What factors contributed to the speaker's **struggles as an immigrant**? How did she deal with them?

4. At three points, the speaker directly addresses her grandchild. How do these three sections indicate a change in her feelings about the story she is telling?

5. How would you describe the speaker's voice, her distinctive manner of expression? What do you think her voice reveals about her personality?

Extending

6. How are the problems of immigrants to the United States today like and unlike those of the speaker?

An allusion *is a reference to a famous person, place, event, or work of literature. In "I Learned to Sew," the speaker makes an allusion to one of the most famous Japanese folk tales, "Urashima Taro":*

Urashima disappeared into the sea
lived in the undersea world
married a beautiful princess
returned to his village
a very old man

1. Why do you think the speaker introduces the folktale of Urashima Taro?

2. What does this allusion add to your impression of the speaker's personality?

3. What do you think this allusion adds to the overall impression created by the poem?

Activities

Writing a Dialogue

This poem is written as dramatic monologue, addressed by an old woman to her grandchild, who never speaks. Recreate the poem as a dialogue. What questions does the child ask of the grandmother? How does the child respond to the grandmother's account of her life?

Creating a Performance

Working with a group of classmates, dramatize this poem. Create a script and cast the various parts (the speaker, her grandchild, her parents, her "picture bridegroom," the immigration man, and so on). Work out the details of stage movement. Decide how you will handle the sound, lighting, setting, costumes, make-up, and props. Perform the play for your fellow classmates.

CAMP HARMONY

by Monica Sone

About the Author

Monica Sone was born in Seattle, Washington, in 1919. In 1942, she and her family were sent to "Camp Harmony," a temporary "assembly center" for people of Japanese descent who were being interned as a result of Executive Order 9066 (see below). Later, they were moved to a camp in Idaho. While she was interned, Sone wrote a series of letters to a friend describing her experiences. After the war, the friend showed the letters to a book editor. He contacted Sone and asked if she would be willing to expand her account of camp life into a book, which was published as Nisei Daughter in 1953.

About the Selection

Following the Japanese attack on Pearl Harbor, there was a widespread anti-Japanese hysteria in the United States. In February 1942, President Roosevelt signed Executive Order 9066, which allowed for the evacuation of people of Japanese ancestry from the Pacific Coast. During the **Japanese-American internment** that resulted, more than 110,000 people, two-thirds of them American citizens, were rounded up. They had to sell their homes and possessions and leave their jobs. They were sent to camps in the western United States that were little better than prisons. As you read "Camp Harmony," note how Monica Sone's experience affects her sense of her identity as an American.

When our bus turned a corner and we no longer had to smile and wave, we settled back gravely[1] in our seats. Everyone was quiet except for a chattering group of university students, who soon started singing college songs. A few people turned and glared at them, which only served to increase the volume of their singing. Then suddenly a baby's sharp cry rose **indignantly**[2] above the hubbub. The singing stopped immediately, followed by a guilty silence. Three seats behind us, a young mother held a wailing red-faced infant in her arms, bouncing it up and down. Its angry little face emerged from multiple layers of kimonos, sweaters, and blankets, and it, too, wore the white pasteboard tag[3] pinned to its blanket. A young man stammered out an apology as the mother gave him a wrathful look. She hunted frantically for a bottle of milk in a shopping bag, and we all relaxed when she had found it. We sped out of the city southward along beautiful stretches of farmland, with dark, newly turned soil. In the beginning we devoured every bit of scenery which flashed past our window and admired the massive-muscled workhorses plodding along the edge of the highway, the rich burnished copper color of a browsing herd of cattle, the vivid spring green of the pastures, but eventually the sameness of the country landscape palled[4] on us. We tried to sleep to escape from the restless anxiety which kept bobbing up to the surface of our minds. I awoke with a start when the bus filled with excited buzzing. A small group of straw-hatted Japanese farmers stood by the highway, waving at us. I felt a sudden warmth toward them, then a twinge of pity. They would be joining us soon.

About noon we crept into a small town. Someone said, "Looks like Puyallup,[5] all right." Parents of small children babbled excitedly, "Stand up quickly and look over there. See all the chick-chicks and fat little piggies?" One little city boy stared hard at the hogs and said **tersely**,[6] "They're bachi—dirty! "

Our bus idled a moment at the traffic signal, and we noticed at the left of us an entire block filled with neat rows of low shacks, resembling chicken houses. Someone commented on it with awe, "Just look at those chicken houses. They sure go in for

---

[1] gravely—seriously.

[2] **indignantly**—angrily.

[3] white pasteboard tag—numbered identification tag worn by the members of all Japanese-American families who registered for evacuation.

[4] palled (pawld)—had a wearisome effect.

[5] Puyallup—town in Washington. "Camp Harmony" was established at a fairgrounds outside the town.

[6] **tersely**—briefly, concisely.

poultry in a big way here." Slowly the bus made a left turn, drove through a wire-fence gate, and to our dismay, we were inside the oversized chicken farm. The bus driver opened the door, the guard stepped out and stationed himself at the door again. Jim, the young man who had shepherded us into the buses, popped his head inside and sang out, "OK, folks, all off at Yokohama,[7] Puyallup."

We stumbled out, stunned, dragging our bundles after us. It must have rained hard the night before in Puyallup, for we sank ankle deep into gray, glutinous[8] mud. The receptionist, a white man, instructed us courteously, "Now, folks, please stay together as family units and line up. You'll be assigned your apartment."

We were standing in Area A, the mammoth parking lot of the state fairgrounds. There were three other separate areas, B, C, and D, all built on the fairgrounds proper, near the baseball field and the racetracks. This camp of army barracks was hopefully called Camp Harmony.

We were assigned to apartment 2-I-A, right across from the bachelor quarters. The apartments resembled **elongated**,[9] low stables about two blocks long. Our home was one room, about eighteen by twenty feet, the size of a living room. There was one small window in the wall opposite the one door. It was bare except for a small, tinny wood-burning stove crouching in the center. The flooring consisted of two-by-fours laid directly on the earth, and dandelions were already pushing their way up through the cracks. Mother was delighted when she saw their shaggy yellow heads. "Don't anyone pick them. I'm going to cultivate them."

Father snorted, "Cultivate them! If we don't watch out, those things will be growing out of our hair."

Just then Henry stomped inside, bringing the rest of our baggage. "What's all the excitement about?"

Sumi replied laconically,[10] "Dandelions."

Henry tore off a fistful. Mother scolded, "Arra![11] Arra!" Stop that. They're the only beautiful things around here. We could have a garden right in here."

> Our home was one room, about eighteen by twenty feet, the size of a living room.

---

[7] Yokohama—joking reference to a Japanese seaport.

[8] glutinous (GLOOT•n•uhs)—sticky.

[9] **elongated**—extended.

[10] laconically (luh•KAHN•ihk•lee)—briefly, concisely.

[11] Arra—Japanese exclamation of surprise.

Kango Takamura's watercolor, *First Impression of Manzanar*, shows Japanese internees arriving at the Manzanar Camp in eastern California.

"Are you joking, Mama?"

I **chided**[12] Henry, "Of course she's not. After all, she has to have some inspiration to write poems, you know, with all the 'nari keri's.'[13] I can think of a poem myself right now:

Oh, Dandelion, Dandelion,
Despised and uprooted by all,
Dance and bob your golden
    heads
For you've finally found your
    home
With your yellow fellows, nari
    keri, amen!"

Henry said, thrusting the dandelions in Mother's black hair, "I think you can do ten times better than that, Mama."

Sumi reclined on her sea bag[14] and fretted, "Where do we sleep? Not on the floor, I hope."

"Stop worrying," Henry replied disgustedly.

Mother and Father wandered out to see what the other folks were doing and they found people wandering in the mud, wondering what other folks were doing. Mother returned shortly, her face lit up in an **ecstatic**[15] smile, "We're in luck. The latrine is right nearby. We won't have to walk blocks."

We laughed, marveling at Mother who could be so poetic and yet so practical. Father came back, bent double like a woodcutter in a fairy tale, with stacks of scrap lumber over his shoulder. His coat and trouser

---

[12] **chided**—scolded.

[13] nari keri's—*Nari keri* is a Japanese phrase suggesting awe and wonder that is often used at the end of a poem.

[14] sea bag—large canvas bag such as sailors use to carry their belongings when at sea.

[15] **ecstatic**—extremely delighted.

pockets bulged with nails. Father dumped his loot in a corner and explained, "There was a pile of wood left by the carpenters and hundreds of nails scattered loose. Everybody was picking them up, and I hustled right in with them. Now maybe we can live in style, with tables and chairs."

The block leader knocked at our door and announced lunchtime. He instructed us to take our meal at the nearest mess hall. As I untied my sea bag to get out my pie plate, tin cup, spoon, and fork, I realized I was hungry. At the mess hall we found a long line of people. Children darted in and out of the line, skiing in the slithery mud. The young stood impatiently on one foot, then the other, and scowled, "The food had better be good after all this wait." But the issei[16] stood quietly, arms folded, saying very little. A light drizzle began to fall, coating bare black heads with tiny sparkling raindrops. The chow line inched forward.

Lunch consisted of two canned sausages, one lob of boiled potato, and a slab of bread. Our family had to split up, for the hall was too crowded for us to sit together. I wandered up and down the aisles, back and forth along the crowded tables and benches, looking for a few inches to squeeze into. A small issei woman finished her meal, stood up, and hoisted her legs modestly over the bench, leaving a space for one. Even as I thrust myself into the **breach**,[17] the space had shrunk to two inches, but I worked myself into it. My dinner companion, hooked just inside my right elbow, was a bald-headed, gruff-looking issei man who seemed to resent nestling at mealtime. Under my left elbow was a tiny, mud-spattered girl. With busy, runny nose, she was belaboring her sausages, tearing them into shreds and mixing them into the potato gruel[18] which she had made with water. I choked my food down.

We cheered loudly when trucks rolled by, distributing canvas army cots for the young and hardy, and steel cots for the older folks. Henry directed the arrangement of the cots. Father and Mother were to occupy the corner nearest the wood stove. In the other corner, Henry

> Lunch consisted of two canned sausages, one lob of boiled potato, and a slab of bread.

---

[16] issei (EES•SAY)—Japanese immigrants.

[17] **breach**—opening.

[18] gruel (GROO•uhl)—thin, watery porridge.

arranged two cots in an L shape and announced that this was the combination living room-bedroom area, to be occupied by Sumi and myself. He fixed a male den for himself in the corner nearest the door. If I had had my way, I would have arranged everyone's cots in one neat row, as in Father's hotel dormitory.

We felt fortunate to be assigned to a room at the end of the barracks, because we had just one neighbor to worry about. The partition wall separating the rooms was only seven feet high, with an opening of four feet at the top, so at night, Mrs. Funai next door could tell when Sumi was still sitting up in bed in the dark, putting her hair up. "Mah, Sumi-chan," Mrs. Funai would say through the plank wall, "are you curling your hair tonight, again?

Do you put it up every night?" Sumi would put her hands on her hips and glare defiantly at the wall.

The block monitor, an impressive nisei[19] who looked like a star tackle, with his crouching walk, came around the first night to tell us that we must all be inside our room by nine o'clock every night. At ten o'clock, he rapped at the door again, yelling, "Lights out!" and Mother rushed to turn the light off not a second later.

Throughout the barracks, there was a medley of creaking cots, whimpering infants, and explosive night coughs. Our attention was riveted on the intense little wood stove, which glowed so violently I feared it would melt right down to the floor. We soon

---

[19] nisei (NEE•SAY)—person born in America of parents who emigrated from Japan.

Another watercolor by Takamura shows Japanese internees at Manzanar making rice cakes for a celebration. ▶

learned that this condition lasted for only a short time, after which it suddenly turned into a deep freeze. Henry and Father took turns at the stove to produce the harrowing[20] blast which all but singed our army blankets but did not penetrate through them. As it grew quieter in the barracks, I could hear the light patter of rain. Soon I felt the *splat! splat!* of raindrops digging holes into my face. The dampness on my pillow spread like a mortal bleeding, and I finally had to get out and haul my cot toward the center of the room. In a short while, Henry was up. "I've got multiple leaks, too. Have to complain to the landlord first thing in the morning."

All through the night I heard people getting up, dragging cots around. I stared at our little window, unable to sleep. I was glad Mother had put up a makeshift curtain on the window, for I noticed a powerful beam of light sweeping across it every few seconds. The lights came from high towers placed around the camp, where guards with tommy guns kept a twenty-four-hour vigil. I remembered the wire fence encircling us, and a knot of anger tightened in my breast. What was I doing behind a fence, like a criminal? If there were accusations to be made, why hadn't I been given a fair trial? Maybe I wasn't considered an American anymore. My citizenship wasn't real, after all.

Then what was I? I was certainly not a citizen of Japan, as my parents were. On second thought, even Father and Mother were more alien residents of the United States than Japanese nationals, for they had little ties with their mother country. In their twenty-five years in America, they had worked and paid their taxes to their adopted government as any other citizen.

Of one thing I was sure. The wire fence was real. I no longer had the right to walk out of it. It was because I had Japanese ancestors. It was also because some people had little faith in the ideas and ideals of democracy. They said that after all these were but words and could not possibly ensure loyalty. New laws and camps were surer devices. I finally buried my face in my pillow to wipe out burning thoughts and snatch what sleep I could.

> ## What was I doing behind a fence, like a criminal?

---

[20] harrowing—tormenting.

Questions to Consider

Responding

1. What do you think is the most disturbing aspect of the **Japanese-American internment** during World War II?

Analyzing

2. What impression do the Japanese Americans form of the internment camp when they first arrive there?

3. How do the attitudes among the people in Camp Harmony differ? What different factors do you think contributed to this?

4. What effect do Sone's experience of internment have on her sense of identity as an American?

Extending

5. What conditions might cause an ethnic group in the United States today to be treated the way the Japanese Americans were? What factors would work against this happening today?

Literature Connection

The **setting** *of a literary work is the time and place of the action. Sometimes the setting is clear and well-defined; at other times, it is left to the reader's imagination. Read the following passage from "Camp Harmony":*

I was glad Mother had put up the makeshift curtain across the window, for I noticed a powerful beam of light sweeping across it every few seconds. The lights came from high towers placed around the camp, where guards with tommy guns kept a twenty-four-hour vigil. I remembered the wire fence encircling us, and a knot of anger tightened in my breast. What was I doing behind a fence, like a criminal?

1. What picture does Sone create with the details of setting she gives?

2. How does setting contribute to the meaning Sone finds in her experience?

Activity

Writing Haiku

The traditional Japanese poetic form known as the haiku consists of three lines. The first and third line each have five syllables; the second line has seven syllables. A writer of haiku uses imagery, comparison, contrast, and association to create a single vivid impression. For example, Monica Sone might have written a haiku contrasting the pleasant sound of rain on the roof with the nasty feel of it on her face:

Pattering above,
or cold drops upon my cheek—
how wetness differs!

Experiment with writing haiku based on Sone's experiences. Don't worry as much about the number of syllables as about creating a strong impression through your poem.

THE Noble Experiment

BY JACKIE ROBINSON

About the Author

Jackie Robinson (1919–1972) was born in Georgia and grew up in California, where he was an outstanding high school and college athlete. He served in the army during World War II, becoming an officer. After leaving the army, Robinson briefly played for the Kansas City Monarchs, a leading team in the Negro Leagues. In October 1945, Branch Rickey, the owner and manager of the Brooklyn Dodgers, signed Robinson to play for the Montreal Royals, a Brooklyn farm team. Two years later, major league baseball's color line was shattered when Robinson was brought up to the Dodgers.

About the Selection

*Although a few African Americans played for major professional teams in the late 1800s, big-league baseball was a whites-only sport by the turn of the century. Until the late 1940s, talented black players could only play in the Negro Leagues or in Latin America, where baseball wasn't segregated. In the mid-1940s, Branch Rickey, the owner and manager of the Brooklyn Dodgers, began to work toward a longtime dream of the **integration of major league baseball**. As you read "The Noble Experiment," note the obstacles that were faced by Jackie Robinson, the first African American to play in the big leagues in the 20th century.*

In 1910 Branch Rickey was a coach for Ohio Wesleyan. The team went to South Bend, Indiana, for a game. The hotel management registered the coach and team but refused to assign a room to a black player named Charley Thomas. In those days college ball had a few black players. Mr. Rickey took the manager aside and said he would move the entire team to another hotel unless the black athlete was accepted. The threat was a bluff because he knew the other hotels also would have refused accommodations to a black man. While the hotel manager was thinking about the threat, Mr. Rickey came up with a compromise. He suggested a cot be put in his own room, which he would share with the unwanted guest. The hotel manager wasn't happy about the idea, but he gave in.

Years later Branch Rickey told the story of the misery of that black player to whom he had given a place to sleep. He remembered that Thomas couldn't sleep.

"He sat on that cot," Mr. Rickey said, "and was silent for a long time. Then he began to cry, tears he couldn't hold back. His whole body shook with emotion. I sat and watched him, not knowing what to do until he began tearing at one hand with the other—just as if he were trying to scratch the skin off his hands with his fingernails. I was alarmed. I asked him what he was trying to do to himself

"'It's my hands,' he sobbed. 'They're black. If only they were white, I'd be as good as anybody then, wouldn't I, Mr. Rickey? If only they were white.'"

"Charley," Mr. Rickey said, "the day will come when they won't have to be white."

Thirty-five years later, while I was lying awake nights, frustrated, unable to see a future, Mr. Rickey, by now the president of the Dodgers, was also lying awake at night, trying to make up his mind about a new experiment.

He had never forgotten the agony of that black athlete. When he became a front-office executive in St. Louis, he had fought, behind the scenes, against the custom that consigned black spectators to the Jim Crow section[1] of the Sportsman's Park, later to become Busch Memorial Stadium. His pleas to change the rules were in vain. Those in power argued that if blacks were allowed a free choice of seating, white business would suffer.

---

[1] Jim Crow section—area where African Americans were permitted to sit. "Jim Crow" refers to the system of customs and laws that discriminated against African Americans. The name comes from a character in minstrel shows, which used low humor to stereotype blacks.

Branch Rickey lost that fight, but when he became the boss of the Brooklyn Dodgers in 1943, he felt the time for equality in baseball had come. He knew that achieving it would be terribly difficult. There would be deep resentment, determined opposition, and perhaps even racial violence. He was convinced he was morally right, and he **shrewdly**[2] sensed that making the game a truly national one would have healthy financial results. He took his case before the startled directors of the club, and using persuasive **eloquence**,[3] he won the first battle in what would be a long and bitter campaign. He was voted permission to make the Brooklyn club the pioneer in bringing blacks into baseball.

Winning his directors' approval was almost insignificant in contrast to the task which now lay ahead of the Dodger president. He made certain that word of his plans did not leak out, particularly to the press. Next, he had to find the ideal player for his project, which came to be called "Rickey's noble experiment." This player had to be one who could take abuse, name-calling, rejection by fans and sportswriters and by fellow players not only on opposing teams but on his own. He had to be able to stand up in the face of merciless persecution and not **retaliate**.[4] On the other hand, he had to be a contradiction in human terms; he still had to have spirit. He could not be an "Uncle Tom."[5] His ability to turn the other cheek had to be **predicated**[6] on his determination to gain acceptance. Once having proven his ability as player, teammate, and man, he had to be able to cast off humbleness and stand up as a full-fledged participant whose triumph did not carry the poison of bitterness.

Unknown to most people and certainly to me, after launching a major scouting program, Branch Rickey had picked me as that player. The Rickey talent hunt went beyond national borders. Cuba, Mexico, Puerto Rico, Venezuela, and other countries where dark-skinned people lived had been checked out. Mr. Rickey had learned that there were a number of

> *He had to find the ideal player for his project, which came to be called "Rickey's noble experiment."*

---

[2] **shrewdly**—wisely; cleverly.

[3] **eloquence** (EL•uh•kwens)—skill and power in speaking.

[4] **retaliate** (rih•TAL•ee•AYT)—pay back (an injury) in kind.

[5] Uncle Tom—offensive term for a black person regarded as too eager to please whites. The name comes from a character in Harriet Beecher Stowe's novel *Uncle Tom's Cabin.*

[6] **predicated** (PREHD•ih•kay•tihd)—based.

black players, war veterans mainly, who had gone to these countries, despairing of finding an opportunity in their own country. The manhunt had to be camouflaged. If it became known he was looking for a black recruit for the Dodgers, there would have been all kinds of trouble. The gimmick he used as a coverup was to make the world believe that he was about to establish a new Negro league. In the spring of 1945 he called a press conference and announced that the Dodgers were organizing the United States League, composed of all black teams. This, of course, made blacks and prointegration whites **indignant.**[7] He was accused of trying to uphold the existing segregation and, at the same time, capitalize on black players. Cleverly, Mr. Rickey replied that his league would be better organized than the current ones. He said its main purpose, eventually, was to be absorbed into the majors. It is ironic that by coming very close to telling the truth, he was able to conceal that truth from the enemies of integrated baseball. Most people assumed that when he spoke of some distant goal of integration, Mr. Rickey was being a **hypocrite**[8] on this issue as so many of baseball's leaders had been.

---

[7] **indignant** (ihn•DIHG•nuhnt)—angry.

[8] **hypocrite** (hihp•uh•kriht)—someone who pretends to have beliefs or values that he or she does not really possess.

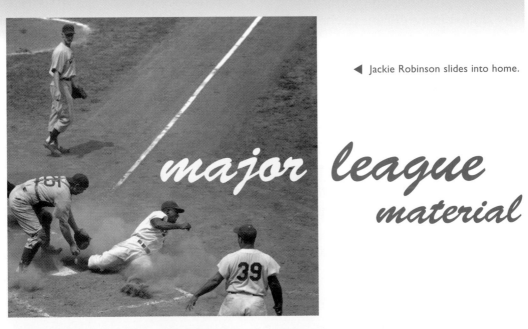

◀ Jackie Robinson slides into home.

major league material

*B*lack players were familiar with this kind of hypocrisy. When I was with the Monarchs, shortly before I met Mr. Rickey, Wendell Smith, then sports editor of the black weekly Pittsburgh *Courier*, had arranged for me and two other players from the Negro league to go to a tryout with the Boston Red Sox. The tryout had been brought about because a Boston city councilman had frightened the Red Sox management. Councilman Isadore Muchneck threatened to push a bill through banning Sunday baseball unless the Red Sox hired black players. Sam Jethroe of the Cleveland Buckeyes, Marvin Williams of the Philadelphia Stars, and I had been grateful to Wendell for getting us a chance in the Red Sox tryout, and we put our best efforts into it. However, not for one minute did we believe the tryout was sincere. The Boston club officials praised our performance, let us fill out application cards, and said "So long." We were fairly certain they wouldn't call us, and we had no intention of calling them.

Incidents like this made Wendell Smith as **cynical**[9] as we were. He didn't accept Branch Rickey's new league as a genuine project, and he frankly told him so. During this conversation, the Dodger boss asked Wendell whether any of the three of us who had gone to Boston was really good major league material. Wendell said I was. I will be forever indebted to Wendell because, without his even knowing it, his recommendation was in the end partly responsible for my career. At the time, it started a thorough investigation of my background.

In August 1945, at Comiskey Park in Chicago, I was approached by Clyde Sukeforth, the Dodger scout. Blacks have had to learn to protect themselves by being cynical but not cynical enough to slam the door on potential opportunities. We go through life walking a tightrope to prevent too much disillusionment. I was out on the field when Sukeforth called my name and beckoned. He told me the Brown Dodgers were looking for top ballplayers, that Branch Rickey had heard about me and sent him to watch me throw from the hole.[10] He had come at an unfortunate time. I had hurt my shoulder a couple of days before that,

> *We go through life walking a tightrope to prevent too much disillusionment.*

---

[9] **cynical** (SIHN•ih•kuhl)—mistrustful of the motives of others.

[10] throw from the hole—throw from deep in the infield to first base.

and I wouldn't be doing any throwing for at least a week.

Sukeforth said he'd like to talk with me anyhow. He asked me to come to see him after the game at the Stevens Hotel.

Here we go again, I thought. Another time-wasting experience. But Sukeforth looked like a sincere person, and I thought I might as well listen. I agreed to meet him that night. When we met, Sukeforth got right to the point. Mr. Rickey wanted to talk to me about the possibility of becoming a Brown Dodger. If I could get a few days off and go to Brooklyn, my fare and expenses would be paid. At first I said that I couldn't leave my team and go to Brooklyn just like that. Sukeforth wouldn't take no for an answer. He pointed out that I couldn't play for a few days anyhow because of my bum arm. Why should my team object?

I continued to hold out and demanded to know what would happen if the Monarchs fired me. The Dodger scout replied quietly that he didn't believe that would happen.

I shrugged and said I'd make the trip. I figured I had nothing to lose.

Branch Rickey was an impressive-looking man. He had a classic face, an air of command, a deep, booming voice, and a way of cutting through red tape and getting down to basics. He shook my hand vigorously and, after a brief conversation, sprang the first question.

"You got a girl?" he demanded.

It was a hell of a question. I had two reactions: why should he be concerned about my relationship with a girl; and, second, while I thought, hoped, and prayed I had a girl, the way things had been going, I was afraid she might have begun to consider me a hopeless case. I explained this to Mr. Rickey and Clyde.

Mr. Rickey wanted to know all about Rachel. I told him of our hopes and plans.

"You know, you have a girl," he said heartily. "When we get through today, you may want to call her up because there are times when a man needs a woman by his side."

*M*y heart began racing a little faster again as I sat there **speculating**.[11] First he asked me if I really understood why he had sent for me. I told him what Clyde Sukeforth had told me.

"That's what he was supposed to tell you," Mr. Rickey said. "The truth is you are not a candidate for the

---

[11] **speculating**—thinking about different possibilities.

Brooklyn Brown Dodgers. I've sent for you because I'm interested in you as a candidate for the Brooklyn National League Club. I think you can play in the major leagues. How do you feel about it?"

My reactions seemed like some kind of weird mixture churning in a blender. I was thrilled, scared, and excited. I was **incredulous**.[12] Most of all, I was speechless.

"You think you can play for Montreal?" he demanded.

I got my tongue back. "Yes," I answered.

Montreal was the Brooklyn Dodgers' top farm club. The players who went there and made it had an excellent chance at the big time.

I was busy reorganizing my thoughts while Mr. Rickey and Clyde Sukeforth discussed me briefly, almost as if I weren't there. Mr. Rickey was questioning Clyde. Could I make the grade?

Abruptly, Mr. Rickey swung his swivel chair in my direction. He was a man who conducted himself with great drama. He pointed a finger at me.

"I know you're a good ballplayer," he barked. "What I don't know is whether you have the guts."

I knew it was all too good to be true. Here was a guy questioning my

courage. That virtually amounted to him asking me if I was a coward. Mr. Rickey or no Mr. Rickey, that was an **insinuation**[13] hard to take. I felt the heat coming up into my cheeks.

Before I could react to what he had said, he leaned forward in his chair and explained.

I wasn't just another athlete being hired by a ball club. We were playing for big stakes. This was the reason Branch Rickey's search had been so **exhaustive**.[14] The search had spanned the globe and narrowed down to a few candidates, then finally to me. When it looked as though I might be the number-one choice, the investigation of my life, my habits, my reputation, and my character had become an intensified study.

My reactions seemed like some kind of weird mixture churning in a blender.

"I've investigated you thoroughly, Robinson," Mr. Rickey said.

One of the results of this thorough screening were reports from California athletic circles that I had been a "racial

---

[12] **incredulous** (ihn•KREJ•uh•luhs)—unable or unwilling to believe something.
[13] **insinuation** (ihn•SIHN•yoo•AY•shuhn)—suggestion, hint.
[14] **exhaustive**—thorough.

agitator"[15] at UCLA. Mr. Rickey had not accepted these criticisms on face value. He had demanded and received more information and came to the conclusion that if I had been white, people would have said, "Here's a guy who's a contender, a competitor."

After that he had some grim words of warning. "We can't fight our way through this, Robinson. We've got no army. There's virtually nobody on our side. No owners, no umpires, very few newspapermen. And I'm afraid that many fans will be hostile. We'll be in a tough position. We can win only if we can convince the world that I'm doing this because you're a great ballplayer and a fine gentleman."

He had me **transfixed**[16] as he spoke. I could feel his sincerity, and I began to get a sense of how much this major step meant to him. Because of his nature and his passion for justice, he had to do what he was doing. He continued. The rumbling voice, the theatrical gestures were gone. He was speaking from a deep, quiet strength.

"So there's more than just playing," he said. "I wish it meant only hits, runs, and errors—only the things they put in the box score. Because you know—yes, you would know, Robinson, that a baseball box score is

▲

Robinson signs a fan's autograph book.

a democratic thing. It doesn't tell how big you are, what church you attend, what color you are, or how your father voted in the last election. It just tells what kind of baseball player you were on that particular day."

I interrupted. "But it's the box score that really counts—that and that alone, isn't it?"

"It's all that ought to count," he replied. "But it isn't. Maybe one of these days it will be all that counts. That is one of the reasons I've got you here, Robinson. If you're a good enough man, we can make this a start in the right direction. But let me tell you, it's going to take an awful lot of courage."

---

[15] racial agitator—negative term for someone who tried stir up trouble between people of different races.

[16] **transfixed**—completely attentive.

He was back to the crossroads question that made me start to get angry minutes earlier. He asked it slowly and with great care.

"Have you got the guts to play the game no matter what happens?"

"I think I can play the game, Mr. Rickey," I said.

The next few minutes were tough. Branch Rickey had to make absolutely sure that I knew what I would face. Beanballs[17] would be thrown at me. I would be called the kind of names which would hurt and infuriate any man. I would be physically attacked. Could I take all of this and control my temper, remain steadfastly loyal to our **ultimate**[18] aim?

*H*e knew I would have terrible problems and wanted me to know the extent of them before I agreed to the plan. I was twenty-six years old, and all my life I had believed in payback, retaliation. The most luxurious possession, the richest treasure anybody has, is his personal dignity. I looked at Mr. Rickey guardedly, and in that second I was looking at him not as a partner in a great experiment, but as the enemy— a white man. I had a question, and it was the age-old one about whether or not you sell your birthright.

"Mr. Rickey," I asked, "are you looking for a Negro who is afraid to fight back?"

I never will forget the way he exploded.

"Robinson," he said, "I'm looking for a ballplayer with guts enough not to fight back."

After that, Mr. Rickey continued his lecture on the kind of thing I'd be facing.

He not only told me about it, but he acted out the part of a white player charging into me, blaming me for the "accident" and calling me all kinds of foul racial names. He talked about my race, my parents, in language that was almost unendurable.

> *Could I take all of this and control my temper, remain steadfastly loyal to our ultimate aim?*

"They'll **taunt**[19] and goad you," Mr. Rickey said. "They'll do anything to make you react. They'll try to provoke a race riot in the ballpark. This is the way to prove to the public that a Negro should not be allowed in the major league. This is the way to

---

[17] Beanballs—pitches aimed at a batter's head.

[18] **ultimate**—basic.

[19] **taunt**—mock, make fun of.

frighten the fans and make them afraid to attend the games."

If hundreds of black people wanted to come to the ballpark to watch me play and Mr. Rickey tried to discourage them, would I understand that he was doing it because the emotional enthusiasm of my people could harm the experiment? That kind of enthusiasm would be as bad as the emotional opposition of prejudiced white fans.

Suppose I was at shortstop. Another player comes down from first, stealing, flying in with spikes high, and cuts me on the leg. As I feel the blood running down my leg, the white player laughs in my face.

"How do you like that, boy?" he sneers.

Could I turn the other cheek? I didn't know how I would do it. Yet I knew that I must. I had to do it for so many reasons. For black youth, for my mother, for Rae, for myself. I had already begun to feel I had to do it for Branch Rickey.

I was offered, and agreed to sign later, a contract with a $3,500 bonus and $600-a-month salary. I was officially a Montreal Royal. I must not tell anyone except Rae and my mother.

In 1982, the U.S. Post Office issued a stamp honoring Jackie Robinson. He was the first professional baseball player to appear on an American postage stamp. ▶

Responding

1. In your opinion, what was the biggest challenge Jackie Robinson had to face in the **integration of major league baseball**?

Analyzing

2. What kind of a person does Jackie Robinson appear to be in this excerpt from his autobiography?

3. Why do you think Branch Rickey wanted to keep his plans for integrating baseball secret?

4. How did Rickey respond to the charge that Robinson had been a "racial agitator" when he was in college?

Extending

5. What role do you think professional sports plays today in promoting racial integration in the United States?

Activities

Writing About a Complex Character

Jackie Robinson was a complex individual, combining aggressiveness with a willingness to hold himself firmly in check. Write about someone in your life who seems to you to have a character that has strongly opposing tendencies such as Robinson's.

Creating a Time Line

Pick a professional sport that interests you and do research on the process by which it was opened up to people of color—and women, if they are or have been involved in

Literature Connection

Conflict is a struggle between opposing forces. In an external conflict, an individual struggles against another person or some outside force. An internal conflict is a struggle within an individual.

1. What were the external conflicts faced by Jackie Robinson?

2. What were some of the internal conflicts he faced?

▲

In 1959, Althea Gibson became the first African American to win the Wimbledon tennis championship.

the sport. Then create a time line that indicates important events in this process. Find pictures of these events to illustrate your time line.

ROSA PARKS

BY RITA DOVE

About the Author

Born in Akron, Ohio, in 1952, Rita Dove was educated at Miami University in Ohio, the University of Iowa, and in Germany. She has written drama, short stories, and a novel, but is best known as a poet. Dove's poetry collection about her grandparents, *Thomas and Beulah* (1986), won the Pulitzer Prize. In 1995, she became the youngest person and the first African American to become Poet Laureate of the United States. Today, she teaches and writes a column on poetry for the Washington Post—part of her goal to bring poetry into people's everyday lives.

About the Selections

From the mid-1950s to the mid-1970s, Americans experienced a period of enormous social change. The most important cause of these changes was the **civil rights movement**. The beginning of the civil rights movement is often seen in the 1955 boycott by African Americans of the segregated buses in the Southern city of Montgomery, Alabama. The boycott was itself sparked by the arrest of Rosa Parks, who refused to move to the rear of a bus when ordered to by the white driver. The Montgomery bus boycott was the start of a heroic era of protest when African Americans—followed by Native Americans, Latinos, Asian Americans, women, and other groups—fought for their rights. As you read "Rosa Parks" and "I Was Born at the Wrong Time" (page 387), think about the advantages and disadvantages if living through such an era.

We know the story. One December evening, a woman left work and boarded a bus for home. She was tired; her feet ached. But this was Montgomery, Ala., in 1955, and as the bus became crowded, the woman, a black woman, was ordered to give up her seat to a white passenger. When she remained seated, that simple decision eventually led to the **disintegration**[1] of institutionalized segregation in the South, ushering in a new era of the civil rights movement.

This, anyway, was the story I had heard from the time I was curious enough to eavesdrop on adult conversations. I was three years old when a white bus driver warned Rosa Parks, "Well, I'm going to have you arrested," and she replied, "You may go on and do so." As a child, I didn't understand how doing nothing had caused so much activity, but I recognized the template: David slaying the giant Goliath,[2] or the boy who saved his village by sticking his finger in the dike.[3] And perhaps it is precisely the lure of fairy-tale retribution that colors the lens we look back through. Parks was 42 years old when she refused to give up her seat. She has insisted that her feet were not aching; she was, by her own testimony, no more tired than usual. And she did not plan her fateful act: "I did not get on the bus to get arrested," she has said. "I got on the bus to go home."

Montgomery's segregation laws were complex: blacks were required to pay their fare to the driver, then get off and reboard through the back door. Sometimes the bus would drive off before the paid-up customers made it to the back entrance. If the white section was full and another white customer entered, blacks were required to give up their seats and move farther to the back; a black person was not even allowed to sit across the aisle from whites. These humiliations were compounded by the fact that two-thirds of the bus riders in Montgomery were black.

> "I did not get on the bus to get arrested," she has said. "I got on the bus to go home."

---

[1] **disintegration**—collapse, falling apart.

[2] David . . . Goliath—characters in a famous story in the Bible. The Israelite shepherd boy David, armed only with a sling and stones, defeats a giant enemy warrior named Goliath.

[3] boy . . . dike—character in a Dutch legend who stops his village from being flooded by using his finger to block a hole in a dike, one of the walls used in Holland to hold back the sea.

Parks was not the first to be detained for this offense. Eight months earlier, Claudette Colvin, 15, refused to give up her seat and was arrested. Black activists met with this girl to determine if she would make a good test case—as secretary of the local N.A.A.C.P.,[4] Parks attended the meeting—but it was decided that a more "upstanding" candidate was necessary to withstand the scrutiny of the courts and the press. And then in October, a young woman named Mary Louise Smith was arrested;

N.A.A.C.P. leaders rejected her too as their vehicle, looking for someone more able to withstand media scrutiny. Smith paid the fine and was released.

Six weeks later, the time was ripe. The facts, rubbed shiny for retelling, are these: On Dec. 1, 1955, Mrs. Rosa Parks, seamstress for the Montgomery Fair department store, boarded the Cleveland Avenue bus. She took a seat

[4] N.A.A.C.P.—National Association for the Advancement of Colored People, an African-American civil rights organization founded in 1909.

in the fifth row—the first row of the "Colored Section." The driver was the same one who had put her off a bus 12 years earlier for refusing to get off and reboard through the back door. ("He was still mean-looking," she has said.) Did that make her stubborn? Or had her work in the N.A.A.C.P. sharpened her sensibilities so that she knew what to do—or more precisely, what not to do: Don't frown, don't struggle, don't shout, don't pay the fine?

At the news of the arrest, local civil rights leader E. D. Nixon exclaimed, "My God, look what segregation has put in my hands!" Parks was not only above moral **reproach**[5] (securely married, reasonably employed) but possessed a quiet fortitude as well as political savvy—in short, she was the ideal plaintiff for a test case.

She was arrested on a Thursday; bail was posted by Clifford Durr, the white lawyer whose wife had employed Parks as a seamstress. That evening, after talking it over with her mother and husband, Rosa Parks agreed to challenge the constitutionality[6] of Montgomery's segregation laws. During a midnight meeting of the Women's Political Council, 35,000 handbills were mimeographed for distribution to all black schools the next morning. The message was simple:

"We are . . . asking every Negro to stay off the buses Monday in protest of the arrest and trial . . . You can afford to stay out of school for one day. If you work, take a cab, or walk. But please, children and grown-ups, don't ride the bus at all on Monday. Please stay off the buses Monday."

Monday came. Rain threatened, yet the black population of Montgomery stayed off the buses, either walking or catching one of the black cabs stopping at every municipal bus stop for 10¢ per customer— standard bus fare. Meanwhile, Parks was scheduled to appear in court. As she made her way through the throngs at the courthouse, a **demure**[7] figure in a long-sleeved black dress with white collar and cuffs, a trim black velvet hat, gray coat and white gloves, a girl in the crowd caught sight of her and cried out, "Oh, she's so sweet. They've messed with the wrong one now!"

Yes, indeed. The trial lasted 30 min., with the expected conviction and penalty. That afternoon, the

> Oh, she's so sweet. They've messed with the wrong one now!

---

[5] **reproach**—disapproval, criticism.

[6] constitutionality—legality.

[7] **demure** (dih•MYUR)—shy, modest.

Montgomery Improvement Association was formed. So as not to ruffle any local activists' feathers, the members elected as their president a relative newcomer to Montgomery, the young minister of Dexter Avenue Baptist Church: the Rev. Martin Luther King, Jr. That evening, addressing a crowd gathered at the Holt Street Baptist Church, King declared in that **sonorous**,[8] ringing voice millions the world over would soon thrill to: "There comes a time that people get tired." When he was finished, Parks stood up so the audience could see her. She did not speak; there was no need to. *Here I am*, her silence said, *among you*.

And she has been with us ever since—a persistent symbol of human dignity in the face of brutal authority. The famous U.P.I. photo (actually taken more than a year later, on Dec. 21, 1956, the day Montgomery's public transportation system was legally integrated) is a study of calm strength. She is looking out the bus window, her hands resting in the folds of her checked dress, while a white man sits, unperturbed, in the row *behind* her. That clear profile, the neat cloche[9] and eyeglasses and sensible coat—she could have been my mother, anybody's favorite aunt.

History is often portrayed as a string of arias[10] in a grand opera, all baritone intrigues and tenor heroics. Some of the most tumultuous events, however, have been provoked by serendipity[11]—the assassination of an **inconsequential**[12] archduke spawned World War I, a kicked-over lantern may have sparked the Great Chicago Fire. One cannot help wondering what role Martin Luther King, Jr., would have played in the civil rights movement if the opportunity had not presented itself that first evening of the boycott—if Rosa Parks had chosen a row farther back from the outset, or if she had missed the bus altogether.

At the end of this **millennium**[13] (and a particularly noisy century), it is the modesty of Rosa Parks' example that sustains us. It is no less than the belief in the power of the individual, that cornerstone of the American Dream, that she inspires, along with the hope that all of us—even the least of us—could be that brave, that serenely human, when crunch time comes.

---

[8] **sonorous** (SAHN•uhr•uhs)—with a full, deep, rich sound.

[9] **cloche** (klohsh)—close-fitting woman's hat with a bell-like shape.

[10] **arias**—solo operatic performances.

[11] **serendipity** (sehr•uhn•DIHP•ih•tee)—unlikely accident.

[12] **inconsequential** (ihn•kahn•sih•KWEHN•shuhl)—unimportant.

[13] **millennium** (muh•LEHN•ee•uhm)—thousand-year period.

I WAS BORN AT THE WRONG TIME

BY ANGELA SHELF MEDEARIS

About the Author

Author and storyteller Angela Shelf Medearis was born in Virginia. Because her father was an Air Force recruiter, her family moved often while she was growing up. Books and reading helped give her a sense of identity and continuity. During this time, she was also developing as a writer, although she did not begin writing professionally until she was 30. She enjoys history, and spends a lot of time researching African-American history for her books.

I had to ask
my mom
to define
a "sit in."
You know, they sit in a place
to protest something,
carry signs, and get arrested.
I had to ask about it
because I was born at the wrong time.

All the excitement is over with.
My mom had already marched for civil rights,
sung WE SHALL OVERCOME,
shouted BLACK POWER,
MARCHED ON WASHINGTON,
had a basketball-sized Afro,
sang sweet soul music,
and cried over
Martin Luther King Jr. and both Kennedys
long before my first birthday.
I wonder if there will be any causes left
to believe in
by the time I'm old enough
to join in the fight?

▲
A civil rights demonstrator is arrested by police in Birmingham, Alabama, in 1963.

Responding

1. What do you think are the most important qualities needed by a hero?

Analyzing

2. What impression of Rosa Parks's personality do you get from Rita Dove's essay?

3. Why do you think Dove mentions David and Goliath and the boy who sticks his finger in the dike?

4. Why does the speaker in Angela Shelf Meadearis's poem feel she was "born at the wrong time"?

5. What do you think would be the advantages and disadvantages of living through a troubled period like that of the **civil rights movement**?

Extending

6. If you could select any era of American history to grow up in—such as the Revolution, the settlement of the West, the Roaring '20s—which one would you choose and why?

Literature Connection

*The **tone** of a literary work expresses the writer's attitude toward a subject. Words such as angry, sad, or humorous can be used to describe tone.*

1. What attitude does Rita Dove seem to have toward Rosa Parks?

2. What words would you use to describe the tone of "I Was Born at the Wrong Time"?

Activity

Writing Oral History

Ask your parents or some other older people to recall their memories of a significant historical event or period they lived through. Use their recollections as the basis for a brief oral history.

One of the tragically memorable events of the 1980s was the explosion of the space shuttle *Challenger*, which exploded shortly after liftoff on January 26, 1986. All seven crew members (shown here) were killed.

Linking Cultures

Struggles for Justice

One important element in the history of the United States has been the struggle of various ethnic groups to gain freedom, justice, and equality with other Americans. These struggles continue today as new groups face some of the old problems.

▲

During the fall and winter of 1838–1839, the U.S. government forced about 16,000 Cherokee to march 800 miles from their homeland in Tennessee and Georgia to what is now Oklahoma. One-fourth died on what became known as the "Trail of Tears" from cold, hunger, and disease.

The U.S. government introduced Native American children to white culture by enforcing military-style discipline in Indian schools.

In the late 1800s, anti-Chinese feeling was so strong in the United States, particularly in the West, that it sometimes led to riots. ▶

Thousand of Chinese immigrants were detained at the immigration station established in 1910 at Angel Island in San Francisco Bay.
▼

In 1892, when three of her friends were killed by a mob, the African-American journalist Ida B. Wells (1862–1931) began a lifelong campaign against lynching.

▲

W. E. B. Du Bois (1868–1963) encouraged African Americans to reject segregation. In 1909, he helped found the National Association for the Advancement of Colored People. Du Bois (center) is shown around 1910 in the editorial office of the NAACP's journal, *The Crisis*.

▲
Segregated public facilities were established by so-called "Jim Crow" laws in the South following the Civil War. These laws remained in force until the civil rights movement of the 1950s and 1960s.

African Americans continued to be the victims of racial violence in the 20th century. During the NAACP's anti-lynching campaign in the 1920s, this banner was hung outside the organization's New York office as a protest. ▶

▲

In the United States during World War II, more than 110,000 people of Japanese descent, two-thirds of them American citizens, were rounded up and sent to camps in the western United States that were little better than prisons.

In the early 1960s, civil rights demonstrators began to stage "sit-ins," like this one in an Oklahoma restaurant, to protest segregated public facilities in the South. ▶

▲

In March of 1965, civil rights activists led by Dr. Martin Luther King, Jr., spent five days walking from Selma, Alabama, to the state capital of Montgomery. The march was a protest against discrimination in voting rights.

▲

The best known Latino civil rights activist was Cesar Chavez (1927–1993), a labor leader who successfully organized migrant farm workers. In March 1966, in the midst of a grape workers' strike, Chavez (center) led a march from Delano, California, to the state capital, Sacramento.

In 2000, a six-year-old Cuban boy, Elían Gonzalez, was rescued when the small boat in which he and his mother were fleeing from Cuba sank. A fierce legal battle developed over whether Elían should remain in the United States or be reunited with his Cuban father. ▶

These Native Americans are participating in a recent memorial ride marking the anniversary of the massacre at Wounded Knee on December 29, 1890.

 ▼

Texts

2 "Home" by Gwendolyn Brooks from *Maud Martha*. Reprinted by permission of The Estate of Gwendolyn Brooks. **6** "Knoxville, Tennessee" from *Black Feeling, Black Talk, Black Judgment* by Nikki Giovanni. Copyright © 1968, 1970 by Nikki Giovanni. Reprinted by permission of HarperCollins Publishers, Inc., William Morrow. **9** "Ellis Island" from *The Remembered Earth*, edited by Geary Hobson, 1979. (Red Earth Press, Albuquerque). Reprinted by permission of Barbara S. Kouts Literary Agent. **11** "The Time We Climbed Snake Mountain" by Leslie Marmon Silko. Copyright © 1981 by Leslie Marmon Silko, reprinted with the permission of The Wylie Agency, Inc. **13** "The Other Pioneers" by Roberto Félix Salazar published in The LULAC News, July 1939. Reprinted by permission of The LULAC National. **16** "Gold" by Pat Mora. Reprinted by permission of the author. www.patmora.com. **19** "Tears of Autumn" from *The Forbidden Stitch* by Yoshiko Uchida, 1989. Courtesy of the Bancroft Library, University of California, Berkeley. **28** "Picture Bride" from *Picture Bride* by Cathy Song. Copyright © 1983 by Cathy Song. Reprinted by permission of Yale University Press. **33** "Exile" by Judith Ortiz Cofer is reprinted with permission from the publisher of *Terms of Survival* (Houston: Arte Público Press—University of Houston, 1987). **36** "Tsali of the Cherokees" from *American Indian Mythology* by Alice Marriott. Copyright © 1968 by Alice Marriott and Carol K. Rachlin. Reprinted by permission of HarperCollins Publishers, Inc. **47** "The Circuit" by Francisco Jiménez from *The Arizona Quarterly* (Autumn 1973). Copyright and reprint permission by the author. **56** "The War of the Wall" by Toni Cade Bambara. Reprinted with permission from The Estate of Toni Cade Bambara. **68** "The Negro Speaks of Rivers" from *The Collected Poems of Langston Hughes* by Langston Hughes, copyright © 1994 by The Estate of Langston Hughes. Used by permission of Alfred A. Knopf, a division of Random House, Inc. **70** "Ancestors" from *After the Killing* by

Dudley Randall. Reprinted by permission of the Dudley Randall Estate. **73** "High Horse's Courting" reprinted from *Black Elk Speaks* by John G. Neihardt by permission of the University of Nebraska Press. Copyright 1932, 1959, 1972 by John G. Neihardt. Copyright © 1961 by the John G. Neihardt Trust. **81** "Tales Told under the Mango Tree . . ." by Judith Ortiz Cofer is reprinted with permission from the publisher of *Silent Dancing: A Partial Remembrance of a Puerto Rican Childhood*. (Houston: Arte Público Press— University of Houston, 1990). **88** "Miss Butterfly" from *The Chauvinist and Other Stories* by Toshio Mori. Copyright © 1979 by Asian American Studies Center, UCLA. Reprinted by permission of the Asian American Studies Center, UCLA. **96** "Legacies" from *My House* by Nikki Giovanni. Copyright © 1972 by Nikki Giovanni. Reprinted by permission of HarperCollins Publishers Inc., William Morrow. **98** "Lineage" by Margaret Walker Alexander from *This is My Century: New and Collected Poems*. Reprinted by permission of The University of Georgia Press. **100** "The Medicine Bag" by Virginia Driving Hawk Sneve, 1975. Reprinted by permission of the author. **112** "Koreans Have a Reason Not to Smile" by K. Connie Kang from *The New York Times*, September 8, 1990. Copyright © 1990 by the New York Times Co. Reprinted by permission. **128** "The Secret Lion" from *The Iguana Killer: Twelve Stories of the Heart /* Alberto Alvaro Ríos; etchings by Antonio Pazos (Hard) by Alberto Alvaro Ríos. Copyright 2000 by Univ of New Mexico Press. Reproduced with permission of Univ of New Mexico Press in the format Textbook via Copyright Clearance Center. **136** "Drenched in Light" as taken from *The Complete Stories* by Zora Neale Hurston. Introduction copyright © 1995 by Henry Louis Gates, Jr. and Sieglinde Lemke. Compilation copyright © 1995 by Vivian Bowden, Lois J. Hurston Gaston, Clifford Hurston, Lucy Ann Hurston, Winifred Hurston Clark, Zora Mack Goins, Edgar Hurston, Sr., and Barbara Hurston

Lewis. Afterword and Bibliography copyright © 1995 by Henry Louis Gates. Reprinted by permission of HarperCollins Publishers, Inc. Originally published in *Opportunity*, December 1924. **148** "Flash Cards," from *Grace Notes* by Rita Dove. Copyright © 1989 by Rita Dove. Used by permission of the author and W. W. Norton & Company, Inc. **150** "Mother to Son" from *The Collected Poems of Langston Hughes* by Langston Hughes, copyright © 1994 by The Estate of Langston Hughes. Used by permission of Alfred A. Knopf, a division of Random House, Inc. **152** "At Last I Kill a Buffalo," from *My Indian Boyhood* by Chief Luther Standing Bear. Copyright 1931 by Chief Luther Standing Bear, © renewed 1959 by May Jones. Reprinted by permission of Houghton Mifflin Company. All rights reserved. **162** "The Journey" by Duane BigEagle from *Earth Power Coming: Short Fiction in Native American Literature*. Copyright © Duane BigEagle 1983. Reprinted by permission of the author. **170** "Epiphany: The Third Gift" by Lucha Corpi, essay was first published in *Latinas: Voices from the Borderlands*, 1992. Reprinted by permission of the author. **181** "Hollywood and the Pits" by Cherylene Lee, 1992. Reprinted by permission of Bret Adams Limited on behalf of the author. **194** "Amigo Brothers" from *Stories from El Barrio* by Piri Thomas, reprinted by permission of the author. **207** "The 'Black Table' Is Still There" by Lawrence Otis Graham from *The New York Times*, Feb 3, 1991. Copyright © 1991 by the New York Times Co. Reprinted by permission. **214** "Mi Familia" from *Sonnets to Human Beings and Other Selected Works* by Carmen Tafolla, 1992. Copyright © 1992 by Carmen Tafolla. Reprinted by permission of the author. **222** "My Mother Pieced Quilts" by Teresa Palomo Acosta. Reprinted by permission of the author. **226** "My Mother Juggling Bean Bags" by James Masao Mitsui. Reprinted by permission of the author. **229** "Those Winter Sundays." Copyright © 1966 by Robert Hayden, from *Collected Poems of Robert Hayden by Robert Hayden*, edited by Frederick Glaysher.

Used by permission of Liveright Publishing Corporation. **231** "My Father's Song" by Simon J. Ortiz, originally published in *Woven Stone*, University of Arizona Press, 1992. Permission to reprint granted by author, Simon J. Ortiz. **234** "Bowling to Find a Lost Father" by Mee Her. Reprinted by permission of the author. **239** "Eva and Daniel" by Tomás Rivera is reprinted with permission from the publisher of Tomás Rivera: The Complete Works (Houston: Arte Público Press—University of Houston, 1992). **246** "Sweet Potato Pie" by Eugenia Collier, originally published in *Black World*, August 1972. Reprinted by permission of the author. **260** "Last Night" by Fae Myenne Ng from *Cosmopolis: Urban Stories by Women* by Ines Rieder. Reprinted by permission of Donadio & Olson, Inc. Copyright 1990 by Fae Myenne Ng. **269** From *Body in Flames/Cuerpo en Llamas* by Francisco X. Alarcón © 1990. Reprinted by permission of Chronicle Books, San Francisco. **271** "Nikki-Rosa" from *Black Feeling, Black Talk, Black Judgment* by Nikki Giovanni. Copyright © 1968, 1970 by Nikki Giovanni. Reprinted by permission of HarperCollins Publishers, Inc., William Morrow. **284** "On Being Asian American" by Lawson Fusao Inada. Copyright © Lawson Fusao Inada. Reprinted by permission. **287** "Saying Yes" by Diana Chang, from *Asian American Heritage: An Anthology of Prose and Poetry*. Copyright © Diana Chang. Reprinted by permission of the author. **289** "The Struggle to Be an All-American Girl" by Elizabeth Wong. Reprinted by permission of the author. **293** "Grandma's Primo" by Leroy V. Quintana from *Hispanics in the United States: An Anthology of Creative Literature*, 1980. Reprinted by permission of Bilingual Press/Editorial Bilingüe, Arizona State University, Tempe, AZ. **295** From "Neighbours" from *A Daughter of the Samurai* by E. I. Sugimoto, copyright 1925, 1928 by Doubleday, a division of Bantam Doubleday Dell Publishing Group, Inc. Used by permission of Doubleday, a division of Random House, Inc. **302** "Like Mexicans" from *The Effects of Knut*

Illustrations

Position of images on a page is indicated by these abbreviations: (T) top, (C) center, (B) bottom, (L) Left, (R) right.

Cover, i © Helen Hardin 1976. Photograph © Cradoc Bagshaw 2002. **iiiT, x–I** © Lawrence Migdale. **iiiC** © Mansell/TimePix. **iiiB** © Christie's Images/Corbis. **ivT** © David Alan Harvey/Magnum Photos. **ivC** © Wade Spees/Black Star. **ivB** © Denver Art Museum Collection, Gift of Sioux Indian Exhibit and Crafts Centre, 1956. **vT** © Susie Fitzhugh. **vC** © Patrick Zachmann/Magnum Photos. **vBL** © David Grossman. **vBR** © Peter Huizdak/The Image Works **viT** © Lawrence Migdale. **viB** Private Collection/Daniel Nevins/Superstock. **viiT** © Spencer Grant/Stock Boston. **viiC** © B. Daemmrich/The Image Works. **viiBL** © Werner Forman/CORBIS. **viiBR** © Susie Fitzhugh. **viiiT** Visions & Motion, Elliot Pinkney, 1997, Los Angeles. From *Walls of Heritage Walls of Pride*, James Prigoff, Robin J. Dunitz. **viiiC** © Howard Terpning 2001, licensed courtesy of the Greenwich Workshop, Inc. **viiiB** The Granger Collection, New York. **ixT** Courtesy, National Museum of the American Indian, Smithsonian Institution, neg. 1000-A. **ixC** © The Image Works. **ixB** © Ben Mangor/Superstock. **2T** © Bettmann/CORBIS. **2B, 5** Weems Photograph Negative Collection 1943/4068-4209, Atlanta-Fulton Public Library System-Research Library. **6** AP/Wide World Photos. **7** © Susie Fitzhugh. **8** Library of Congress. **9T** Courtesy Carol Bruchac. **9B, 10** © Christie's Images/CORBIS. **10** © Christie's Images/CORBIS. **11** © Robyn McDaniels. **13, 14** Seaver Center for Western History Research, Los Angeles County Museum of Natural History. **16** © Miriam Berkley. **17** © Lynn Radeka/SuperStock. **19T** Courtesy of the Bancroft Library, University of California, Berkeley. **19B, 21** © Mansell/TimePix. **26** © M. Koga/Bishop Museum. **28** © John Eddy. **29** © Bettmann/CORBIS. **30** © M. Koga/Bishop Museum. **31T** © CORBIS. **31B** © David Grossman. **32** Courtesy Christie's Images, New York, 2002. **33** University of Georgia Public Affairs. **34** © David M. Grossman. **36, 39** National Anthropological Archives, Smithsonian Institution, neg. 1000-A. **40** Courtesy, National Museum of the American Indian, Smithsonian Institution. Photo by Carmelo Guadagno. **44** #33072, Collection of The New-York Historical Society. **46** Library of Congress. **47T** Courtesy University of New Mexico Press. **47B** © Michael Rougier/TimePix. **49** © Bernard Hoffman/TimePix. **50** © Michael Rougier/TimePix. **55** © Lawrence Migdale. **56T** © Bill Gaskins. **56B** Feed Your Child the Truth, Bernard Williams, 1994, Chicago. From *Walls of Heritage-Walls of Pride*, James Prigoff, Robin J. Dunitz. **59** Tuzuri Watu (We Are a Beautiful People), Brooke Fancher, 1987, San Francisco. From *Walls of Heritage-Walls of Pride*, James Prigoff, Robin J. Dunitz. **62** Feed Your Child the Truth, Bernard Williams, 1994, Chicago. From *Walls of Heritage-Walls of Pride*, James Prigoff, Robin J. Dunitz. **66-67** © David Alan Harvey/Magnum Photos. **68T** © Hulton/Archive/Getty Images. **68B** The Detroit Institute of Arts, USA/City of Detroit Purchase/Bridgeman Art Library. **69** The Metropolitan Museum of Art, The Michael C. Rockefeller Memorial Collection, Gift of Nelson A. Rockefeller, 1965 (1978.412.309) Photograph © 1983 The Metropolitan Museum of Art. **70** Courtesy Vivian Randall **71** © Wade Spees/Black Star. **72** Photofest. **73T** National Anthropological Archives, Smithsonian Institution, neg. 3303-C. **73B** Milwaukee Public Museum. **75** Milwaukee Public Museum. **79** Denver Art Museum Collection: Native Arts acquisition fund, 1948.156 © Denver Art Museum 2002. **81T** © Miriam Berkley. **81B** © Seattle Art Museum/CORBIS . **83** Reprinted with permission of the publisher, Children's Book Press, San Francisco, CA. *Honoring Our Ancestors: Stories and Pictures by Fourteen Artists*, edited by Harriet Rohmer. Illustration copyright © 1999 by Maya Christina Gonzalez. **86** Courtesy Christie's Images, New York, 2002. **87** © Jonathan Blair/CORBIS. **88T** Courtesy Steven Mori. **88B** © Ben Mangor/Superstock. **91** © Ben Mangor/SuperStock. **95** © Joel Gordon. **96T** © Hulton/Archive/Getty Images. **96B, 97** © Susie Fitzhugh.

Susie Fitzhugh. **274** © Lawrence Migdale/Stock Boston. **275T** © Lawrence Migdale/Stock Boston. **275B** © Ellen Senisi/The Image Works. **276L** © Joel Gordon. **276R** © John Berry/The Image Works. **277T** © Lawrence Migdale. **277B** © Susie Fitzhugh. **278** © Joel Gordon. **279T** © Lori Adamski Peek/Getty Images/Stone. **279B, 280L** © Susie Fitzhugh. **280R** © Copyright Smithsonian American Art Museum, Washington, DC/Art Resource, NY. **281T, 281B** © Susie Fitzhugh. **282-283** © Spencer Grant/Stock Boston. **284T** © Paul Schraub. **284B, 286** © Joel Gordon. **287** © Gordon Robotham. **288** © Rhoda Sidney/Stock Boston. **289T** Courtesy of the author. **289B** © Lawrence Migdale. **292** © Lawrence Migdale. **293** Courtesy Leroy V. Quintana. **295T** Photo by Ichiro Tori, courtesy Dr. Charles J. G. Kiyooka. **295B** © Sharon Hoogstraten. **297** © Bettmann/Corbis. **299** Janette Ostier Gallery, Paris, France/Giraudon, Paris/SuperStock. **301** © PhotoDisc. **302T** © Janjapp Dekker/Used by permission of Gary Soto. **302B** © Susie Fitzhugh. **304** © Susie Fitzhugh. **307** © PhotoDisc. **309T** © Bill Gaskins. **309B** Schomburg Center for Research in Black Culture, Art & Artifacts Division, The New York Public Library, Astor, Lenox and Tilden Foundations. **312** © D. Wells/The Image Works. **315** Library of Congress. **316** Schomburg Center for Research in Black Culture, Art & Artifacts Division, The New York Public Library, Astor, Lenox and Tilden Foundations. **318T** © PhotoDisc. **318B** © D.Wells/The Image Works. **319T** © Miriam Berkley. **319B** © B. Daemmrich/The Image Works. **320** © Susie Fitzhugh. **321** Reprinted with permission from Arte Publico Press . **322** © Michael Yamashita/CORBIS. **323T** Courtesy of the author. **323B** Library of Congress. **328** T.C. Cannon, "Collector #5 or Osage with Van Gogh," IAC 1953, Heard Museum, Phoenix, Arizona. **331** © Werner Forman/CORBIS. **333** © PhotoDisc. **334-335** Visions & Motion, Elliott Pinkney, 1997, Los Angeles. From *Walls of Heritage-Walls of Pride*, James Prigoff, Robin J. Dunitz. **336T** © Hulton/

Archive/Getty Images. **336B** Library of Congress. **337** © Howard Terpning 2001, licensed courtesy of The Greenwich Workshop, Inc. **338** © CORBIS. **340T** From the Ann Petry Collection in the Special Collections at Boston University, © Carl Van Vechten, with permission from the Van Vechten Trust. **340B** © Copyright Bennett College. All rights reserved. **343** Schomburg Center for Research in Black Culture, The New York Public Library. **346** © Judith Bloom Fradin, courtesy Oberlin Senior Center. **349** Verelst, John/National Archives of Canada/PAC-123708. **351** © Copyright Bennett College. All rights reserved. **353, 355, 356** Photofest. **358T** © Miriam Berkley. **358B, 361** Bishop Museum. **363T** Courtesy University of Washington Press. **363B** © Hulton/Archive/Getty Images. **366, 368** Department of Special Collections, Charles E. Young Research Library, UCLA. **371T** © 1997 PhotoDisc, Inc. All rights reserved. Images provided by © 1997 C Squared Studios. **371C, B** © Bettmann/CORBIS. **374** © Bettmann/Corbis. **378** AP/Wide World Photos. **380** The Granger Collection, New York. **381** © Bettmann/CORBIS. **382T** © Hulton/Archive/Getty Images. **382B** AP/Wide World Photos. **384** AP/Wide World Photos. **387** Courtesy of the author. **388** © Bruce Davidson/Magnum Photos. **389** © CORBIS. **390, 391T** The Granger Collection, New York. **391L** © Bettmann/CORBIS. **391R** Courtesy of the Library of Congress. **392L** The Granger Collection, New York. **392R** © Underwood & Underwood/CORBIS. **393T** The Granger Collection, New York. **393B** The Granger Collection, New York. **394T** © Hulton/Archive/Getty Images. **394B** © Bettmann/CORBIS. **395** © Hulton/Archive/Getty Images. **396** © Gerhard Gscheidle/Magnum Photos. **397T** © AFP/CORBIS. **397B** © Ted Wood.

Index of Authors and Titles